Praise for the greatest untold story of the Second World War

"READ IT . . . YOU'LL WEEP, THAT THESE THINGS WERE ENDURED BY MEN."
Edward L. Beach, author of
RUN SILENT, RUN DEEP

"If survival itself is heroic, the survivors whose tale is told in RETURN FROM THE RIVER KWAI deserve humanity's highest honors. The assembled recollections inexorably cut through the minutiae and into our hearts and guts, far more than most fiction can . . . the suspense is exquisite."
Los Angeles Times

"A READABLE, MOVING BOOK . . . IT IS A MEASURE OF THE FASCINATION OF THE STORY THAT THE READER WANTS TO KNOW STILL MORE. NOT EVEN THE BEST WAR FICTION OFTEN DOES THAT."
Washington Star

Return
FROM THE
River Kwai

Joan and Clay Blair, Jr.

BALLANTINE BOOKS • NEW YORK

To Anne Shields

Library of Congress Catalog Card Number: 79-531

ISBN 0-345-29007-0

This edition published by arrangement with Simon and Schuster

Manufactured in the United States of America

First Ballantine Books Edition: January 1981

Contents

Acknowledgments

We extend our deepest gratitude to the hundreds of people worldwide who assisted us in the preparation of this book.

In the United States: Dean C. Allard, head, Operational Archives Branch, Naval Historical Center; his assistants Geraldine K. Judkins and Bernard Cavalcante; Robert J. Cressman, Ships' History Division, Naval Historical Center; Submarine Veterans of World War II: Anthony J. A. Alamia; Roy Anderberg, Clarence G. Carmody; Harry G. Fisher, editor, *Polaris* magazine; Anthony C. Hauptman, Charles Levine, Paul Pappas, C. E Whitten. In addition: Joseph C. Bates, Colin Dangaard, Edward and Myrna McGinnis, Eleanor and Frederic Sherman, Anne Shields, Hank, Alma and Cathy Walker. And the scores of other ex-submariners from *Barb, Pampanito, Queenfish* and *Sealion II* whom we interviewed or who sent letters, documents, photographs and other material. They are listed in the Source Notes.

In the United Kingdom: The able staff of the Public Records Office (now computerized!) in Kew Gardens; L. B. Duncan, Ministry of Defence; S. Stephenson, Department of Health and Social Security; A. G. Davey, Army Records Center; A. L. Denholm, Far East POW Fund, London. The many officers of the Far East POW Association in England and Scotland who helped find survivors, especially: Bryn Roberts, London; H. Hughes, Edinburgh; G. W. Harrison, Leeds; and C. Middleton, Oldham. Also the "Thames at 6" television show in London: Andrew Gardner, Carole Brown, Rosemary Forgan and Sandie Perrins. And the dozens of survivors who freely gave of their time and provided documents, diaries, manuscripts, newspaper clippings, photographs, letters, etc. Especially: Norman Ashworth, Wilfred Barnett, Roy A. Hudson and Thomas Pounder. Other survivors interviewed are listed in the Source Notes. Special thanks to a princely Englishman, Alan D. Gerrard, friend and mentor.

In Australia: Geoffrey McKeown, Australian War Memorial, Canberra; Sandra Bardwell, Australian Archives, Melbourne; Alan Payne, secretary-treasurer, Naval Historical Society of Australia; J. M. Mackenzie, historian, Navy Officer, Department of Defence, Melbourne. Jack and Odette McNiven and the staff of the Manhattan Hotel, Sydney; Robert W. Brack and James Montgomery, Melbourne. The many officers of the Returned Servicemen's League who helped find survivors, especially Sir Colin J. Hines, Frank Gow and Marjorie Page in Sydney. The representatives of the media who helped enormously in the search, especially: Thomas H. Farrell and Tim Dare of the Sydney *Morning Herald,* Douglas Blaikie of the Brisbane *Courier Mail,* Michael Gough of the Melbourne *Herald* and Michael Wilkinson of the Melbourne *Sun* (and Ray Terry, chief librarian). Radio host Bob Rogers and his assistant Bernadette Funnell. Television talk show hosts Mike Walsh, Maggi Eckardt and Don Lane. And the scores of survivors who freely gave of their time and provided documents, diaries, manuscripts, letters, newspaper clippings, photographs, etc. Especially: Arthur Bancroft, Philip J. Beilby, M. Robert Farrands, Victor R. Duncan, Francis J. McGovern, Dr. Rowland Richards (and his wife, Beth), J. Russell Savage, R. Neville Thams and Walter G. Williams Other survivors interviewed are listed in the Source Notes.

Joan and Clay Blair, Jr.

Foreword

In 1954 the French writer Pierre Boulle published a novel, *The Bridge over the River Kwai,* which was later made into a tremendously successful film, *The Bridge on the River Kwai.* These were fictionalized accounts of the horrors endured by Allied prisoners of war who were enslaved to build a bridge for a Japanese railway running through the jungles of Burma and Thailand. In the climax of the novel, a commando team attempts, unsuccessfully, to blow up the bridge. In the film the team succeeds. This, of course, was purely imaginary.

However, the story was set in a real milieu Allied POWs did build such a railway partly along the River Kwae Noi (Kwai), under horrifying conditions, with enormous loss of life. There were many bridges along the road, but none was ever destroyed by a commando team. One of these POW-built bridges, a modern eleven-span steel and concrete structure at Tamarkan, Thailand (adjacent to Kanchanaburi), has now become a popular tourist attraction and is called the Bridge over the River Kwai. Nearby is a huge cemetery where thousands of POWs who died on the railway are buried.

This book is nonfiction, a factual account of what happened to 2,218 Australian and British POWs—and a lone American—who survived the railway. They returned from the River Kwai to face an even more terrifying experience.

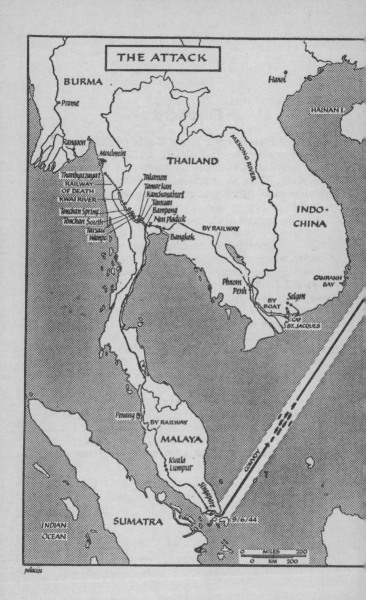

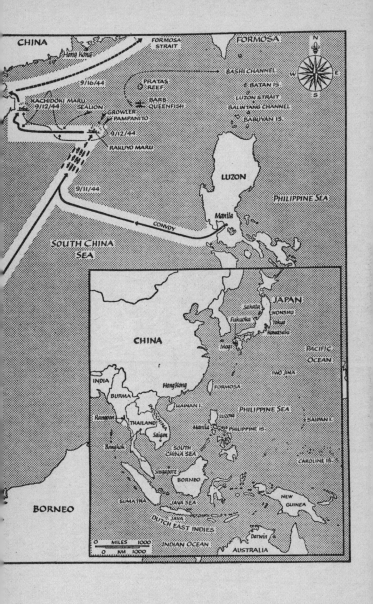

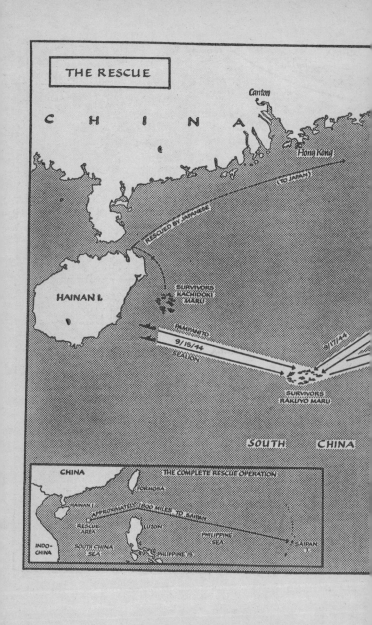

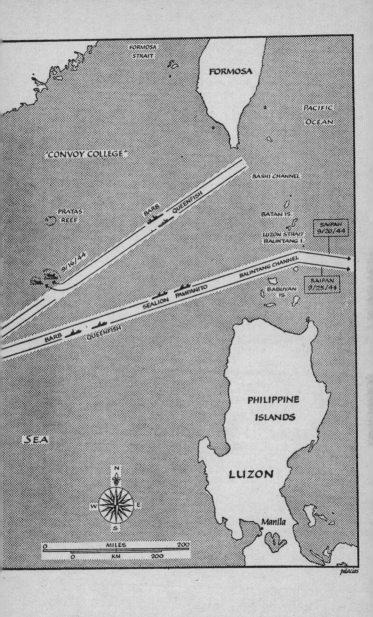

PART ONE

Saigon

PART ONE

Saloon.

(1)

At Tamarkan, Thailand, a miserable Japanese prisoner-of-war camp near a bridge over the River Kwai, the news struck like a thunderclap. In the broken English of the camp guards, it was: "All fit men go Nippon."

The several thousand prisoners at Tamarkan, all Australian, fell out on the bare dirt parade ground for medical inspection. There was hardly one "fit" man in the lot. They were skeleton-thin, hollow-eyed, ravaged by malaria and dysentery, many with open sores on their bodies. They were dressed in tatters or in simple loincloths they called "Jap-happies." A few wore rotting boots, but most had only wooden clogs that they had fashioned by hand. Some still wore rakish digger hats, but these were now filthy and misshapen.

These Australians were a portion of the survivors of the "Railway of Death," one of the least known but most savage atrocities of World War II, a horror story second only to the Holocaust. The Japanese had impressed some 61,000 Allied POWs (the majority Australian and British), together with some 250,000 Asian natives, to build, literally by hand, a 265-mile military railway through the dense jungles and rugged mountains of Thailand and Burma. Lashed on by brutal and sadistic Japanese and Korean guards, reduced to starvation rations, denied proper housing and medical care, for fourteen months the men had toiled like the slaves on the Egyptian pyramids. They had done the job, but at fearful cost in human suffering. About one-fifth of all the white men—12,568—had died, plus an estimated seven times that number of Asian coolies All but a handful had been struck down by jungle diseases or those caused by malnutrition and starvation. Now, the railway finished, Tokyo had decreed that 10,000 of the most "fit" of these wretched men be shipped to Japan, to help alleviate the

3

acute shortage of labor in the mines and war production factories.

Ordinarily the Japanese camp commander left the details of selecting work parties to the POW officers. Not this time. It was soon made clear that selection of this "Japan Party" was a very special, even somewhat historic, occasion. As the POWs stood uneasily in tattered rows, a white-coated Japanese "medical officer" (actually a dentist) and his retinue walked up and down making the choice. All older men and those with dark skin (or even freckles) were automatically excluded. All others who could stand unaided, had no apparent physical infirmities, such as broken or amputated limbs, festering skin ulcers or malarial seizures, were chosen. That day 900 names went on the list. By any rational standard no more than 5 percent of these could have been considered "fit."

This moment was one more in a seemingly endless parade of traumatic events in the lives of these prisoners. Heretofore the Australian officers had managed by one means or another to keep the various military units intact. Most of these units, regionally recruited, were composed of men who, if not lifelong friends, at least knew one another fairly well. This closeness, together with unit pride, had helped sustain many through the ghastly ordeal of the railway. But now, the Japanese chose at random—often, it seemed, capriciously—without regard to military unit. On that day, unit integrity disappeared and many intimate, life-saving friendships were abruptly disrupted. Even some relatives were separated

There were deeply mixed feelings about going to Japan. Many men welcomed the idea of getting away from the terrible diseases, starvation and brutality of these jungle camps. They reasoned that life in Japan could not possibly be worse and might even be considerably better. But many had strong doubts. It was March 1944. They knew from the clandestine radios in camp that the Pacific war had now turned decisively in favor of the Allies. In Thailand, an advanced and vulnerable area, they might look forward to early liberation; whereas in Japan, they might languish behind barbed wire for untold more years. Moreover, word had reached the POWs that Allied submarines were now taking a fearful toll of Japanese naval and merchant marine vessels. The odds were good that the Japan Party would be torpedoed and lost at sea "Better

4

the devil you know than the devil you don't know," said one of the doubters.

Following the selection parade, the members of the Japan Party received yet another surprise. Befitting the historic air of the occasion, they were issued a new set of clothing, the first in their two years of captivity. It consisted of a green tunic, a white T-shirt, green or khaki cotton drill shorts, undershorts and socks, a green straw hat and Japanese rubber boots, with a separate niche for the big toe. Very little of the new "kit" fitted properly; most of the shoes, designed for smaller Japanese feet, were three or four sizes too small. Even so, the men of the Japan Party examined the new issue with a sense of wonderment and awe, as though they had come into a fabulous and wholly unexpected inheritance.

(2)

The senior Allied POW officer in Burma and Thailand at this time was Australian Brigadier Arthur L. Varley, fifty, a civilian-soldier of impressive bearing and courage. A World War I hero, Varley had left his cattle and real estate business in the Australian bush country to lead one of two brigades of the Australian 8th Division against the Japanese in Malaya His son, John A. Varley, twenty-three, had commanded a platoon. Both had fought with distinction. After the surrender of Singapore, both had been incarcerated in the infamous Singapore POW camp Changi, along with tens of thousands of other Allied prisoners.

When the Japanese launched the Burma-Thailand railway construction, drawing on Changi for the bulk of the manpower, Brigadier Varley was detailed to command the 10,000 mostly Australian POWs working in Burma. His son Jack had accompanied him as a staff officer. During his fourteen months in Burma, Brigadier Varley had fearlessly confronted the Japanese at every turn, demanding more-humane working conditions for his men. Few of these demands were met, but Varley's efforts had made him a legendary figure among the prisoners.

By then, most of the senior Allied POWs in Burma, Thailand and Malaya had been sent to special POW camps in Formosa and elsewhere. Brigadier Varley either had been overlooked or had been kept in Burma owing to his administrative talent Whatever the case, now that the railway was finished, he was to be transferred to a senior officers' camp in Formosa. He would travel with this first Japan Party as a supernumerary. Because of his presence, the Party would later be referred to, in some military circles, as the "Varley Party." In fact he did not actually command the Party.

The commander, or tactical POW leader, was Australian Captain Arthur B. Sumner, twenty-nine, a spirited infantry company commander who was liked and respected by the men. Under Sumner the 900 men in the Japan Party were organized into six units of 150 men each, called *kumis* and labeled with a number from 35 to 40. Each *kumi* was led by a *kumicho*, an Australian officer. Captain Sumner, wearing two hats, tactically commanded the Party and also *Kumi* 35 The other *kumi* leaders were lieutenants. Each *kumi* was assigned a medical attendant. In *Kumi* 35, he was Captain Rowland "Rowley" Richards, a doctor who was not quite twenty-eight and looked twenty or less. The senior medical officer, Major John S. Chalmers, a Tasmanian, was assigned to *Kumi* 38. *Kumis* 36, 37, 39 and 40 had only enlisted medical orderlies. A chaplain was designated to go with the Party, but he was found "not fit" physically. Since no other could be found, the Japan Party had no formal religious adviser.

The Japanese officer designated to lead the Party was one Lieutenant Yamada. The POWs considered this a fortuitous choice In appearance, Yamada was "rather grim and forbidding." Yet he was considered "one of the best" Japanese officers on the railway, a soldier of rare humanity. He had exercised "intelligence and tolerance" in the supervision of the POWs in his care, often going toe to toe with his superiors in the prisoners' behalf. Whenever possible, he had stretched the rules, even to the extent of inviting POW musicians to his hut for concerts and whiskey. He confided to them that he felt he was as much a prisoner as they. One POW remembered that Yamada publicly whipped one of the Korean guards for an inexcusable assault on a POW. It had been nearly seven years since he had seen his wife and children in Japan. Now, at last, he was going home.

After Yamada's appointment, the men noted a distinct

6

change for the better in the attitude of the hated Korean guards who would accompany the Party. One who noted this change was an Australian sailor, Arthur Bancroft, twenty-two. He was one of about forty-five navy men in the Japan Party who had managed to survive when their ship, the cruiser *Perth,* had been sunk early in the war. Bancroft, a bank clerk before the war, was nicknamed "Blood" on account of his flaming red hair. He was, against all rules, keeping a detailed diary of his terrible experiences (noting, especially, atrocities), complete with penciled drawings. At first Bancroft was "puzzled" by the new attitude of the guards, but later he learned, and noted, that the guards "had been given strict instructions to look after the welfare" of the Japan Party. Clearly, Yamada and others intended that the Party arrive in Japan in as good physical shape as possible and with no external signs of past brutalities. This was very welcome news indeed, and the POWs on the Party facetiously dubbed themselves "The Chosen Men."

But the guards were not above a little good-natured teasing. Perhaps giving voice to their own inner fears, they repeatedly harped on the dangers of submarine attack during the sea voyage ahead, declaring it was most unlikely the Japan Party would ever reach Japan and that all the POWs would become "fish food." Half-believing this assertion, and fearful of a thorough search before they left Tamarkan, Bancroft and others decided to turn over their "valuables" to those who would not be making the trip. Bancroft's most valuable possession was his diary. Giving it to a sailor friend, Marcus Clark, Bancroft told him to bury it should he be assigned to a later Japan Party.

(3)

For the trip to a seaport to board a ship, the 900-man Japan Party was split into two groups of 450 men, considered a trainload. The first three *kumis,* 35, 36 and 37, departed Tamarkan on the afternoon of March 27, 1944. The leave-taking was a formal event, of sorts. The Japanese camp commandant ordered all men, except those in the hospital, on parade. The Japanese themselves turned out in full uniform with swords. The Japan Party, decked out in new kits, lined up in neat rows to hear a farewell speech from the commandant.

One of the POWs listening carefully to this rambling, colorful oration was a corporal of the 8th Division, M. Robert Farrands, twenty-one. A short, stocky lad with clear blue eyes and blond hair, Farrands had been an auto mechanic. Now he was something of a minor legend among his mates. A while past, at a railway work camp in Burma, Farrands had emerged the winner in one of the most remarkable events ever staged in this, or any other, POW camp in World War II. This was the simulation— on a rare holiday—of a famous Australian horse race, the Melbourne Cup.

It was an extraordinary day-long spectacle, with a musical concert, a "fashion parade" of POWs dressed as females, coffee and tea bars, betting stalls and other festivities. The big race itself was a bizarre contest. "Jockeys," such as Farrands, rode "horses" named for real Melbourne Cup winners (but with obscene pedigrees) made of bamboo, over a two-mile circular course. "Riding" Wanger (out of Wet Dream by Rice Bubble), Farrands came in first. His prize was a small silver cup, later suitably engraved. It was now tucked in the ragged, dirty haversack slung over his shoulder. It was his most valuable possession—intrinsically and sentimentally—and he was determined to hang on to it and place it in an honored place in his home in Australia.

The thrust of the commandant's speech was forever stamped in Farrands' mind:

All men should be honored to know they are going to a land of peace and tranquility, where even the birds can nestle on the hunter's hand and will not be harmed. Where the snow covers the land in winter and the warm sun of spring melts it, leaving the country clean. A land of milk and honey. In Japan, it is a sin to eat and not work, so to prevent all men from becoming sinners, we shall put you to work.

When at last the commandant concluded his speech, Captain Sumner ordered the Japan Party to attention. Then, after a thorough search that produced no contraband, the three *kumis* moved smartly toward the main gate of the camp, giving an "eyes left" salute to the cluster of

Japanese. Close mates and relatives, separated by the cruel selection process, waved farewell and wiped away tears. These included the Varleys. The Brigadier's son Jack would remain behind. Then the Party was gone, bound to face a devil it did not know.

(4)

The Party marched four miles to the railway yard at Kanchanaburi. There it formed up beside a train made up of small, open flatcars. The 450 POWs and the guards boarded the train quietly. Then slowly the train pulled out onto the main line. As it jolted along beneath the hot sun, Blood Bancroft, who had begun a new diary, recalled: "Little was said, but it can be safely assumed that everyone's thoughts were of those they had left behind."

With each passing mile, the train took the men farther from the dismal jungles and horrors of the Railway of Death, into civilized and populated countryside. The reentry was a profoundly moving experience. It had been nearly two years since most of them had left Singapore for Burma. In all the time since their capture they had lived in unspeakably filthy, primitive bamboo huts, surrounded by hostile jungle. They had seen no white men other than themselves, and no white women. The ordinary appurtenances of civilization, such as automobiles and buildings, roads and farms, were only vague memories. Now, seeing these once again, they stared in hushed silence, drinking in the details.

One man on the train was all but oblivious to these new sights and sounds. This was R. Neville Thams, twenty-six, assigned to Lieutenant H. Lester Stupart's *Kumi* 36. Thams had worked in his family's cinema before the war. His new Japanese shoes did not fit; he had marched the four miles in old wooden clogs. Worse than sore feet was a double-headed abscess on his back. It was swelling steadily and painfully with each passing mile. The medical orderly in this *kumi* could do nothing to help. It was too early to lance the abscess, and he had no medicine to treat it or relieve the pain. Neville Thams could only grit his teeth and wonder if anywhere along the journey he might find proper medical care.

9

After a short journey, the train arrived at a rail junction, Non Pladuk, near Bampong. Here there was yet another POW camp containing about 10,000 Australian, British and Dutch. The *kumis* detrained to await a connecting train to Bangkok. Befitting its exalted status, the Party was billeted in a group of transient huts off limits to the resident POWs. The men were astonished and pleased to find yet another sign of civilization: fresh water wells sunk deep into the earth. The resident medical officer had declared these wells free of "wogs" (germs) and the water safe to drink. For the first time in almost two years, the Australians had water without the laborious process of chlorinating and/or boiling, a wondrously satisfying experience. They drank "the cool refreshing natural beverage" until they were bloated.

The Party remained at Non Pladuk for several days. During that time, the other three *kumis* came from Tamarkan. On April 1, now staging in groups of 300 men, *Kumis* 35 and 36 entrained for the short trip to Bangkok. The massive railway yards in cosmopolitan Bangkok impressed one and all. The men gawked at huge American- and German-built locomotives and "luxurious" parlor cars and coaches—superior even to those in Australia. Everywhere there were Japanese troops and troop trains, en route to the front lines in Burma over the railway the POWs had recently finished. There had been several Allied air raids on Bangkok, but there was little or no evidence of this in the railway yards.

Some of the men had assumed that the Party would board ship in Thailand. They were wrong. The destination of the Party was now revealed to be Saigon, Indochina, the principal Japanese naval and merchant marine terminus in the area. The Party would travel about 400 miles by rail to Phnom Penh, the capital of Cambodia, and thence 150 miles by riverboat on the Mekong River to Saigon. After a meal of rice, served by a railside kitchen catering to Japanese troop trains, the Party re-embarked on yet another train in late afternoon. This one was made up of steel cattle cars. The POWs swept out the hay and manure, then crowded sixty-two men into each car. The six guards per car staked out one-third of the total space for themselves in "first class" accommodations near the open sliding doors.

Once again the Japan Party was off. It traveled nonstop until eight o'clock the following morning, when the train pulled off at another railside kitchen. After eating, Strachan M. White recalled, the POWs obtained permission from the guards to bathe under a water pump used to fill the engines.

They traveled all that day, passing through vast rice paddies. They stopped again at the Cambodian border to eat and to exchange the Thai engine for a French one. (Though occupied by the Japanese, Cambodia was still a French colony.) White: "The trip was becoming a very trying one on account of our cramped positions and lack of sleep." Near midnight the train rolled into cosmopolitan Phnom Penh. The men climbed out of the wretched cars. Many promptly lay down on the cinders between the rails and fell into deep sleep. Others, agonized by thirst, gulped down tea and, later, a rice meal, provided by another railside kitchen.

After dawn the Party was rousted out and marched from the rail yards through downtown Phnom Penh to the river docks. Here the re-entry shock was severe. The broad tree-lined streets were crowded with beautiful French and Eurasian women and girls wearing lovely dresses. The POWs, Bancroft remembered, "stared wide-eyed and open-mouthed." These French, ostensibly loyal to the Nazi-dominated Vichy government, were for the most part secretly aligned with or sympathetic to the Free French. They made their feelings known with friendly sidelong glances and smiles. A few flashed a V (for Victory) sign with their fingers. These expressions of friendship were thrilling and heartwarming. Some of the wide-staring eyes filmed with tears.

Arriving at the docks on the broad, muddy Mekong River, the Party was pleased when it saw the next means of transportation. It was the *Long Ho,* a clean, modern, 300-ton river steamer. They marched aboard, crowding into a forward hold. When that was filled to capacity, the overflow was permitted to remain topside on the bow. The new quarters were not "unduly cramped," at least not like the cattle cars. All the men would recall the "river cruise" as a "very pleasant" experience, one of the highlights of their long captivity.

Some of the POWs topside made contact with a native and obtained a full bottle of rice wine. For many of these soldiers it was the first taste of this appurtenance of civilization since before the surrender in Singapore. Ian A. MacDiarmid, twenty-three, a farm equipment salesman,

11

remembered that he got "stinking drunk." Alfred D. Winter, thirty, who had been a schoolteacher and was one of the few Australians in this group who was married and had a son, recalled that everybody had "a whale of a time singing and dancing." The guards looked on faintly amused, either not aware of this flagrant violation of POW rules or uncaring. At the end of the trip, two of the celebrants were so drunk they had to be carried off the steamer. When the guards inquired what was wrong with them, Alf Winter lied gravely: "Malaria."

The voyage on the Mekong River was over all too quickly. After thirty hours, on April 4, the *Long Ho* docked at a modern concrete quay on the Saigon waterfront, amid the teeming Japanese shipping. The Japan Party debarked, gaping at the bustling activity. Until sea transportation could be arranged, they would be temporarily billeted in yet another POW camp, close by the waterfront. As they were marched along the docks to their new quarters, the Australians lustily sang their favorite song, "Waltzing Matilda."

(5)

The new camp was better, by far, than any other they had ever seen. Before the Japanese occupation, it had been a French Foreign Legion cantonment. The well-made wooden barracks were equipped with unheard-of luxuries, such as tile roofs, concrete floors, double-tiered bunks with mosquito netting, and—wonder of wonders—electricity and toilets. Outside there were concrete bathing troughs with continuous, clean, free-flowing water, a volleyball court and a miniature golf course. Most astonishing of all, there was a canteen, offering for sale, at modest prices, food and fruit of all kinds, as well as soap, talcum powder, toothbrushes and paste and tailor-made cigarettes.

Following the surrender at Singapore, this camp had originally been inhabited by a party of 2,000 British POWs, brought up from Changi to work as stevedores on the Saigon waterfront. The majority of these had subsequently been drafted to work on the railway. There were now only about 250 British remaining in the camp.

In the mistaken belief that the Japan Party was made up of fellow Britons, the resident British POWs had prepared a sumptuous welcoming dinner. The Australians devoured it with gratitude.

During the meal the Australians listened in utter disbelief to accounts of POW life in Saigon. For, all this time, the British POWs had been well fed, well housed, lightly worked and decently treated by the Japanese guards. Only one or two POWs had died—of natural causes. Beyond that, they had established surreptitious contact with the sympathetic Free French in Saigon. The French had clandestinely supplied them with money, medicine, food, tobacco, sweets, soap and accurate news on the progress of the war. Many British POWs had "gone under the wire" at night, slipping into Saigon in civilian clothes provided by French friends. They had visited French homes, nightclubs, cinemas and brothels. At one time, so many British were going under the wire that venereal disease became a problem in the camp. The men who got it had to slip back into town to be treated by sympathetic French doctors.

For their part, the Australians shocked the "Pommies" (as they usually referred to the British) with grim accounts of life on the railway. The diseases and the appalling death rate. The atrocities. The hideous living conditions. The punishing and dangerous work. At first the British refused to believe, but as the Australians piled detail upon detail, atrocity atop atrocity, they saw that it was true and realized that by the luck of the draw they might have escaped a ghastly fate. So depressing and relentlessly anti-Japanese were these accounts that the British officers requested that the Australians not discuss the railway further. The talk was upsetting and demoralizing the British, many of whom had close friends and relatives assigned to Burma and Thailand.

Several days later, during the early part of Easter Week, word came to the Japan Party that sea transportation had been arranged. The Party would embark downriver at Cape Saint Jacques, where the Japanese convoys staged. On Easter Sunday, April 9, the advance elements of the Party packed up and moved out, boarding motorized barges. The men carried sufficient rice—and firewood for cooking it—for a trip to Japan. One man was left behind: Neville Thams, who had checked into the British-operated camp hospital to have the painful double-headed abscess lanced. It had not healed and Thams was in no condition to travel.

The trip downriver took almost eleven hours. At Cape Saint Jacques, there was a Japanese convoy in the process of forming up. The barges pulled alongside a large, fairly new freighter anchored in the roadstead. The men climbed aboard the vessel by means of rope ladders and cargo nets slung over the side. Three men, Harold T. Bunker, twenty-three, Edward W. "Andy" Anderson, twenty-eight, and Frederic C. Mills, twenty-six, looked down into the water and were appalled to see several massive sharks, estimated to be thirty or forty feet in length. At that moment, Andy Anderson, who was married and had been a golf pro in civilian life, had another cyclic attack of malaria. His was the "vomiting" strain. As he hung there, throwing up and breaking into sweat, his strength ebbed rapidly. Fearing he might let go and fall among the sharks, Anderson gave a final mighty effort and reached the deck.

The POWs were pleasantly surprised at the condition of the ship. It was spotless. The Japanese crew, a decent and not unfriendly lot, directed the men to an area on the forward deck. Apparently there was no space available in the holds. They would make the trip to Japan in the open. Later the crew prepared and served a good meal of rice and beans. After that, the men bedded down for the night, believing that on the morrow a new and perilous leg of the journey would begin.

The next morning the Party awoke to astounding news: "All men back to Saigon." The captain of the ship had refused to take the POWs to Japan. By now the Allies had imposed a massive submarine blockade against Japanese shipping, beginning just outside Cam Ranh Bay. It extended through the South China Sea to Formosa Strait, to the East China Sea, to Japan. One could "walk to Tokyo on the periscopes." The captain would not endanger the operation of his vessel by hauling so great a human deck cargo. Nor would he accept responsibility for the inevitable loss of life that would ensue if the ship was torpedoed.

This was a strange and baffling turn of events. What was to happen to them now? The Japan Party repacked and debarked, climbing back into the hastily resummoned barges. After a day-long trip back up the river, the barges arrived where they had started, at the Saigon waterfront.

The Japan Party marched back to the ex-French Foreign Legion barracks. Apparently they would wait there while Lieutenant Yamada arranged some other means of sea transport.

Corporal Donald F. McArdle, twenty-two, a greyhound dog race trainer, received the shock of his life. Strolling through a barracks, he stopped and did a double-take. There, on a bunk, sat his older brother James, twenty-six. James had been assigned to one of the unluckiest outfits in the Australian army, the 2nd Pioneers. It had fought hard—and well—in the Middle East with the British, suffering high casualties. On the way home to Australia in January 1942, it was diverted to Java in a futile eleventh-hour effort to stop the Japanese. The entire outfit was captured and most of them were sent from Java to work on the railway.

Don had seen James once in Burma, hardly more than a glimpse. A guard had allowed them to exchange "a few words." Now, in this unlikely place, the brothers were united after many years. James was amazed to see that Don was alive. Don had been assigned to a work force on the railway that was known to have suffered about 40 percent casualties. But it was now Don's turn to worry about James. In spite of the superior living conditions in Saigon, and the availability of medicine, James was severely ill with dysentery and malaria.

(6)

The Japan Party, facing an uncertain future, settled down in uneasy company with the resident Pommies. As on the railway, the two nationalities were billeted separately. There had never been any love lost between the two. The Australians considered the British effete, smug, humorless, lazy and unclean. They were deeply resentful that the British high command had failed to reinforce Singapore adequately with air and naval power, forcing an early surrender. The British viewed the Australians as raw, uncouth, undisciplined, a pack of thieves and brigands. They resented the resourcefulness of the Aussies, their cheerful capacity to survive, often quite well, the meanest adversities.

15

After a few days, the Australians were divided into small work parties that sallied forth daily all over Saigon. Some men went to the docks, some to the airfields, some to the hospitals, some to random, ever-changing tasks. Compared with the work on the railway, these daily chores were not taxing. Most men looked forward to the work as a diversion, an opportunity to make money, to see the sights of the city, to make contact with the Free French or to steal.

The dock parties worked hardest, loading and unloading barges and ships. A large part of this coolie work consisted in unloading very heavy (200 pounds or more) bags of rice from the river barges and storing them in the go-downs (warehouses) or moving them from the go-downs to the outgoing ships. The men had to master the knack of balancing so great a weight on their backs while in motion. Once mastered, however, the work was not very difficult and it was performed at a leisurely pace. Since the men were now eating well, marvelously well compared with the railway standards, most believed the dockwork helpful in getting back into good physical condition. Many men volunteered for the dock parties.

The opportunities for thieving on the docks were endless. The Australians had become masters at the game. They "pinched" not only rice but also salt, sugar, canned foods of all types (meat, condensed milk, sweets, etc.)— anything that could be eaten or "flogged" (sold or traded) to the natives. On the railway they would have been severely punished—beaten—for such wholesale larceny, but in Saigon the Japanese guards were casual. Ian Mac-Diarmid recalled how brazen the Australians became: "They [the guards] used to search us every night when we returned to camp. But if you looked like you were in a kitchen work party and walked right in with a case of tinned meat on your shoulder, they wouldn't search you or even stop you. One time some blokes made off with a whole case of hand grenades and sold them to the natives."

One day one of the better-natured Japanese guards on the docks decided he would lecture the Australians about this rampant thievery. No one who was present would ever forget the scene. He lined the men up, then held up a can of condensed milk. As Philip J. Beilby, thirty-four, a mechanic and amateur musician, recalled, he said: "You think Nippon not know what go on here? This is what Australian do." He pantomimed a POW carefully looking first one way and then the other, then slapped his cap over the can to conceal it. Again he looked one way and the other. Then he reached for his cap and the can of milk. To his astonishment, the milk was gone. A POW had swiped it in midlecture. As the POWs broke up with laughter, the flabbergasted guard gave up, laughed himself and said: "Okay, you win."

The man who had swiped the milk was Pat Linnane. His best mate, another accomplished thief, was Roydon C. Cornford, who celebrated his twenty-second birthday in Saigon. Cornford recalled that later in the day Linnane, to avoid possible retribution on the whole group, returned the can of milk. "The guard grinned and carried it back to camp. Then he called Pat out and gave it back to him."

Earlier, during the fall of Singapore, Roy Cornford had very nearly escaped. He and a group of mates commandeered a sampan and reached the *Empire Star,* one of the last ships to leave Singapore before the surrender. En route to Batavia, the ship was bombed and many soldiers aboard it were killed. In Batavia the ship's captain maintained that Cornford and his mates had "shot and forced" their way onto his ship. Cornford and others were yanked off the ship (which then sailed for Australia) and jailed. Eventually the group escaped to the hills, where they hid out for two months, until compelled by the Japanese to surrender.

On another occasion, a less-good-natured Japanese guard pulled a surprise inspection, an unusually determined one. One POW, notably short in stature, was about to be caught with two large cans of meat. With cunning born of necessity, he took a place in line between two tall mates, then stood on the two cans. Intent on his search, the guard failed to notice the cans or that one of his charges had grown a full foot. Later, the cans were smuggled into camp, a nice addition to the evening meal.

The men assigned to work at the nearby airfields built concrete revetments for the planes, filled in bomb craters and, in some cases, armed and fueled the aircraft. J. Russell Savage, twenty-three, an accountant, was one of the regulars on the work parties at the airport. He and a mate who held a pilot's license seriously considered stealing an airplane and escaping. But they finally gave up the scheme, doubting that the plane had range enough to reach Allied lines. Another regular, Raymond W.

Wheeler, twenty, did his bit for the war effort by contaminating the aircraft fuel drums with sand, sugar and even emery powder. Two other airport regulars, Reginald J. Harris, twenty-seven, and Ronald C. Miscamble, twenty-seven, found the better-educated Japanese airmen rather sympathetic. Harris: "The Jap airmen felt sorry for us because we were so thin. They gave us food and cigarettes."

An English-born carpenter, Victor Clifford, twenty-seven, one of the luckless 2nd Pioneers, was assigned to work at a naval hospital. He detected a similar attitude among the Japanese naval personnel: "The Jap sailors were not a bad lot. We'd pull out an old mangy cigarette butt and ask for a match. They'd feel sorry and give us a new cigarette. We got about eight smokes a day with that old butt. Not only that, we were reasonably fed at the hospital—if you can believe it—better than the camp."

The men assigned to random chores in Saigon had some remarkable and amusing experiences, often involving the Free French. William M. "Mac" McKittrick, twenty-seven, an English-born merchant seaman, was assigned to help paint a Japanese colonel's house in the suburbs. Every morning he was there, a Free Frenchman whizzed by on his bicycle and surreptitiously slapped a cigarette package in McKittrick's hand. The package always contained a little paper money, an underground news sheet with important war news and a cigarette or two. On one occasion, another French sympathizer absconded with McKittrick's canteen and later returned it brimming with fine red wine.

Frank J. Coombes, twenty-three, a cabinetmaker, and his mate, Ronald Jones, were detailed to go into the city with two Japanese truck drivers to pick up the camp vegetables. When the party arrived in town, the Japanese announced they were going sightseeing. They gave Coombes and Jones a note stating that they were POWs and authorized to be out of camp, then took off. The POWs, left alone and hugely enjoying this first taste of "freedom" in a long while, wandered around Saigon, passing "thousands of Japs" and stopping to talk with the "lovely" French, some of whom bought them drinks. The Japanese returned from sightseeing in the afternoon, carrying a "huge" bottle of sake. The four men—two guards, two prisoners—sat on the curb and gulped down sake until they were all "pretty drunk." Somehow they managed to find the vegetables and returned to camp. The Japanese were in the front of the truck "singing their heads off"; Coombes and Jones were in the rear, passed out cold atop the vegetables.

The men who were too ill to go on work parties, such as Neville Thams, back from the hospital, were required to help reduce the vast annoying fly population inside the camp. The daily quota was one hundred carcasses. One of these men, Harold G. Ramsey, twenty-two, a salesman, who had accidentally opened up an old ulcer on the first day of his work party, recalled: "There were ways to get around the fly quota. One of the Dutch POWs had built an ingenious fly trap. He'd sell you one hundred flies for ten cents. But I had a cheaper way. An Australian sergeant major in our hut was in charge of counting flies. Every day at the same time he took a nap. While he was asleep, I'd sneak in and steal one hundred flies. Then, when he awoke, I'd turn in my quota." Strachan White: "Some days there would be between twenty thousand and thirty thousand flies killed."

Many POWs devoted much time, thought and ingenuity to turning a quick dollar. One group discovered that the large cloth borders of the mosquito netting could be manufactured into quite presentable shorts, prized by the natives. After the group had exhausted the material in the barracks, it broke into the warehouse where the netting was stored and got more. Harry Picket, twenty-eight, a musician, and his mates made 3,000 piasters selling these homemade shorts. Ray Wheeler removed the brass bushings from the barracks doorknobs, sawed up scrounged brass pipes and manufactured "gold" rings, which he sold to the natives. Some of his more artful creations had "precious stones" inset, made from old toothbrush handles. A Scottish-born jeweler stamped many of these rings with fake "gold" content in karats. Vic Clifford made real-looking fake watches from scrap metal. He sold them to the natives by holding his own (real) watch to the buyer's ear to hear the ticking, then, with a clever bit of sleight of hand, substituted the fake for the real watch.

The money earned in these various endeavors, plus the considerable money slipped to the POWs by the French, was spent mostly at the camp canteen on food (eggs, crackers, bananas, pineapples, etc.) and cigarettes. The Japanese who supervised the canteen was a precise accountant. He soon noted that the POWs were spending vastly larger sums than they earned in legitimate POW work. When he raised the point with the POWs, they shrugged it off, saying that his arithmetic was wrong or that they had saved money on the railway or that a generous Japanese colonel who pitied them had given them thousands of dollars. That the deception was not pursued was almost surely due to the influence of Lieutenant Yamada. He had no reason to complain. Each day, the Japan Party in his charge was growing stronger and fatter, far better specimens to deliver to Japan.

(7)

Transportation from Saigon was evidently hard to come by—or nonexistent. Weeks dragged by. In off-duty hours the Japan Party whiled away the time with musical concerts (instruments, including violins, drums and a piano, donated by the French) or athletic contests (including formal boxing matches) or reading carefully hoarded books, which the men traded or sold back and forth. Ray Wheeler brushed up his high school French by reading Saigon newspapers slipped into camp. Roy H. Whitecross taught the senior medical officer, Major Chalmers, shorthand.

The Japanese further amazed the POWs when, one day, they distributed blank forms, inviting the Japan Party to fill them in for radio broadcast to their parents and loved ones. This had never happened before. Most POWs were skeptical and stowed the forms to use as toilet paper, but some filled them out. One was Walter G. "Wal" Williams, twenty-two, a factory worker, who penciled this message: "Hello Dad . . . I'm sending you all best wishes and love. I'm in good health and spirits. Max [H. Maxwell, a *Perth* survivor] Campbell is with me and quite okay. Best of love to the whole team." The messages were actually broadcast later and picked up by a ham operator in Australia—with complicating results.

One night in the first week of June, the idyllic POW life was rudely shattered. Shortly after "lights out," the waterfront air raid siren began a mournful wail. Allied bombers were on the way to make a low-level attack on the shipping and warehouses. There were no air raid shelters in the POW camp. The men rolled out of their bunks and lay flat on the concrete floor—all but Thomas R. Moxham, thirty, a grazier, who became hopelessly enmeshed in his mosquito netting. Lieutenant Campbell E. Smith, *kumicho* of *Kumi* 39, stood calmly in the barracks doorway describing the action: "He's making another run. . . . He's circling. . . . Heads down! He's coming right over the top!" The nearby waterfront ack-ack batteries and shipboard guns blazed away at the enemy planes. Alf Winter remembered that an infuriated Japanese officer climbed a tower and fired at the planes with his pistol.

One bomb fell, with a fearful explosion, within a hundred yards of the camp. The concussion shook the earth —and the barracks. Shrapnel whizzed through the roofs. The next day the POWs learned that this bomb had flattened a nearby tobacco warehouse, scattering tobacco leaves all over the area. The POWs resourcefully collected the leaves and rolled them into cigars. Along with the rakish digger hats, a big, jutting, somewhat ragged cigar now became the hallmark of the Japan Party. However, the raid had been a sobering experience, and the Party wanted very much to get away from the Saigon waterfront.

Not long after the raid, the Free French slipped newspapers into the camp containing momentous war news. The Allies had invaded Nazi-occupied France in Normandy. Ray Wheeler translated the details for his deliriously happy mates. Everyone was certain the war would now be over—and they would be free—in a matter of a few weeks. Mac McKittrick was sure he would be back in Australia for his twenty-eighth birthday, September 30. Fears and doubts about going to Japan evaporated.

The euphoria was short-lived. About one week after the Normandy invasion, a Japanese guard started a new and depressing rumor: "All men go Singapore catch ship." The rumor proved to be true. Lieutenant Yamada had given up trying to get the Japan Party on a ship in Saigon. The submarine blockade was too tight. However, definite arrangements were being concluded in Singapore. Again, they would stage in groups of two *kumis*. *Kumis* 35 and 36 should prepare to move out at once, the other *kumis* to follow by twos, shortly.

21

So ended the easy life of the Japan Party in Saigon. The first two *kumis* of the Party set off on the backward trek to Phnom Penh, Bangkok and Bampong on June 24. It was a very different-looking group of men. After two and a half months in Saigon, most had regained lost weight and were in good health. A few of the sick were left behind. Also left behind was James McArdle, who was still very ill with malaria and dysentery. It was a difficult and emotional parting for the brothers. Don was certain he would never see James alive again.

Marching off to the river steamer for the trip to Phnom Penh, the Australians were in a jaunty mood. They sang French barracks-room songs, such as "Mademoiselle from Armentières." They flashed furtive V signs with their fingers to the French. The boyish-looking doctor in *Kumi* 35, Rowley Richards, remembered that one Frenchman returned the signal in a most extraordinary manner. He dashed out on his lawn in his pajamas, stood on his head and opened his legs in a clearly delineated V.

The river steamer awaiting them was the *Tian Guan,* similar in size and lines to the *Long Ho.* But this time the river voyage was not so pleasant. It was now late June. Saigon is only about 10 degrees north of the equator. It was insufferably hot in the hold, aired by only a half-dozen portholes. Whitecross remembered that the stench of three hundred sweating bodies, mixed with that of the cargo, which included dried fish, was soon "thick and foul."

In Phnom Penh they were forced to wait three days for a train. In the interim, they camped in an abandoned POW compound next to a golden-roofed pagoda. Here Brigadier Varley and a camp cook, Sergeant D. William Cunneen, twenty-eight, a farmer, had an interesting, and nerve-racking, contact with an Allied intelligence agent. Approaching the POWs under the very eyes of the Japanese guards, the agent brought medicine and further encouraging war news: Saipan island had been invaded. He inquired about who the POWs were and where they were bound. Varley explained that they were a Japan Party en route to Singapore to catch a ship. He gave the agent a complete list of names of the men in the Party, written on a roll of toilet paper, urgently requesting that the agent get the list through to Australia. The agent promised that he would do so—leading to an interesting aftermath. Then he revealed his identity. He was the chief of police of Phnom Penh. Brigadier Varley and the others were rendered speechless. Then they noted well his name and address, each officer in the Party memorizing one word or number of it.

At last the train arrived. The first two *kumis* moved out on June 27. They marched to the main railway station singing "The Marseillaise" and other French songs. "The French seemed very pleased," Bancroft recalled. But when the POWs saw the train, the merriment ceased abruptly. It was a string of tiny (18 by 18 by 8 feet) steel boxcars, each car already half full of bags of rice. The cars were like ovens, the steel sides too hot to touch. The Japanese decreed that thirty men, plus their guards, would occupy the remaining small space in each car. The men crowded in "like sardines in a tin," sitting with knees drawn under their chins, sweating bodies pressed together. The guards, as usual, took the prime space near the open sliding doors.

Soon after the train jolted off, Rowley Richards, the doctor, found he had a serious medical crisis on his hands. Sergeant Peter Britz had come down with—of all things—pneumonia. Richards, revered by the men for his remarkable and selfless service on the railway (Varley had put him in for a high award), had left Tamarkan with only a stethoscope (in which was concealed a six-page distillation of the diary he had been keeping). In Saigon he had improved his medical kit somewhat, but now he could find only four sulfa tablets for Britz. He administered these and did everything possible to keep Britz cool. Remarkably, Britz survived the crisis.

The wretched train paused briefly in the Bangkok railway yards. This time the Australians were pleased to find much evidence of recent Allied bombing attacks. Where before the yards had been a beehive, now they were all but deserted. The Thais in the yard—in contrast to the French—were sullen and hostile, apparently expressing anger over the air raids. Some threw stones at the POWs. When the train at last pulled out, the POWs were happy to leave Bangkok behind.

At the Bampong rail junction, the train switched to the southbound tracks, creeping slowly toward Malaya. In one car Harry Pickett was enlisted to help with another medical crisis. One of the men had developed a big abscess

23

on his bottom. A medical attendant operated, lancing the swelling with one swift stroke of his scalpel. Pickett ripped up a tunic and swabbed the wound. He remained by the man's side for the rest of the trip, doing all he could to ease his agonizing pain.

The train chugged slowly southward into the jungles of Malaya. It stopped once or twice a day at railside troop kitchens. The prisoners debarked, ate, filled canteens with water and went to the toilet in the woods. In the larger cities, such as Penang and Kuala Lumpur, they were shocked to find the throngs of natives in rags and starving. The economy of Malaya, they learned, had suffered a drastic decline during the long, rapacious Japanese occupation. The country was destitute. There was little or no rice reaching it from Thailand or Indochina. The Australians gave the natives rice, receiving in turn clusters of bananas and other fruit. Seeing this impoverishment, the prisoners were very glad they were only briefly passing through.

Finally the ghastly trip was over. On July 4—American Independence Day—the train crossed the causeway onto Singapore island. The men debarked at the main station, again touched by the appalling poverty and hunger of the natives, the gloom hanging over once-gay Singapore. From the station they marched listlessly through the steaming hot city to a transient POW compound, called River Valley Road.

PART TWO

Singapore

(1)

At Tamuan, Thailand, an all-British POW camp a few miles east of Kanchanaburi, an electrifying pronouncement swept the camp: "All fit men go Nippon." A few days later, there was a medical inspection, almost a duplicate of that the Australians had endured earlier at Tamarkan. The Japanese subjected the British to the same cruel selection process that destroyed unit integrity and severed close friendships. Formed, like the Australians, into 150-man *kumis,* with officers in charge and medical attendants, the British were told to prepare for early movement to Singapore, where they would catch a ship to Japan.

The British POWs had carried out the major share of the work on the Railway of Death in Thailand. They had first built the so-called "Bridge over the River Kwai" near Kanchanaburi, then pushed the railway up the banks of the Kwai River toward the Burma border, where they linked up with the Australians. They had suffered cruel losses, far worse than the Australians had in Burma. Two outfits, "F Force" and "H Force," comprising about 10,000 men of all nationalities, had been devastated. Of the 6,000 British POWs in these two units, 2,742 had died—an appalling death rate of 45.7 percent. About one-fifth of these had been struck down by the dreaded cholera (a severe, usually fatal form of dysentery), which was more prevalent in Thailand than in Burma. That many more British had not died in Thailand was a tribute to the human will, an extraordinary and compelling desire to live. These survivors—pathetic scarecrows all—were withdrawn from the railway and sent to "rest camps" and "hospitals" near Kanchanaburi. Tamuan, like Tamarkan, was a "rest camp."

Many of these POWs were members of the 17,000-man British 18th Division. Originally designated for duty in the Middle East, the 18th had been diverted to Singapore in another ill-conceived and futile eleventh-hour attempt to stop the Japanese. Hurled into the shambles of the retreating Allied forces, the division had been sacrificed to no purpose. No sooner had it debarked and deployed than the British General, Arthur E. Percival, surrendered. There had been no time for the division to build unit pride and solidarity in combat. The men, mostly green conscripts, were justifiably bewildered, disillusioned and resentful, not the best frame of mind for confronting the ordeal that lay ahead as POWs. Hundreds had died.

One of the survivors was Alfred G. Allbury, thirty-one, an aspiring writer, married and the father of one child. Held in Changi until October 1942, like most of the British, Allbury had come up to Thailand in a 600-man work party. He had survived fourteen months of brutality and starvation in the British camps at Tarsao and Tonchan and at Tonchan Spring, which was struck by a devastating cholera epidemic. Allbury had buried—or burned—the bodies of most of his friends. Toward the end, he had been lucky to get a job as cook for the Japanese and Korean guards. He ate well and recovered some of his strength, arriving at Tamuan in fairly good shape.

Having left these hideous slave camps behind, Allbury gaped "in wonderment" at the sight of Tamuan. Neat rows of well-made bamboo huts. Shade trees. Banana groves. Vegetable gardens. A swimming beach at the river. Good cooking facilities. Plenty of rice and even, occasionally, meat. Other than camp maintenance and expansion, there was no work of consequence, nothing to compare with the punishing ordeal on the railway. The hated Korean and Japanese guards from the railway were there, but their sadism and brutality were not so intense, and in this crowded camp, it was far easier to avoid the worst ones.

In one of the huts, Allbury was pleased to find an old buddy whom he had not seen in two years. He was Theodore Jewell, twenty-four, a carpenter, who, with his happy-go-lucky brother Reginald, twenty-one, had been assigned to the luckless 18th Division. Ted and Reggie had worked in a camp "up-country" near the Burma border. The camp had been hit by cholera. Ted had barely survived, but Reggie had died. Ted had dug his brother's grave and buried him. Now, Ted was very happy to see Allbury still alive. The two men became "muckers," or buddies, once again.

Another survivor at Tamuan was Thomas Pounder, thirty-one, onetime hotel clerk. Pounder had slaved at the British camps Tarsao, Wampo South, Kai-Saio and Takanum. Two of these camps had been hit by cholera. Pounder had suffered from dysentery, malaria and beri-beri (a vitamin deficiency that causes the body to itch unbearably or swell grotesquely). Once he had been beaten nearly to death by a sadistic Korean, "Black Bastard." He had arrived at Tamuan without a mucker, but soon he and Douglas Spon-Smith, twenty-five, a meat dealer, struck up a friendship. Spon-Smith had left a pregnant wife in England. He had not heard from her. He had survived thirty-two attacks of malaria on the railway and, compared with Pounder, was in pretty fair shape, and growing stronger every day at Tamuan.

Still another was Sergeant G. R. "Roll" Parvin, twenty-five. He, too, had left a pregnant wife in England, but he had received a letter from her in Singapore and knew he had a daughter. Roll Parvin and his mucker, Harry Currie, had worked at Tarsao and Tonchan. Parvin had nearly died of malaria and dysentery. He had had the good luck to be one of the first evacuated to the base "hospital" at Chungkai, near Kanchanaburi. He had lain near death for six months; then, almost miraculously, he had recovered. Finally considered "fit," he had been discharged from Chungkai and transferred, along with hundreds of others, to Tamuan. He, too, was pleasantly surprised at what he found at this "rest camp."

Yet another was Sergeant Henry W. "Johnny" Sherwood, a famous sports celebrity in England (pro football). A big man physically, Sherwood was married to a beauty queen and had one son. He was probably in better shape than any other POW in Thailand. Like Allbury, he had wrangled a cook's job on the railway and gorged himself to 238 pounds—70 pounds over his normal weight. But he had lost that job, become ill with dysentery and arrived at Tamuan a walking skeleton like most of the others. Since then, he had been building himself up at an astounding rate. He recalled: "This rest camp was built right in the middle of a banana plantation. . . . Did we eat! It was nothing for us to eat nearly a hundred bananas a day." Duck eggs could be purchased from the natives "for almost nothing." He recalled that he and his mucker, Benjamin Russell, were eating "over a hundred duck eggs a day." They improvised a frying pan and cooked omelets. "Just imagine a twenty-five-duck-egg omelet! Did we look well." Once again Sherwood's weight had zoomed. Now it was 252 pounds!

Another sergeant was Harry Jones, twenty-eight. Son of a regular army man, Jones, too, had joined the regular army, becoming a radio specialist in the Signal Corps. He had been posted to Singapore in 1937 and captured with the fall of the city. Against all rules, Jones had built, during his months of imprisonment, four or five radios. These radios, secreted from the Japanese, had provided the POWs at Changi, and later on the railway, their principal source of news of the outside world. In addition, to his mechanical talents, Jones was an intelligence specialist who spoke several native dialects. He, too, was keeping a diary, especially noting possible Allied bombing targets. He was convinced that sooner or later he would escape and the information would be valuable.

All these survivors—Alf Allbury, Ted Jewell, Tom Pounder, Doug Spon-Smith, Roll Parvin, Harry Currie, Johnny Sherwood, Benjamin Russell and Harry Jones—were chosen for the British Japan Party. They, too, had mixed reactions. Most of them feared a submarine attack at sea and did not want to go. Sherwood remembered that the news was a "crushing blow." Alone among them, Harry Jones was eager to go. He believed that somewhere along the journey, perhaps even at sea, he would make good his escape.

Like the Australians, the British were amazed to learn they would be issued a new kit for the trip. Theirs turned out to be a bizarre and colorfully mismatched collection of clothing: captured Dutch army green tunics, captured British army white T-shirts, cotton gym shorts (bright pink, blue, yellow or green, some with floral patterns) of completely mysterious origin, white undershorts and socks, green straw hats and Japanese rubber shoes. The gay shorts evoked earthy comments and gales of laughter. The speculation was they must be Chinese women's bloomers. The colorful garb set the Japan Party apart, giving them a special air, like "The Chosen Men" of the Australian Japan Party.

A few days later, word passed through the huts for the

Japan Party to pack and parade. It would leave immediately for Singapore. The leave-taking at Tamuan, like that at Tamarkan, turned out to be a rigidly formal and touching ceremony. The entire camp was ordered out. The Japanese, wearing full uniforms and swords, stood fiercely erect on a reviewing platform in front of the administration office. A six-piece British band took up position beside the platform.

The Japan Party paraded and counted off by *kumis* in Japanese. Again, amid much bowing, official orders were handed over and the columns began to move out. The band struck up "The Colonel Bogey March," a traditional British army song. (Years later it would be made world-famous by the defiantly whistling POWs in the film *The Bridge on the River Kwai.*) When the columns approached the Japanese dignitaries on the platform, the British officer in charge commanded: "Eyes left." As they filed past the Japanese, eyes dutifully left, the POWs broke into song: the insultingly obscene words of "The Colonel Bogey March." The words were unmistakably directed at the solemn, uncomprehending Japanese.

This moment was forever impressed on the mind of Alf Allbury. Ten years later he recalled: "There was a confused blur of pinks and yellows and greens, the bobbing of broad straw hats, the clatter and din of pots and pans tied onto our packs, as triumphantly we passed through the gate still raucously paying tribute to our conquerors. It was for everyone, including those left behind, one of the most uniquely moving moments of the war. Whatever tomorrow might bring, today had been ours."

(2)

The Party marched to the railway, where a special POW train was parked on a siding. It was a string of small, steel boxcars. The British POWs knew these dreadful cars well. They had come up from Singapore in them a year and a half ago. As before, they were jammed in, thirty men to a car. Although the prisoners were now more accustomed to deprivation and discomfort, the rice cars in the heat of an equatorial summer were not easy to take. They were filthy and airless, the steel walls sizzling to the touch.

The train moved onto the main line. It ran the short distance to the junction at Bampong and turned south toward Malaya—and Singapore. Harry Jones made a note of the many new workshops and sidings at the junction. These, too, were deserving of Allied bombs.

By this time, there was intense fighting in Burma. A steady stream of Japanese reinforcements was coming north in troop trains. From Bampong these trains would go over the railway to Burma. The POW train was frequently shunted to sidings to make way for the higher priority troop trains. Observing the Japanese soldiers—they looked like mere boys—the hardened POWs sneered inwardly. They hoped and prayed that one of the shaky bridges or trestles they had built would give way and plunge these soldiers to a hideous death.

One of those wishing the Japanese the worst possible fate was Roy A. Hudson, thirty-one. Hudson had been a gardener for the Duke of Devonshire at his famous Chatsworth estate, later a foreman at the Royal Botanic Gardens, outside London. He was married. He had a prized souvenir in his tattered haversack: a fine portrait by fellow POW Ronald Searle, twenty-four, an artist, later to gain great fame. Hudson had paid Searle about fifty cents to do the portrait. He kept it rolled in a bamboo tube, like a Japanese scroll.

Another sneering POW was Albert E. B. Hall, twenty-five, a Welshman, who, like Johnny Sherwood, had been a famous pro football player before the war. He, also, was married and had children. Hall was recklessly hot-tempered, a troublesome prisoner, one of the most punished on the railway, who lived to tell about it. He had been repeatedly "bashed" with bamboo sticks, picks and rifle butts. He had been buried up to his neck for three days and tied to a tree for a like time. But the Japanese had not yet tamed Albert Hall. He hated Japanese with every ounce of his considerable strength. Many of his fellow POWs feared Hall, believing that he took unnecessary risks and that he might someday bring the roof down on all their heads.

The train crept south into Malaya, the British, too, were shocked at the destitute condition of the natives Harry Jones recalled: "Gone were the smiles of old and the cries of children playing in the streets. . . . Instead I now saw a silent hollow-eyed populace with skeleton-like children crying for food from even POWs who had little enough themselves. One or two prisoners could not resist giving a portion of their meager ration to a few children. . . . Unfortunately this was seen. One little girl did not get away quickly enough. One of the Korean guards brutally kicked the poor child in the stomach."

The train rolled into Kuala Lumpur. The station, once as clean and beautiful as a sultan's palace, was now, under Japanese management, filthy and seedy. A Japanese sergeant ordered Jones to carry rice from the railside kitchen to the POW cars. However, the Japanese cooks had not yet got the rice ready Jones: "The Japanese sergeant was so mad he knocked the cook in charge into a vat of boiling water. The man's screams could be heard all over the station. If he's still alive, I'm sure he bears the scars to this day." While waiting, Jones, seeking intelligence information, struck up a conversation with a Tamil. For that, he was viciously bashed in the face.

The following day—the fifth en route—the train crossed the causeway into Singapore. It stopped at Singapore station, near the Keppel Harbor docks. Jones, noticing there were few ships in the harbor, recalled: "Apparently business was not too good or the Allied submarines had perhaps been taking a heavy toll of Jap shipping." From Singapore station, the POWs marched in the sweltering heat to a transient camp This time they did not sing. Allbury remembered that the party was "disheveled, tired and irritable, with our gay shirts filthy and torn and our straw hats battered beyond all recognition."

The transient camp was one of the worst they had ever seen. It consisted of row after row of dilapidated open-sided bamboo huts with attap roofs, the whole surrounded by a high wooden fence. A filthy stream (the "River") cut the camp in half. On one side it was known as River Valley Road, on the other as Havelock Road. The camp had been built before the war to house native refugees. But even they had spurned it. Since the war, the Japanese had used it for temporary housing Long deserted, it was now filling up with the transient Japan Parties coming down from Thailand. The British were distributed between the two camps.

A POW who was billeted on the Havelock Road side, Geoffrey P. Adams, remembered that his hut was rat-infested. The men organized a rat-killing program with small cash prizes. Adams: "A perfect massacre followed. The rats had become overconfident, boldly scampering all over our sleeping platforms and up and down the bamboos supporting our three-decker shacks, and the winning team killed over four hundred. Some of them seemed big as cats."

Of much greater concern to the POWs than the vermin-infested huts was the food situation. It was soon apparent that the severe scarcity of food observed in up-country Malaya also prevailed in Singapore. The POWs were reduced to the starvation-level rations they had been issued on the railway. These consisted of one mug of fish- or vegetable-flavored rice three times a day and, occasionally, a mug of watery stew. Allbury: "Tamuan, with its abundance of rice, vegetables and bananas, became a tormenting reminder of a paradise to which there could be no return." Those who had recovered their health at Tamuan began to sink again.

Hoping to sail any day from this wretched place, the British were sorely disappointed. On the day after their arrival, the men were divided into small working parties and sent to the Singapore docks to load and unload ships alongside the native coolies. Tom Pounder welcomed the work, to break the monotony of the waiting. Compared with their labors on the railway, the work on the docks was not difficult He said that "there was no rush, no 'speedo,' and the work . . . was quite leisurely." They loaded ships with tin, lead, rubber, loose cement, coal, copra and ton after ton of scrap iron of every description.

Among the British dockworkers fresh from Thailand was Ernest S. Benford, twenty-two. He had an unusual family saga to tell. His father, a World War I veteran, was a career army man Long before the war, he had been posted to Singapore. On the eve of the hostilities he was still there with his wife and Ernest's younger sister. Ernest, who had joined the army in 1936, arrived in Singapore with his unit in late November 1941. The unit was rushed north before he could make contact with his family. Later he spent a day with his mother and sister in Kuala Lumpur but had yet to see his father, who was based in Changi. War came. Ernest was wounded in the fighting. By then, dependents were being evacuated, but Ernest's mother refused to go because Ernest had been wounded. Then Ernest was advised that *he* would be evacuated to England. He in turn refused to be evacuated because his mother would not leave.

Later, in mid-January, Ernest had been transferred to a makeshift hospital in Singapore. From his bed he saw his father for the first time, walking along the sidewalk. Ernest called out. His father, who was then a captain quartermaster, was shocked speechless to find his son wounded and hospitalized. Ten days later his mother and sister were ordered out on the *Duchess of Bedford*. Father and son saw them off. (The ship was bombed by the Japanese, limped into Sumatra for repairs and eventually reached England.) Ernest and his father took up quarters in a house The house received a direct bomb hit and was destroyed. Ernest moved to another hospital, which was bombed out, then finally to a high school converted to a medical facility.

After the surrender, father and son had met in a Singapore POW camp. Ernest's father's unit was ordered to Thailand to work on the railway. Although still recovering from his wound, Ernest, then nineteen, volunteered to join his father's work unit. They were together at camps Kanu and Kanu II. But in January 1943 the senior Benford came down with amebic dysentery and was sent to an isolation "hospital" near Kanchanaburi. Ernest was sent north. In June he learned that his father had died in April. On the docks in Singapore, Benford met a marine who had been with his father when he died. "Whilst they were talking, Father asked for a drink of water. The marine went to the end of the hut where the drinking water container was kept. When he returned, Father was dead. He gave me the last note Father had written: a request to his superiors for an advance on the salary due him, so he wouldn't have to go into the isolation hospital without any money." Ernest had put the note among his pitiful valuables.

Like the Australians in Saigon, the British soon became adept at stealing food: rice, sugar, cocoa, beans, peanuts and even palm oil, which they used for frying and as a flavoring for rice. The guards were not so casual as the guards in Saigon. Each night there were thorough searches before the men returned to the camp. Anyone caught suffered severe punishment.

Allbury remembered the time four men were caught stealing a piddling quantity of rice. The Japanese were furious: "They dragged them out of the ranks and gave them the most savagely brutal beating-up. Sweating and grunting, their vicious yellow faces distorted with rage, they continued to thud their heavy boots into the prostrate figures on the ground long after the men had lost consciousness."

Albert Hall, the pro football player, in league with some others, made a marvelous find. One go-down was packed with cases of cigarettes. As Thomas Smith, twenty-three, a haberdashery salesman, remembered, Albert Hall led a break-in. The men smashed open the cases and crammed their pockets with packages of this valuable commodity. But the Japanese discovered the theft in progress Most of the gang managed to heave the cigarettes into the water, but Hall was caught with his. His punishment, Smith recalled, was a severe bashing and, worst of all, he was put on reduced rations for several days.

Even so, the men continued to steal food. Since they wore little clothing, concealment was difficult until one POW came up with an ingenious solution. He soldered a partition across the interior of his canteen, making a "dry" false bottom with a second corked hole for access. During the day he filled the bottom of the canteen with loot. At the evening inspections he removed the cork from the top ("wet") end of the canteen and poured the residue of water on the ground to prove the canteen did not contain contraband. Other POWs copied this invention and it was soon the universal method of concealment. The deception was never discovered by the Japanese

Some of the POWs found another source of food at the docks, an odd one. There were at that time two German vessels in Singapore—a submarine and a freighter. Christopher T. "Paddy" Dunne, thirty, an Irish-born regular army man, remembered that the German naval personnel on the freighter despised the Japanese and were openly sympathetic with the POWs. A work party was assigned to load supplies on the freighter. Dunne recalled that when the POWs were below decks—out of sight of the Japanese guards—the Germans invited the POWs to help themselves to food. The prisoners devoured black bread and butter, bully beef and cheese. For some time the Germans on this ship (and on the submarine as well) continued to supplement the diet of the British POWs.

Still, there was never enough to eat. *In extremis,* the

men stalked or laid traps for the many cats and occasional dogs that strolled through camp. They had no luck with dogs, but Pounder recalled they managed to trap about "one cat every week until the supply ran out." They skinned them and stewed the edible portions. Pounder: "The results were remarkably like boiled chicken and to us just as delicious and satisfying."

The distribution of the meager rice ration at mealtimes became an exacting, touchy business. Allbury recalled that "animalism and bad temper began to creep back into meal queues." Pounder remembered that the men watched the servers like hawks and if one thought another got slightly more, "an argument ensued." It reached the point that the men elected the servers by popular vote. Pounder's mucker, Doug Spon-Smith, was usually a popular choice.

Soon the men began to weaken and fall ill with the vitamin deficiency diseases that had weakened so many on the railway: beriberi, pellagra, acute dermatitis, dysentery and malaria. The queues at sick call grew longer daily. The "hospital" expanded from a "tiny hut" to infinitely larger quarters. Soon the small quantity of hoarded or stolen medicine was exhausted. Allbury remembered that the medical officer in his *kumi* could do nothing for the men "apart from sympathetic words and ordering men back to their blankets." Allbury came down with a "frightful" attack of dengue fever. He was bedridden, nearly delirious, for three full weeks, during which time he ate nothing at all and soon became skeletal.

Into this dismal scene, on July 4, 1944, Brigadier Varley's Australian Japan Party arrived from Saigon. It was an unforgettable moment. Allbury recalled: "They were an unruly, undisciplined, happy-go-lucky mob. 'Hot, sweet and filthy' [tea or coffee] came swinging through the huts again. Traders came padding among us hawking their boots, spoons and other superfluous items in exchange for a wad of tobacco. Unused huts disintegrated, and little fires with tins and cans bubbling over them again lit dark corners of the camp. Even at Havelock Road, they still found something to brew, boil or fry. There is nothing quite so unquenchable as a 'Digger.' Havelock Road was a brighter place for their presence."

37

(3)

The Australians were shocked by the appalling conditions they found at River Valley Road. Shabby, vermin-infested attap huts. Starvation rations. Canteens with a few goodies—but prices so inflated no one could afford to buy anything. Vicious and sadistic guards. The Australians could not leave this place fast enough. Even the perilous sea voyage to Japan was preferable.

But there was no sign of a ship to transport them to Japan. Again, something had gone wrong. Like the British —also awaiting transport—the Australians were assigned to dock work parties. Here, as in Saigon, the Australians engaged in wanton thievery of food to supplement the meager official ration. And, like the British, they soon sensed the sympathetic mood of the Germans on the freighter and submarine. Ray Wheeler, John Wade, twenty-six, a salesman, and many others availed themselves of this curious hospitality.

Alas, the bonanza was short-lived. One day a Japanese guard mistook one of the German submariners lounging on the dock for a POW. He gave the German a swift kick. The German leaped up in a rage and, as John Wade recalled, "threw the Jap about twenty-five feet into the sea." This provoked a tense confrontation between Germans and Japanese, with the POWs scurrying to the sidelines, silently cheering the Germans. Thereafter, Wheeler remembered, "the sub and freighter were shifted over to the old coaling pier—quite a way off"—beyond reach of the POW work parties.

Not many ships called at Singapore now. Many of those that did, arrived badly damaged by torpedoes, hardly a reassuring sight for the soon-to-be-passengers. The Japanese guards blithely dismissed the damage as due to "collisions in the fog" or other noncombatant causes. However, the Chinese and Malay coolies working on the docks knew better. They told the POWs frankly

38

that the cause was the American submarine blockade. Many ships left Singapore, but "Americana boom-boom" destroyed them at sea. Very few reached Japan, maybe one in ten.

When a ship did reach Singapore, the dockworkers loaded it with tin, rubber and scrap metal. It appeared that everything in Malaya made of metal had been torn down or salvaged and sent to the docks. Stanley J. Manning, twenty-seven, a gold assayer before the war, was astonished by one particular load of scrap: "The Japs had called in all the metal currency in Malay, Thailand and Indochina and issued paper money. One day a whole trainload of these coins arrived at the dock. Thousands and thousands of bags of coins, being sent to Japan as scrap metal, we assumed. We loaded them on the ship along with the tin and rubber."

Life at River Valley Road camp was miserable in the extreme. The food—after Saigon—was awful and never enough. R. Douglas Hampson, twenty-nine, a gold miner, recalled: "In the morning we got a half cup of pap—boiled rice stirred until it was soup. Lunch was a fourth of a cup of rice. Supper was a half-cup of rice and dried fish about the size of your index finger. If no fish, we got boiled wild bananas—they turned purple—about as big as your thumb."

The Australians scrounged through the camp, searching for anything edible. They ate grass and frogs from the filthy river. Harold Ramsey recalled that he and four of his mates ("the five biggest thieves in the camp") had many misadventures and close calls with the guards. One night Ramsey and his mates stole a chicken. "Our chap grabbed the chicken by the ass instead of his neck. It made a terrible noise. A Jap guard approached. We let the chicken go. Then I told all the chaps to kneel down and fold their hands and close their eyes. When the guard reached us, I told him that every night at that time the five of us met at that spot to pray. So it was okay. He left us alone."

By this time, all the huts were in disrepair, sagging badly and dangerously unstable. The men lived in fear that a hut would collapse. One night in mid-July, this fear became reality. A British hut fell over with a terrific crash. The Australians rushed from their huts. They saw the British madly tearing at the debris to free those who had been buried under the bamboo and the attap roof.

Tom Pounder and Doug Spon-Smith were in this hut. They slept on the top row of the double tiered sleeping platforms. When the hut collapsed, they were fortunately buried only by the attap roof. The men in the lower sleeping platforms were crushed beneath the weight of the top platforms, the men on the platforms and the roof. Pounder and Spon-Smith and two dozen others slowly lifted the massive roof and extricated those trapped under it. Luckily, no one was killed, but "twenty or thirty" were seriously injured, several knocked unconscious. The following day, the most seriously injured of the men—perhaps a dozen—were transferred to Changi hospital. Pounder remembered it well: "They were lucky in one respect—they would be taken off the draft for Japan."

The Australians and British took measures to prop the other huts firmly, but still the men lived in fear of another collapse. A few nights later a loud—never explained—noise touched off a panic. Roy Whitecross recalled: "Men still half asleep rushed headlong from each hut, trampling down others in their path. Those sleeping on the upper platforms jumped pell mell to the ground, and many of them sprained ankles; one broke a bone in his foot when he jumped into the drain dug alongside the hut."

There was one moment of relief in this tedious, unhappy—and uncertain—existence. The Japanese inexplicably doled out a few of the thousands of Red Cross packages and mailbags they had confiscated over the years since the war had begun. The Red Cross packages contained Spam, chocolate, sugar, condensed milk, crackers, dried fruit and cigarettes. Leslie J. Bolger, twenty-three, a sporting goods manufacturer, recalled that eight to ten men shared each of the Red Cross packages. His share was one can of Spam. The mail was eighteen months to two years old. Not all of it was cheery. Mac McKittrick remembered that two of his close mates received very depressing news from their mothers. One mate's wife had died; the other was running around with a "Yank." The two men became very depressed and "just seemed to give up. They went downhill fast after those letters."

Brigadier Varley, back in Singapore after an absence of twenty-one months and expecting to sail for Japan at any hour, was extremely anxious to make contact with the

40

senior Allied POW at Changi, Major General "Black Jack" Callaghan. Varley, too, had been keeping a diary, which he still had, along with POW muster rolls and several secret reports on Japanese atrocities on the railway. Fearing he might not get back to Australia, he wished to turn these documents over to Callaghan and to make an oral report on his activities since he had left Changi. But how to make contact with Callaghan?

John Wade, now serving as a medical orderly, agreed to be the go-between. Wade recalled: "In our outfit, we had twenty or thirty men who'd come down with what appeared to be blackwater fever. We arranged to have these men transferred to Changi hospital. I went along as medical orderly and took Varley's papers with me. At Changi I got word to General Callaghan. He came to see me and took the papers. Then he told me to tell Varley to request dental treatment at Changi. That was arranged and thereafter Varley was in close contact with Callaghan." After making his reports, Varley buried his diary at Changi, revealing its location to several officers who were ordered to dig it up after the war should he not return.

Rowley Richards, the young doctor, followed Varley's example. Richards was an obsessive pack rat and record keeper. At this point he had a complete roster of his original outfit, the 15th Battalion, on which he had noted deaths and other pertinent personal data. He contrived another medical reason for visiting Changi hospital and, while there, turned these over to trusted authorities. He returned to camp to discover that a majority of the Australian Japan Party was to move once more—not to Japan but to yet another location in Singapore, for a very special work detail.

(4)

The new home for the majority of the Australians was even worse than River Valley Road. It was a small island, Damar Laut, in the southwest section of Keppel Harbor. It had no facilities, no water, little food, nothing to steal and an obnoxious, sadistic commandant whom

41

the Australians derisively nicknamed "The Jeep" owing to his squat, pudgy build. The Australians renamed the island in his honor: "Jeep Island."

The new work assignment was more coolie labor: assisting some natives who, under Japanese supervision, were digging a graving dock (a shore-based dry dock facility) on the shore opposite Jeep Island. The proposed dock was to be enormous: 525 feet by 100 feet, with a depth of 45 feet, almost big enough for a battleship. The natives and other POWs had been working on it for two years. It was now about 20 or 25 feet deep. Three shifts a day of one thousand men each (mostly natives) were employed at this task. Most of the Australians were assigned to a night shift. They commuted to work from Jeep Island in motorized barges.

The Australians detected at once that this project, "a bloody big hole in the ground," did not have a high priority. Nothing like the frantic pace on the railway. They set to work with picks and shovels on the night shift—under poor lights—at an almost comically slow pace. They slowly filled the winch-drawn line of cars at the bottom of the pit. At every possible opportunity they derailed the cars, laughing uproariously as the little train crashed back down, spilling the dirt back into the hole. One POW estimated that at the rate they were progressing it would take four more years to finish the dock—sometime in 1948!

The Japanese resorted to every known means to speed up the work. First, minor force. Doug Hampson, who celebrated his thirtieth birthday on Jeep Island on August 2, recalled: "One Nip lieutenant used to spend his time sitting on the bank throwing stones at us." Then the Japanese shifted to the carrot-and-stick method. Hampson: "He got the idea of giving cigarettes or fruit to the team that did the most work. That didn't help either. We got our heads together and decided your turn today, our turn tomorrow."

The food shortage on Jeep Island was severe. The Australians, fattened up at Saigon, now began to waste away and the sick queues in Rowley Richards' medical hut grew longer each day. The men foraged in the trees for coconuts and along the seashore for shellfish or anything else edible. The schoolteacher, Alf Winter, son of a planter, had grown up in Ceylon and could scale a coconut tree like a monkey. Although strictly forbidden, he harvested many coconuts. Vic Clifford, engaged at this one day, was warned that a guard was approaching. In near panic, he slid down the tree trunk, burning raw the skin of his chest, arms and legs.

The foraging on the beach for shellfish resulted in tragedy. Unknown to the men, the water was polluted. Several of them, including William E. T. Mayne, twenty-three, became violently ill: "I had to go to the toilet so often I just lay down beside it." One man, Corporal S. R. Gorlick, died. It was the first death in the group since the railway, and the shock was profound. He was buried with appropriate military honors in a "lonely" grave on the island.

The Jeep took exception to the growing lists of sick. He suspected malingering. One morning he arrived in the "hospital" and insisted, over Rowley Richards' protests, on inspecting the men himself. Stopping at Maurice Barkley, who was not only feverish but also had a bad case of beriberi, The Jeep demanded that Barkely report to work the following day. Richards explained that Barkley had almost died three days past and that he would not be fit for work for a long time.

The Jeep was livid. He harangued Richards for ten minutes in broken English. Richards, unyielding, fired a shot reserved for very special occasions: "If you send this man to work, he will die! After the war I will speak to my government. My government will speak to your government and you will be tried for murder."

Screaming in rage, The Jeep lunged at Richards with a piece of wood. He bashed him on the head and beat him with his fists, chipping the doctor's teeth and causing his lips to swell. Richards endured the beating, determined not to fall down, "because then he'd get me with his boots." Finally The Jeep stalked out, huffing and red-faced, muttering Japanese imprecations.

Quixotically, The Jeep returned a few minutes later carrying a bowl of tea and three small rice balls. He offered these to Richards and said, "So sorry. Now all okay?" Richards replied no, pointing to Barkley, reminding The Jeep that the issue was as yet unresolved. The Jeep yielded. Barkley would not have to work. When The Jeep had left, Richards smiled grimly through swollen lips and said, "We won!" Maurice corrected him:

"You won." They shared the curious offering, Richards taking the tea, Barkley the rice balls.

The Australians assigned to Jeep Island spent a hungry, miserable five weeks, from July 27 to September 3. That last day, with no previous warning, The Jeep announced: "All men go Nippon." They would be returned to River Valley Road that day, rejoin the other Australians and ship out the very next day. The Australians greeted this pronouncement with considerable skepticism. It had now been almost six months since they had first heard those words in faraway Tamarkan. They had traveled thousands of seemingly aimless miles. Was this another false alarm or was it for real? Dr. Richards thought it might be true this time. He distilled to one page the six-page summary of the diary he had left at Tamarkan and concealed it in his stethoscope. He buried the six-page summary in Corporal Gorlick's lonely grave, a place that would be easy to find after the war.

PART THREE

The Convoy

(1)

At dawn on September 4, the River Valley Road–Havelock Road camp complex throbbed with excitement and activity. Japanese guards strode imperiously through the huts shouting: "All men go Nippon. All men go Nippon." Evidently it was for real. Two cargo-transports at the Singapore docks—ships some of the POWs had loaded with tin, rubber, copra and the usual scrap iron—had been designated for the trip. They would embark and sail this very day.

The Japan Party assigned to these ships would consist of 2,250 men. The majority—1,500—were to be British, taken from the *kumis* that had been coming down from Tamuan since late May. Some had been at the River Valley Road–Havelock Road complex for three months. Others had only just arrived. The remainder of the Party—some 750 men—would be the original Australian Japan Party less *Kumi* 40, for which there was no room. Several other recently arrived Australian *kumis* were also left behind.

The deletion of *Kumi* 40 caused distress among some Australians of the original Japan Party. Again, close friends were separated: for example, Roy Whitecross and James Campbell, both of the Australian 8th Division Headquarters Staff. Campbell, a cheery lad with a mustache and a gap between his front teeth, limped from an ankle injury sustained in peacetime maneuvers and severely aggravated on the railway. Whitecross, who was staying behind, had a premonition that the convoy would be sunk but that somehow Campbell would be rescued and returned to Australia. The premonition was so compelling he advised Campbell to stay topside on the ship at all times. He asked Campbell to look up his family when he reached Australia. "Tell them I'm okay, Jimmy. Don't tell them I've been sick, just say I've been lucky."

47

The Britisher Charles J. Armstrong, twenty-five, a devout Catholic from Liverpool and a physical-fitness fanatic, had had a similar premonition about himself: "I had visions of being sunk on a Jap ship and then being picked up. I dreamed this same dream three nights before we left. I wanted to go very much and take a chance." He believed, like the British Sergeant Harry Jones, that somehow he would be rescued.

Ray Wheeler also believed he would be sunk at sea—but was not so sure he would survive. This led him to give a valued and highly dangerous possession to Reginald Josephs, a mate remaining behind. After the surrender, in violation of POW rules, Wheeler had kept his small German-made camera. In Burma he had shot all the film he possessed—three rolls of sixteen frames each. Among the exposures was proof of one of the most-remembered Japanese atrocities on the railway: pictures of the graves of eight Australian soldiers of the 4th Anti-tank Regiment, executed, without trial, for attempting escape, as a "lesson" to others. Wheeler had thrown the camera away long ago, but he kept the exposed rolls wrapped in silver foil and raw rubber in the bottom of a shaving stick holder. Josephs willingly took possession of the hidden evidence, promising to safeguard it and turn it over to authorities after the war, if he lived and the film survived.

At 0700 hours the Japan Party paraded for a final inspection and head count. There was hectic confusion in all *kumis*. Some men, still packing their pitiful belongings or, like Wheeler, passing contraband and valuables to mates, were late for formation. Others were too ill to leave the huts. Medical officers, wherever permitted, disqualified the gravely ill. (Other sick were subdivided into "walking sick" and "riding sick.") The men were forced to count off, in Japanese, again and again. At length the British mustered the full quota of 1,500 men, drawing odd lots from other *kumis*. The Australian Kumis 35 to 39 inclusive had been reduced by attrition from 750 men to 718, but no effort was made to fill the gaps from *Kumi* 40 or other sources. Thus the final head count before leaving camp was 2,218 men.

This day there was no formal leave-taking ceremony, no bands, no speeches. The men marched quietly out of camp in one long line. For the most part, they were far from being the "fit" men Tokyo had requested almost six months past. The temporary physical buildup at Tamuan and Saigon—an interlude that had saved many lives—had been wiped out by the weeks of waiting on starvation rations in Singapore. All too many men were once more ravaged by malaria, dysentery, beriberi, pellagra. New kits had been issued some of the British, but most of the men—and all the Australians—wore tattered clothing.

Alf Allbury, suffering from dengue fever, which had turned his "legs to water," had been designated "riding sick." But no transport materialized. He and other "walking sick" trailed along behind the main formation, struggling to keep up, while a Korean guard "ran from one end of the column to the other snarling and yapping like a bad-tempered dog at the heels of a herd of cattle." The sick did not "march" the three miles to the dock but rather "tottered and reeled there, grasping thankfully at the cool drinks that the sympathetic Chinese gave us en route."

The two ships waiting at the quay were the passenger-cargo vessels *Rakuyo Maru* and *Kachidoki Maru*. They were similar in appearance, size, tonnage, accommodations and age. Each had cargo holds, masts, and cranes fore and aft, a commodious passenger area amidships (about one-third the length of the ship), from which a single tall smokestack protruded. Each had about a dozen lifeboats, most on the boat deck in the midships passenger area but some on the raised stern deck, or poop. The *Rakuyo Maru*, 477 feet overall, displaced 9,500 tons; the *Kachidoki Maru*, 524 feet overall, displaced 10,500 tons. Both ships were twenty-three years old—launched and placed in service in 1921. The *Rakuyo Maru* had been built by the Mitsubishi Shipbuilding Company in Nagasaki, Japan; the *Kachidoki Maru* by the New York Shipbuilding Company in Camden, New Jersey. Both were painted battle gray, both flew the "Rising Sun" merchant marine flag (a red ball in the center of a white field). Neither was marked with a red cross or any other indication that it was transporting prisoners of war.

The American-built *Kachidoki Maru* had a checkered history. She first entered service as a passenger-cargo liner on the North Atlantic run, owned by the United States Lines and christened *Wolverine State*. Later she was owned by the Dollar Line. Still later, she was acquired by the American President Lines, renamed *Presi-*

dent Harrison and transferred to the Pacific routes. Just before the war, she was chartered by the U.S. Navy to help transfer naval personnel and marines from Shanghai to the Philippines. When war came, she was overtaken by a Japanese cruiser off the China coast. In an effort to prevent the ship from falling into enemy hands, her Naval Reserve crew ran her onto the reefs and tore her bottom out. The crew was captured and imprisoned. The Japanese salvaged the ship and rechristened her *Kachidoki Maru.*

The rushed departure from the POW camp complex evolved into an old and familiar army exercise: Hurry up and wait. The ships were not yet ready for the POWs to embark. Each was still taking on the last of a cargo of rubber. The POWs fell out of formation, tossed gear onto the dock and sat or lay down in the blazing sun, already feeling hunger and thirst.

As they waited, natives engaged in loading the two ships strolled over to chat. They had little to offer but gloom and doom. A Chinese asked the Britisher Ernest Hughes, thirty-two, a coal miner (many of the British POWs were coal miners), where they were bound. When told Japan, the Chinese said: "You'll never get there." He drew a diagram in the dirt, depicting the extent of the submarine blockade. A Malay told Sergeant Harry Jones: "Live today, perhaps tomorrow you die." Jones was encouraged by this, believing it implied the Allies would have intelligence on the convoy and destroy it, thus opening the way for Jones to make good his escape and rescue.

The Japanese passed the word that no tobacco could be carried on board the ship; there would be no smoking whatsoever. The British POWs got the word and took it literally. The Australians either did not get the word or, typically, ignored it. The Britisher Thomas Smith, twenty-three: "We had a glorious time smoking up everything we had. Every Britisher went on board devoid of cigarettes. But the Australians had plenty of smokes— even big cigars. During the whole trip, we had to scrounge our smokes from them."

One Britisher, Charles A. Perry, thirty-one, a cabinetmaker who was married and had one daughter, had a special concern this day. On the railway, Perry had become a shrewd entrepreneur, buying, selling, trading. Early in the game, he hit on a scheme for making taffy candy from brown sugar and nuts. He was soon famous as "The Peanut Taffy Man." The candy sales had helped him survive the railway.

Now Perry was worried about $15,000 in Malayan currency he had wrapped in a cloth in his haversack. He had obtained the money one day while assigned to a work party that was burning huge piles of Malayan paper money that had been withdrawn in favor of Japanese occupation currency. He'd kept the money all this time for its curiosity value. Then, on arrival in Singapore, he had found to his astonishment—and glee—that it was still good, exchangeable at a favorable rate. Worried now that someone would steal the money, he decided to entrust it to the care of his *kumicho,* Lieutenant F. Keyes.

Perry might have believed that he was the richest POW in the history of warfare, but he was bush leaguer compared with a couple of hustling Australians, Francis B. "Frank" Johnson, twenty-six, and his mate Maxwell W. Curran, nearby on the dock. In league with a third POW, Curran and Johnson had accumulated the incredible sum of $70,000. They had begun to amass this money immediately before the surrender of Singapore when, as Johnson recalled, "You could just walk into a bank and help yourself." Johnson and his mates helped themselves to a goodly sum of Malayan dollars. On the railway, believing, as did Charlie Perry, that it was "play money," they had recklessly gambled with it, betting "as much as five hundred dollars on the turn of a card." After "scheming, trading and gambling" for two and a half years, they had run the stake to $70,000 in large-denomination British, U.S., Dutch and Malayan bills. Like Perry, they were thunderstruck to find the Malayan money still valuable. Johnson had stowed the money in a screw-top jar in his haversack. Nothing on earth could have persuaded him to turn it over to an officer for safekeeping. It was his—and his two pals'—postwar grubstake.

(2)

Hours passed. The hungry and thirsty POWs became more impatient and irritated. Finally the ships completed the loading of rubber and secured the booms. After that, the Japanese passengers began to arrive in a variety of vehicles. There were soldiers (including many wounded from the Burma front); female nurses in blouses and baggy trousers tied off at the ankles; civilians, including women and children. These went aboard the two ships (most of the wounded on *Kachidoki Maru*) with only slight delay. Then the Japanese guards shrilly ordered the POWs to fall again into *kumi* formation on the dock. At last, it appeared, this was it.

For what seemed the tenth time that day, the POWs lined up and counted off in crisp, staccato numbers: *"Ichie. Ni. San. Shi. Go . . ."* It was an impressive performance, one that Alf Allbury thought would have done credit to a crack Japanese regiment. The Japanese, including Lieutenant Yamada, looking down from the bridge of the *Rakuyo Maru,* nodded and gave "grunts of approval." After the count-off a Japanese on the dock divided the men between the two ships: 900 British (6 *kumis*) for *Kachidoki Maru,* 600 British (4 *kumis*) for *Rakuyo Maru,* all 718 Australians (5 depleted *kumis*) for *Rakuyo Maru.*

At the last moment, there were some minor adjustments in the head count. Two more Australians were disqualified physically and eliminated, reducing the total to 716. One Britisher assigned to *Rakuyo Maru* dropped out, leaving 599. Three senior officers joined the *Rakuyo Maru* POW group. These were Brigadier Varley; a British aviator, Group Captain James Winter Carmichael More; and an American Air Corps colonel, Harry R. Melton, Jr. This again brought the total POWs embarked on *Rakuyo Maru* to 1,318, of whom eight were officers. The total on *Kachidoki Maru* remained 900, including about eight officers. Total on both ships: 2,218.

The British aviator, Group Captain More, holder of the Order of British Empire Medal and a Distinguished Flying Cross, had been a POW for nineteen months. Based in Maungdow, Burma, on January 22, 1943, he had led a successful attack on the railway station in Prome, Burma. While he was pulling away, flak had hit More's Hurricane and he was forced to crash-land southwest of Prome. A fellow pilot reported seeing More standing on the ground outside the demolished aircraft looking at his leg, giving the "impression that he was wounded."

The lone American, Colonel Harry Melton, had been commander of the U.S. Army Air Corps' 311th Fighter-Bomber Group, a unit of the Tenth Air Force, based in eastern India. The unit had arrived in India eleven months earlier, in October 1943. A month later, November 27, Colonel Melton, flying a P-51 Mustang fighter, escorting bombers during a raid on the Insein locomotive works, just outside Rangoon, Burma, was shot down. His fellow pilots saw him bail out and, in their official reports, stated that he had landed "in territory where natives were generally friendly." But Melton had been captured and for the last eight months he had been confined to various Japanese POW camps. Like Varley, More and Melton were being transferred to senior officer POW camps.

Now, at last, it was time for the POWs to board their designated ships. On the way to the gangways, they were led through a go-down where great piles of raw rubber were stored. The Japanese issued each POW a shaped block of raw rubber about the size of a large attaché case (2 feet by 2 feet by 1 foot). A "handle" of rubber had been molded into the blocks. The Japanese explained to the puzzled POWs that the blocks of rubber were "life pre-servers." Charlie Perry hefted his rubber block doubtfully. He estimated it weighed perhaps thirty pounds. He doubted it would float, let alone support the weight of a man. He and others concluded rightly that the issue of these worthless "life preservers" was simply a clever way of cramming more rubber on the ships.

The *Rakuyo Maru* took aboard her POWs first: Brigadier Varley, Group Captain More, Colonel Melton, then the British and Australian *kumis*. As he edged toward the gangway, the Britisher Wilfred "Barney" Barnett, twenty-two, another coal miner, saw half a dozen young but homely, Japanese women standing at the rail.

He judged by their appearance that they were, in POW parlance, "jig-a-jig" girls, prostitutes supplied the Japanese army. The prostitutes gazed down suddenly, and when the POWs came within range, the prostitutes spat on them. Said Barnett: "You can imagine what language we came out with."

Kumi by *kumi* the POWs shuffled up the gangway onto the forward deck of the ship, herded along by Korean guards with sharply pointed bamboo sticks. The POWs saw that there were three large cargo loading hatches forward. Number 1 and Number 3 were "battened"— closed over with long planks with canvas lashed over these. Number 2 was not battened. The planks (or hatch boards) were stacked beside the large opening. Peering down into the upper level of Number 2 hold, a dark, hot, airless chasm about eight or nine feet deep, they saw this upper space had been converted for transporting Japanese troops. By the looks of things, this would be quarters for the men.

Although it was clear they were expected to occupy the hold, no one made the slightest move to do so. On the contrary, the men avoided the forbidding space and spread into every nook and cranny of the deck in surging confusion. Allbury described it: "Rope lockers, winches, the narrow stairway leading down into the hold, everywhere and anything that men could hang on to, lean against or squat on was seized, argued over and unwillingly shared. . . . The sloping hatch-cover on the forward hold, raised above the level of the deck, became a heaving sea of jostling humanity." The Australians bunched port, the British starboard. Allbury and his mate, Ted Jewell, crawled under a greasy winch, "an excellent spot." A "phlegmatic calm" settled over jam-packed decks as the men dozed, read or played cards, all the while growing hungrier and thirstier.

The toilet facilities, of necessity, were soon discovered. These consisted of six small wooden platforms with sides lashed outboard of the forward deck lifelines, three starboard, three port. To reach these, the men had to climb over the lifelines, a difficult task for the weaker ones with dysentery—those who required the facilities most urgently. There, thirty feet above the water, in open view of all on the ship, they squatted, the excrement falling through a slit in the floor of the platform. It lacked dignity and privacy, but it was functional. For the rest of the journey there would always be long queues at these six facilities.

As the hours passed, the men grew intensely thirsty. Those with canteens shared, but the canteens were soon dry. The Korean guards could provide no water to refill them. Apparently the fresh water supply on *Rakuyo Maru* was severely limited. Scrounging about for a water source, Jewell and Allbury went to the fo'c'sle, where some Japanese sailors who manned an ancient wheeled army field gun on the bow were billeted. The gun crew had a fresh water tap in their quarters. For a price—one Dutch guilder—they allowed Jewell and Allbury to refill their canteens. When word of this tap spread, other POWs converged there, paying with whatever they had. Allbury remembered: "Regimental badges, woolen hose tops, foreign coins; all the trifling items that had never up to now had a market were suddenly produced. . . . Inside a few hours they had a bucketful of the most incredible junk." For those who could pay, thirst was temporarily slaked.

The matter of occupying the hold was left unresolved for some time, but finally, in midafternoon, the POW officers came forward with the grim news. Allbury remembered that Captain Warner, a British *kumicho*, climbed onto the hatch boards and said: "The orders are for you to be accommodated in the hold. You are to occupy it at once. There will be no food or water available until all of you are in it. I'm sorry, chaps, I've been trying to get some improvement on that, but there was nothing I could do."

Ted Jewell voiced the opinion of the majority: "Damned if they'll get me down. I've stood a lot so far, but this is the bloody limit." His mate Allbury elucidated: "Up to now we had always obeyed an order by our officers; we were still, in spite of all the Japs had reduced us to, soldiers; and to a British soldier, however bedraggled, thirsty, hungry and tired, and even after these soul-destroying, fantastic years, an order up to now had been an order. But not this one. This was an outrage . . . a challenge to whatever spirit we had left in us."

No one moved. The atmosphere became suddenly tense. The POWs were angry, sullen, obstinate. The menacing Korean guards advanced with their pointed sticks and their rifles with fixed bayonets. They pricked and jabbed. The POWs cursed, jumped up, backed away. Slowly, reluctantly, the men were pressed back toward the deckhouse door leading to the hold companionway. Those already inside braced their feet against the bulkheads. The Koreans, returning curse for curse, now let go in full fury, bashing and pummeling with rifles and bamboo sticks. Some men were badly hurt and bleeding.

Inevitably, men gave way and slowly went down the ladder. William H. R. Emmett, twenty-three, remembered that they were derisively *"baaaaing"* like sheep. He noted a plaque in English: "This space is designed for 187 third class passengers." The upper hold—an area about half the size of a football field—had been horizontally subdivided by a temporary wooden deck. This, in effect, doubled the "livable" space—to 374 third class passengers. But between the decks, there was only four feet of head room, not nearly enough to stand, except in the open area immediately beneath the hatch. (This area permitted loading of the lower hold, now sealed off with planks.) It was dark in the hold and insufferably hot. The first men down were instantly soaked with sweat and became light-headed. Some of them passed out. Barney Barnett said: "It was like throwing a load of pigs down there. It was horrible to see."

Quite soon the men below broke into open revolt, fighting back up the stairs against the press of oncoming humanity, carrying or dragging those who had passed out. This upstream pressure—and the shouting, cursing and screaming—forced everyone back out on deck, heedless of the furiously prodding sticks and bayonets. It was now near-open rebellion. Sergeant Harry Jones remembered: "We really got mad and broke out on deck. We kept well to the forward end of the ship to show the captain that while we did not intend to mutiny, our plight was serious." The guards, perhaps fearful of what might happen if they further provoked 1,318 angry and desperate men, backed off and held their distance.

This impasse forced a hasty conference between the Japanese and the senior POW officers. Those conferring included the ship's captain, Lieutenant Yamada, Brigadier Varley, the British and Australian *kumichos* and the medical officers. The upshot was a small but important victory for the POWs. It was agreed that all seriously ill POWs and up to one-third (about 400) of the "fit" POWs could remain topside, the fit to be rotated in a system devised by the *kumichos*. Those topside would remain forward of the bridge superstructure (and passenger area), leaving a clear fore-and-aft passageway for the crew members. Some hatch boards would remain off for ventilation. However, in event of a storm or enemy action, all men would return to the hold and the hatch would be fully battened.

The captain, addressing the POWs in English, sought to reassure them. The POWs should not worry. he said. He had made the trip from Singapore to Japan "eighteen times without trouble." An Australian, shattering the solemnity of the moment, piped up: "Yes, matey, but Ajax went down on the nineteenth." The Australians roared with laughter. Ajax was a famous race horse that had won eighteen straight starts and lost on the nineteenth.

With the last laugh going to the POWs, the confrontation dissolved. Some 900 men with gear filed slowly below. The sick and about 400 others remained topside, staking out small bits of territory.

(3)

As the 900-man all-British POW contingent prepared to board *Kachidoki Maru*, Tom Pounder shuddered when he caught sight of the Japanese officer who would be in charge. He was the notorious Lieutenant Tanaka, one of the most sadistic camp commandants on the railway. A year earlier, at Kai Saio camp in Thailand, Pounder had seen Tanaka cause the death of four sick British POWs for the grave offense of failing to salute him from their sickbeds in the hospital. Tanaka had forced these men from their beds, beat them and then ordered them to work. In a few days, all four were gone.

The POWs, carrying the raw rubber "life preservers," mounted the gangway to the forward deck. A Korean guard led the line to a small deckhouse at the foot of the forward mast. A door gave onto a companionway leading down to Number 2 hold. As on *Rakuyo Maru,* the upper level of this hold had been converted to carry Japanese troops. It, too, had been subdivided with a temporary wooden deck, giving head room of less than four feet on the two levels. The guard indicated that the POWs should descend the ladder and occupy this forbidding space.

There now occurred a scene similar to, but not so explosive as, that on the *Rakuyo Maru*. The front ranks of the queue descended the stairway into the fetid, dimly lighted space. It was like entering a blast furnace. The men were instantly drenched in sweat. Some passed out. Soon the hold was jammed with a sea of wet closely pressed bodies with nowhere to go, the men scarcely able to breathe. The procession stopped. The passed-out men were lifted out, passed overhead from man to man, then laid out on deck. Roll Parvin: "Their clothing was dark and wet as though they had just come from the sea."

The Korean guard prodded the stalled queue with a pointed stick. Pounder heard a POW cry out: "How the bloody hell do they expect to get all of us down the same hold? There's still a good half of us here and the damned hold is full." The Korean responded in broken English: "Orll men down, speedo, speedo, orll men down."

Lieutenant Tanaka, incensed by the delay, let fly "a storm of abuse." Two more Korean guards reinforced the first, prodding and pushing. Again a tense moment as these POWs hovered at the point of open rebellion. Finally they yielded and resumed the slow shuffle into the hold.

Walter G. "Wally" Mole, thirty: "At first I felt like a kid going on a Sunday school outing, but that soon changed. We were pushed up the gangway, and when we got on deck we were greeted by a crazy guard who was striking at everybody with a bamboo stick. My fears grew when I saw our quarters. Hundreds of men were being forced into the hold. . . . As I reached the entrance to go down . . . the stench from the perspiring human cargo below was unbearable. No wonder the lads below were shouting and trying to prevent any more from entering. There wasn't any more room—or at least that is what we thought until a few guards forced their way through and used their persuasive measures. They fitted us in like a jigsaw puzzle."

Pounder and his mate Doug Spon-Smith were among the last group to enter, and this was Pounder's description: "The inside was like nothing I had ever witnessed before. The steps leading down into the depths of the hold were crowded with sprawling human forms. To get down meant having to clamber over them. From the moment we entered, there was a danger of becoming submerged in the mass of bodies. The stink was horrible and the heat suffocating. From the center of the rafters hung a solitary low-wattage light bulb, but the far walls and corners of the hold were in darkness."

Roll Parvin was at the very tail end of the queue. He and his mates descended the ladder, hard put to find a place: "I fumbled and found a spot where I sat with knees drawn up under my chin and my head craned forward to avoid knocking it on the underside of the overhead."

L. A. George Huitson, twenty-seven, who had worked in the grocery business, had this reaction: "It was a frightening experience. People were crowding down after you and there seemed to be no end to it, trying to find places on the shelves. The group who went in first took the upper spaces. I was on the bottom. We on the lower spaces were annoyed because sweat from the chaps above was running down like water on us."

The British officers protested these inhumane living quarters. Here, too, there was a conference. The upshot —curious, considering Tanaka's vicious reputation—was a set of rules more generous than those on *Rakuyo Maru*. The hatch would not, as feared, be battened. After the ship left Singapore, all POWs would be allowed topside on the forward end of the deck during daylight hours. They would stay well clear of Number 3 hold, which was full of wounded Japanese soldiers. A passageway would be left open, fore and aft, to permit the crew access to the fo'c'sle. At night, when it was cooler, all men would be confined to the hold, hatch open, with access to the latrines on request. If the POWs did not adhere exactly to these rules, they would be confined to the hold, hatch battened for the entire trip.

Later, a British officer elaborated on the rules for use of latrines at night: "We will be allowed up during the night to the *benjo* [toilet]. But queues are to be formed on deck at night. Any men coming up for this purpose must be quick about it and get below at once."

In the afternoon, *Kachidoki Maru* and *Rakuyo Maru* got under way and moved out in the roadstead to await the formation of a convoy. The men topside on *Rakuyo Maru* were astounded by the vast number of Japanese ships they saw in Keppel Harbor. Many men counted these ships, but they could not agree on an exact figure. The consensus seemed to be forty ships, including many tankers, both empty and fully laden. The men assumed the ships were bottled up in Singapore by the submarine

59

blockade and wondered how it was possible that they could leave when the other ships could not.

One of the Australians, William R. Smith, twenty-eight, recalled a curious and moving scene as they left the harbor: "When we passed the German submarine, the crew we'd gotten friendly with lined the rails and gave us a British salute."

(4)

They remained in the roadstead about thirty-six hours. Then, on the morning of September 6, at 0700, *Rakuyo Maru; Kachidoki Maru;* two other passenger-cargo vessels, *Nankai Maru* and another; and two heavily laden tankers, thought to be "brand new," slipped their moorings and got underway. They formed into a boxlike convoy. Four escorts joined the formation. These were the 2,000-ton fleet destroyer *Shikinami* and three 800-ton frigates (roughly equivalent to a destroyer escort or large patrol craft). The *Shikinami* took position at the head of the formation, the frigates on the port and starboard flanks and astern. Two seaplanes continuously circled overhead. The army POWs were impressed—and reassured—by the extent of the protection. They mistook the destroyer for a cruiser, the frigates for destroyers.

Setting a northeasterly course for Formosa Strait, the convoy proceeded at about 11 knots. Every six or seven minutes, on signal from *Shikinami*, it zigged radically off the base course to befuddle submarines. The *Shikinami* occasionally zipped back and forth, evidently investigating possible sonar contacts. The two aircraft swept vigilantly overhead, searching the clear tropical seas for the dark shadow of a submarine hull at periscope depth. It was a beautiful, clear, sunny day; the pewter seas were gentle, almost placid.

A few hours after leaving the roadstead, the convoy passed a Singapore-bound convoy close aboard. Again the POWs counted ships. There were four transports and two tankers escorted by several destroyers and frigates and a small aircraft carrier with eight planes parked on deck. The carrier was a queer-looking vessel. She had no "island" superstructure like most carriers above her flight

60

deck, not even a smokestack, leading Roy Cornford to believe she had been "badly damaged" (she hadn't). She was the *Unyo,* an escort carrier of 20,000 tons, one of four recently assigned to shepherd convoys through the South China Sea. Later—in quite different circumstances —a few of the POWs would be called upon to recall all the details of this vessel.

By now, the POWs on both ships were slowly adjusting to the miserable circumstances into which they had been thrust. At sea, the holds were a little cooler but still ghastly. On *Kachidoki Maru,* Roll Parvin: "The stench of . . . fiercely sweating unwashed men crammed against each other in a small space rapidly became almost tangible; but fortunately again, the nose quickly becomes adjusted even to the most revolting of smells and ceases to worry about them."

In daytime all men left the hold on *Kachidoki Maru.* Parvin: "The whole forepart of the deck, from the sheer, wall-like end of the bridge and superstructure up to the narrow bows was ours to roam in. . . . Men swarmed up the ladder to the sunlit, fresh air above; and the green uniforms and brown bodies lay like a patchwork quilt over every inch of deck space and every piece of gear. From rail to rail in the high narrow bows, nothing could be seen of deck, winches, capstans, coils of rope or hatches. Everything was obscured by the living blanket of green and brown." Armed guards patrolled to see that the men did not stray out of the assigned area. No POW strayed, or even attempted to stray, fearing the drastic punishment: all men back in the hold, hatch battened.

Thomas H. Parrott, twenty-four, recalled that one item on *Kachidoki Maru's* forward deck evoked much comment and speculation. This was the ship's bell. It was clearly marked "President Harrison." Parrott and his mates wondered where on earth the Japanese had gotten an American ship's bell. Others, including Tom Pounder, speculated that "either she had been sold to the Japs by the Americans before the war or the Japs had captured the vessel from them."

The topside scene on *Rakuyo Maru* was similar—except that at all times two-thirds of the men were confined to the horrid hold. Charles Armstrong: "Each man had a space of two square feet, just enough room to sit down in. Men had to rest on each other. It was stifling hot . . . hard to breathe. Many men were ill and just lay moaning, wanting to die." Roy Hudson: "Conditions in the hold were appalling. People were ill with dysentery. They couldn't get up to the toilet. So the stench was absolutely unthinkable." Britisher Sidney Johnson, twenty-five, thought it was "the Black Hole of Calcutta all over." An Australian, Hilton G. "Harry" Weigand, thirty-five, a former peacetime navy man, now in the army, thought Winston Churchill had been right when he said the human body could stand more punishment than brick and mortar.

Time dragged slowly in the hold. The men dozed or talked—usually about the food they would have when they finally reached freedom, occasionally about "taking over the ship." The POWs far outnumbered the Japanese. In a concerted rush—some argued—the Japanese could be overwhelmed. But what then? How would they peel out of the convoy without being challenged by an escort? This fantasy consumed many hours for some, but nothing ever came of it. Armstrong: "We had a bit of sense left and we gave it up."

Occasionally some played musical instruments or sang. Phil Beilby, the amateur musician, had a clarinet in his haversack. He played in the style of Benny Goodman and his favorite tune was "Moonglow." Leslie J. Bambridge, twenty-six, a big farmer from the Midlands, whose younger brother Albert was also a POW but not on *Rakuyo Maru*, remembered that one man had a homemade banjo. "He'd play and we'd sing—English songs, army songs, dirty army songs. The guards went wild. They said we were making too much noise. But we kept it up anyway." No guard would dare come into the hold to impose discipline.

On both ships, the men suffered acutely from hunger and thirst. The cause was probably not calculated or arbitrary Japanese sadism, more likely a shortage of facilities for providing food and water. Neither ship had ever carried such a large human cargo. Both were overflowing in the passenger sections. The addition of 1,318 POWs on one ship and 900 on the other must have severely taxed the limited fresh water capacity, forcing the captains of both vessels to impose drastic rationing on the POWs— about one pint per man per day. There was no shortage of rice; each ship carried countless bags on the deck. But the cooking facilities were not adequate for so many people, and, again, severe rationing was imposed.

On *Rakuyo Maru*, there had been a dispute between the British and Australians over who would do the cooking. The Australians won hands down. The chief responsibility fell on the shoulders of big Bill Cunneen, assisted by a half-dozen others, both Australian and British. The POW cookhouse (and the rice) was located on the aft end of the ship. It was a roofed-over shack with two big cast iron cauldrons for cooking rice, ingeniously heated by steam pipes from the ship's boiler room. (This to avoid tell-tale smoke or flame.) Also aft were coops containing chickens and ducks, but these were reserved exclusively for the Japanese.

For security reasons, Cunneen could cook only during the daylight, or about twelve hours a day. Limited to the two pots, there was simply no way he could cook enough rice to satisfy the hunger of 1,318 men. The best he could do was two meals a day, each man receiving about one pitifully inadequate mug of rice and, occasionally, an added dollop of watery fish stew. It was delivered in tin cans to the men on the deck and in the holds. Allbury recalled: "By that time the more ravenous were in a state bordering on cannibalism. . . . When the food did arrive there was complete chaos . . . near panic at the feeding points . . . a lot of queue-jumping and a lot of bad language." Paddy Dunne, the Irish-born artilleryman, said: "At mealtime, there was a free-for-all, fighting for it. We were like savages." Because of the fresh water shortage, about half the rice was cooked in salt water. Some thought this intensified their thirst and gave the rice a peculiar, unappetizing flavor. But in that heat, the extra salt might have been beneficial. Allbury thought the rice was "well cooked."

Cunneen and his helpers remained aft the whole time. The shipboard scenery here was more intriguing and diverting. The senior officers—Varley, More, Melton—were billeted aft. Cunneen talked with Varley (who seldom went forward) and the others occasionally. Some of the Japanese soldiers and the "jig-a-jig" girls were billeted in one of the aft holds. Cunneen kept his distance but was able to report to his mates with authority that the girls "wore no underpants," and other intimate details.

Men on *Rakuyo Maru* took extreme risks to find water. One night Hugh F. "Tug" Wilson, twenty-eight, slipped by the guards into the passenger section and broke into a stateroom, only to come face to face with a Japanese sailor. Fearing for his life, Wilson clutched his stomach and, pretending he was lost in delirium, moaned "*Bioki. Benjo. Benjo.*" ("Sick—need toilet.") Then Wilson bolted, losing himself in the crowd on the forward deck. Later he repeated this audacious foray, returning with a full water bottle. The gravely ill were issued chits to receive extra water. One prisoner forged a chit, signing Dr. Chalmers' name. It backfired. An angry Australian officer called him on the carpet and said: "If you're going to sign Major Chalmers' name, you better learn how to spell it." Others drained water from the small winch and crane engines on deck. It was oily but thirst-quenching.

On *Kachidoki Maru* the pro footballer Sergeant Johnny Sherwood, designated to fetch the food for the POWs, recalled: "After a few days men were feeling rough and almost begging for water. I went to the galley three times a day with four men to collect food. I managed to take six canteens with me on every trip and fill them up with drinking water. They were for the officer in charge of us who was nursing the sick men, one for myself which I kept for emergency—when anyone passed out. The others went to the men in the hold. But all day and night the men were crying out for water."

On both vessels the medical attendants set up "aid stations" topside. Each day, as the men's health sank steadily from hunger and thirst, more and more of the old familiar diseases returned: dysentery, malaria, beriberi, pellagra. The newly ill on *Kachidoki Maru* included Tom Pounder, stricken with severe dysentery. Other than provide chits for an extra water ration (a quarter- or half-cup), there was nothing much the medics could do. After only one or two days, Rowley Richards, on *Rakuyo Maru*, began to wonder seriously how many men could survive the voyage.

(5)

The convoy steamed steadily northeastward day after day. The weather remained fair and blistering. Allbury: "All around, the sea was burnished by the harsh rays of the sun. There was not a cloud. The sky, until it darkened into the horizon, was a fierce white glare. There was no wind.

My body, long the color of mahogany, began to take on a fresh angry red. It was fiendishly hot, far hotter than we'd ever known it before. . . . We welcomed the cool of the evening when the fire of the sun was spent and it plunged in a blaze of glory below the horizon, and the other ships became ever darkening silhouettes melting into the shadow of night."

As the days slipped by, the Japanese and Korean guards appeared to take a more relaxed attitude toward the POWs. On *Rakuyo Maru,* the one-third topside, two-thirds in the hold rule was not strictly enforced. No one bothered to count. On some days as many as six hundred men were topside, greatly thinning the congested space below. (Some men *preferred* the stinking hold to the blazing sun topside.) At night on *Kachidoki Maru,* more and more men came up to the *benjo*—and stayed, hiding in the shadows. The guards did not seem to care.

Some of the men struck up casual, guarded relationships with the Japanese. Johnny Sherwood made friends with one who spoke reasonably good English in the *Kachidoki Maru*'s galley. He gave Sherwood cigarettes. Sherwood did not smoke. but he was glad to pass them on to the men in the hold who did. "I used to tell him Japan Number One country in the world. He loved it. Every time I told him, he gave me more cigarettes."

After several days at sea, the men were so filthy and rank they could no longer stand their own bodies. Delegations of officers on both ships petitioned for and obtained permission for the men to bathe with the topside salt water pumps utilized for hosing down the decks. On *Rakuyo Maru* these were located aft of the passenger section. Allbury had a vivid recollection of what else he saw. "On the way to wash we passed the windows of the dining salon. The tables were set with sprays of blossoms; tablecloths, white, still creased from their laundering; carafes of water; glasses, clean and sparkling: it was another world. A world whose existence we had almost forgotten. It was something even to look at it." While they washed naked under the salt water, the "jig-a-jig" girls watched and giggled teasingly. Roy Cornford laughed himself as he explained: "They held their hands apart to show what size they saw."

On the fifth afternoon at sea, September 10, fresh water came in unexpected abundance. A torrential rain fell on the convoy. On both vessels the POWs topside danced naked with joy, mouths agape, letting the stinging, pure water assault their faces and bodies. The men filled canteens and set mess tins, or anything else that would hold water, on the decks and drank greedily. For the first time since leaving Singapore, thirst was not a problem. After sunset, the rain fell off to a steady drizzle, sweeping the decks and blotting out the stars. Then it became suddenly cold, so cold the men topside on *Rakuyo Maru* even considered returning to the hold. Most didn't. Allbury and Ted Jewell, "as dejected as a couple of half-drowned cats," nestled close together for the night, for once eagerly anticipating the searing heat of the sun.

On the following day, September 11, as they approached the middle of the South China Sea, there was a significant change in the makeup of the convoy. The ever present land-based air cover was terminated. The convoy was too far from land for the planes to operate efficiently. Six other ships—three empty freighters, three frigates—merged into the group. The guards told the POWs the new ships had come from Manila. The convoy was reshaped into three columns of three ships with the destroyer *Shikinami* in the van and three frigates on each flank. The two tankers, laden with valuable oil, took up position in the center column, shielded by the other ships. *Rakuyo Maru* became the last ship in the starboard column. One of the frigates steamed close off her starboard beam.

On both prisoner ships, the POWs could feel tension rising. More Japanese lookouts with powerful binoculars appeared on the bridge structures and bows. The gun crew on the ancient fieldpiece on the bow drilled diligently and packed sandbags around the wheels. The guards confided nervously that the convoy was now approaching the most dangerous leg of the voyage, Luzon Strait, where U.S. submarines were as thick as schools of tuna. They would be without an air screen for another day or so—until aircraft from Formosa or Takao, a small island west of Formosa, could effectively reach them. On *Kachidoki Maru* a Japanese gave Tom Parrott the shivers when he said: "This is the day we sink." The feeble jokes about men becoming "fish food" ceased.

All the POWs began to give urgent thought to shipwreck survival. On *Kachidoki Maru* the men turned up an enormous stock of life preservers in the lower hold. After one had been distributed to each man, there were still scores left over. On *Rakuyo Maru,* caches of life preservers were found in the upper hold and topside. All available preservers were distributed, but there were only about one thousand. Twenty-five percent of the men had to do without. Those with preservers wore them during daytime and used them for pillows at night.

Of all the POWs on *Rakuyo Maru,* those best trained to meet a shipboard emergency were, of course, the *Perth* survivors in the Australian contingent. Within this group, which kept pretty much to itself, the senior man was the capable Victor R. Duncan, twenty-nine. An electrical artificer with the rank of chief petty officer, Duncan had been assigned to Lieutenant Laurie J. Phillips' *Kumi* 37, with the simulated army rank of sergeant major. Owing to Phillips' dislike of paperwork and discipline, Duncan had literally been running the *kumi* since Tamarkan. He was an intelligent and fair man who quickly won the respect and admiration of the army men under his supervision.

Born in Dundee, Scotland, son of a carpenter who had emigrated to Australia, Duncan had joined the Royal Australian Navy in 1937, age twenty-two. After several years' sea duty, he had been assigned to *Perth* for a rugged combat tour in the Mediterranean. When *Perth* returned to Australia for refit, Duncan was married. He was then shipped out again. During the battle in which *Perth* was torpedoed and sunk in Sunda Strait, Duncan was knocked unconscious and seriously injured, but he survived to become a prisoner and to work on the railway. He had kept himself in excellent physical condition and was something of a medical oddity: he never contracted dysentery and an entire year went by before he came down with malaira.

On *Rakuyo Maru,* Duncan became the chief adviser to Captain Sumner and the other *kumichos* on abandon-ship procedure. It was he who had found the kapok life preservers, distributed them and briefed the men on how to don them and jump into the water—taking care to fold arms over the chest kapok block so it wouldn't slam up and strike the chin. He led the officers to the wooden life rafts on deck (sixty altogether, in lashed-down stacks; and gave instructions on how to launch and board them. He inventoried everything on the forward deck that would float—hatch boards, chests, ladders, even the overhanging *benjos*—and drew up a plan for getting those over the side in a hurry. He devised a method of quickly emptying the hold of men by lowering the long hatch boards into the hold.

Again and again Duncan briefed small groups on the rudiments of abandon-ship procedure: "Don't panic. Fill your canteen, if possible. Get rid of your shoes or boots. Keep your hat or head covering—tie it with a string, if possible. Don't abandon ship until you're sure the ship is sinking. Don't throw a raft or hatch board on somebody already in the water, and be sure the water is clear of people and rafts when you jump. If there is a torpedo hole in the ship, go over the opposite side so you won't be sucked down with it. Swim away from oil or flame on the sea surface; with—not against—the current, if at all possible. Try to keep the rafts together. The bigger the group, the more likely you'll be found. *Don't drink salt water.*" And so on.

A few of the British soldiers could contribute advice based on their misadventures at sea. Joseph Bagnall, twenty-eight, and George K. J. "Dagger" Ward, twenty-four, both ex-coal miners in the Sherwood Forester Regiment, had been evacuated from the beaches at Dunkirk before getting shipped to Singapore. Charlie Perry, Tommy Smith and Edward G. Starkey, twenty-six, had all survived the bombing and sinking of the troopship *Empress of Asia* as she approached Singapore to land part of the ill-fated 18th Division.

Rowley Richards, the doctor, was a man not only of courage and obstinacy but also of considerable independence and self-reliance. He attributed this in part to his upbringing. His father, a draftsman and cartographer, had been born deaf and dumb. His mother was deaf as a result of diphtheria. This had placed a special responsibility on Richards at a very young age. He participated in family decisions and often became its chief spokesman to the outside world. This had matured him rather rapidly and given him a tough-minded outlook. Despite his boyish appearance, he was a realist. It had been he, more than anyone else, who had demanded that the seriously sick remain topside.

Now, with the convoy entering dangerous waters, Richards was gravely concerned about what might happen to those seriously sick if *Rakuyo Maru* were to be torpedoed. There were about one hundred in his care, most of them bedded down on top of Number 1 hatch. He had provided them life preservers, but how were they to get over the

68

side? In consultation with Vic Duncan and others, principally a devoted new assistant, Jack J. McKone, Richards drew up a plan. Under its terms, neither Richards nor McKone nor certain other designated medical orderlies would leave the ship until the last of the seriously sick had been evacuated.

Beyond that, Richards worried about what might happen to all these undernourished men if they were compelled to survive for a long period of time in the ocean. Water, he reasoned, would be the crucial factor. Even if sufficient water could be obtained, they had no means of storing it on the rafts or hatch boards or other floating debris. Most men would abandon ship with only a canteenful, if that. One day in the hot sun would exhaust whatever water the men could take. These men, already dangerously dehydrated by dysentery, would require far more water than the average survivor.

It was far from being the ordinary survival situation, and Richards' thinking led him far from conventional survival doctrine. "I had had a lot of experience in the work camps with salt intake, measuring the physiological impact when men were salt-depleted and salt-saturated and so on. It seemed to me that with strict discipline, one could drink salt water in moderate amounts without catastrophe. Underline *moderate amounts*. So I devised this experiment on the ship, using myself and a small group. We started off drinking one-third salt-water, graduating to one-half, then to straight salt water. No one got sick. It's a case of accommodating your body to it." However, this radical—and dangerous—doctrine was not disseminated outside the group.

On the night the ships from Manila joined the convoy, September 11, the weather was cloudy but not disagreeable. The cook, Bill Cunneen, after another killing day's work, looked toward a long, sound sleep. He was soon disabused of this notion. The Japanese had discovered that someone had stolen some sugar. Cunneen and three other POWs assigned to him were ordered to guard the sugar bags (as well as the rice bags) stored near the ladder leading to the poop. If anything was missing on the morrow, Cunneen would be held personally responsible. Cunneen, cursing his luck (and the sugar thieves), set up a watch on the aft deck, noting that the gun crew on the ancient wheeled gun on the poop seemed more alert, edgier, than usual.

The two culprits who had stolen the sugar were Alf Winter and a mate in his *kumi*, Walter V. "Wally" Winter—no kin. That night they were in a moral quandary. Alf Winter told their story: "We broke a lock and got into a hold. We pinched a thirty- or forty-pound bag of sugar and distributed it in our *kumi*. Everybody gulped it down raw. The Japs found out and made inquiries—to no avail, of course. So they announced that if the people who stole it didn't own up, the whole lot would be punished." They lay side by side, painfully discussing whether or not to confess.

That same night, Reg Harris and Ron Miscamble, unaware of the tightened security everywhere on the ship, decided to slip aft and sleep with the cooks, in order to see what they might steal to eat. No sooner had they settled down than a Japanese guard came along and demanded an explanation. They replied they were "kitchen pickets." When the guard went off to check out this story, Ron Miscamble ran like mad to the Number 2 hold. But Reg Harris was too slow. The angry guard returned, cried, "You speak no good," and slammed him with his rifle. Harris limped back toward the hold feeling lucky to get off without more severe punishment.

By midnight the perambulations had ceased and most POWs on *Rakuyo Maru* were asleep—in the hold or topside. The ship's bow rose and dipped in the gentle swell. The deck officer on the blacked-out bridge was absorbed with the tricky chore of keeping the ship in column, maintaining the required distance behind the ship ahead. The lookouts on the bridge wings, the bow and high in the superstructure strained to spot danger against the clouded horizon. Since the ship had no radar—so rare in the Japanese maritime forces that only the most important vessels were equipped with it—the lookouts were quite literally the eyes of the ship. On them might depend the lives of more than fifteen hundred men and women.

PART FOUR

Convoy College

(1)

On the hill overlooking the naval base at Pearl Harbor, Hawaii, there stood a new, singularly nondescript building, innocuously marked "Fleet Radio Unit, Pacific" (FRUPAC). It was enclosed by a high chain-link fence; a thicket of radio antennae rose from the roof. Armed marines patrolled the fence and manned the single gate. Few Navy men knew what went on in the building; fewer still had ever been admitted through the tight security. The building housed an important division of the Navy's most valuable and closely held intelligence operation in World War II: the Japanese codebreakers.

Since the 1920s a handful of brilliant, dogged and somewhat eccentric naval officers and civilians had been working at the difficult task of breaking Japanese codes. In the 1930s they had made remarkable progress. Because the Japanese had maintained strict radio silence prior to the attack on Pearl Harbor, the codebreakers had been unable to warn of that operation and suffered an undeserved black eye. Ever since then, however, they had provided a priceless flow of detailed information on Japanese ship movements and military plans and, as a consequence, had recouped their lost reputation. From the spring of 1942 onward, the strategy and tactics of the Pacific war had been heavily based on the output of the anonymous codebreakers, working behind an absolute wall of security.

By the summer of 1944, what had once been a small personalized intelligence operation had grown into mammoth impersonal bureaucracy. There were a thousand men and women working in the FRUPAC building on the hill, thousands more in Washington, D.C., and Australia. The outfit now even had formal divisions: Cryptanalysis. Call Signs. Traffic. Translation, etc. Some of the important solutions were being found with the aid of clacking I.B.M. machines. All the effort was still directed toward one goal: providing the Commander in Chief, Pacific Fleet, Admiral Chester W. Nimitz, Jr. (and his opposite in the Southwest Pacific, General Douglas MacArthur), with the latest and most reliable facts and insights into Japanese war plans and operations.

One branch of FRUPAC concentrated exclusively on Japanese merchant marine convoys. Fortunately for the U.S. Navy, the movement of most of these convoys was controlled by a single monolithic shipping agency in Japan. This agency not only routed most convoys but also assigned a series of "noon positions" to which the convoys would rigidly adhere. These encoded instructions, widely disseminated by radio to the convoys, local Japanese military commanders and others concerned with ship movements, were, almost without exception, intercepted and decoded by FRUPAC. The information was passed along to Admiral Nimitz's headquarters, thus enabling the Commander, Submarines Pacific Fleet, Vice Admiral Charles A. Lockwood, Jr., to position his limited number of submarines to intercept shipping in the vast reaches of the Pacific in the most telling manner.

In early September 1944, FRUPAC intercepted and decoded a convoy instruction. The exact text is still classified, but the gist may be stated. An "important convoy" of six ships (four passenger-cargo, two tankers) plus undetermined escorts would depart Singapore September 6 for Japan. It would be joined on September 11 by three additional vessels plus undetermined escort from Manila. Other data included precise noon positions for the ten-day voyage utilizing the Japanese grid system for subdividing the ocean, a system that was thoroughly understood by the codebreakers, Lockwood and others with a "need to know." There was no indication whatsoever in this dispatch that two of the ships would be transporting POWs. Nor had there been a request from the Japanese for the "safe passage" of these ships, as was sometimes requested for Red Cross or hospital ships. Such requests were invariably honored by Lockwood, even though he suspected that the Japanese deceptively used such ships for transporting war matériel. Had the Japanese requested safe passage for *Rakuyo Maru* and *Kachidoki Maru* on grounds they were transporting POWs, it certainly would have been granted.

By this time, formal communications channels between FRUPAC and Admiral Nimitz's headquarters had been short-circuited. There now was a secure "hot line" between FRUPAC and Submarine Headquarters on the second floor of the torpedo shop in the submarine base. Lockwood's subordinate for receipt of such calls was Captain Wilfred J. "Jasper" Holmes. He was a Naval Academy graduate and peacetime submarine skipper who had been beached for a physical disability but recalled to shore duty after the war. It is not likely that any man on the Allied side knew more about the Japanese navy and merchant marine than Jasper Holmes.

Straightaway, Holmes took the message down the hall to the office of Lockwood's Operations Officer, Commander Richard G. Voge. A legendary figure in the U.S. submarine force, Voge had made four patrols early in the war as skipper of *Sailfish* before being handpicked to be Lockwood's chief planning officer for the conduct of the submarine war. A small, tightly wound man, on call twenty-four hours a day (as was Holmes), Voge was considered a technical genius by his peers and by the submarine skippers under Lockwood's command. They had absolute faith in his professionalism and judgment.

Holmes and Voge consulted the top-secret plotting board on the wall in the Operations Room, a large map of the Far East, dotted with metallic black silhouettes of American submarines on patrol. They roughly laid out the northeasterly course of the convoy from Singapore and its predicted noon positions. It would first come through the South China Sea to Formosa Strait, passing through a submarine patrol area in and west of Luzon Strait code-named "Convoy College." There was no literal submarine blockade there, as the Japanese believed, but there were three wolf packs in Convoy College. These were code-named for the nicknames of the tactical commanders: "Donc's Devils," "Ben's Busters" and "Ed's Eradicators." The question was, Which of these wolf packs should be assigned to intercept this important convoy?

In making this decision, Voge weighed several factors. Size of the wolf pack—that is, the number of boats. Total torpedoes expended, total torpedoes remaining. Aggressiveness and dependability of the skippers, traits well known to Voge. And a human factor: Who was most deserving of this plum? In this instance his decision was further complicated because all three wolf packs

75

had been permanently or temporarily reduced from three boats to two. In Ed's Eradicators, *Tunny* had been badly bombed by aircraft and withdrawn. In Donc's Devils and Ben's Busters, *Spadefish* and *Sealion II*, respectively, had shot off most of their torpedoes in earlier attacks and had put into Saipan to reload from the tender *Holland*. Could either get back to Convoy College in time?

After considerable discussion, Voge reached a decision. He would send two of the depleted wolf packs against the convoy. Ben's Busters, comprising *Growler* and *Pampanito*, would get first crack at it. If the third boat of this pack, *Sealion II*, could get back to Saipan in time for the action, so much the better. But this was doubtful. For that reason, and others, Voge would backstop the Busters with Ed's Eradicators, *Barb* and *Queenfish*. That would be a total of four boats strung out along the convoy's path. Five, if *Sealion II* made it.

Voge and his staff now plotted the rendezvous points. For Ben's Busters they decided on 115° east longitude, 18° 40′ north latitude. This was a point ahead of the convoy's predicted course almost precisely in the middle of the South China Sea. The point was as far from Japanese aircraft bases as it was possible to be: 280 miles east of Hainan Island, 300 miles west of Luzon, 280 miles south of Hong Kong. There was one other consideration in the choice of rendezvous. Lockwood's submarines were not permitted to operate south of an east-west line at 18° 30′ north latitude. Territory south of the line was patrolled by submarines of the Seventh Fleet, operating under control of General MacArthur and his submarine commander, Rear Admiral Ralph W. Christie. The rendezvous Voge selected for the Busters was 10 miles north of the boundary. The second two-boat wolf pack, Ed's Eradicators, would be positioned about 70 miles northeast of the Busters. What the Busters failed to sink, the Eradicators would intercept. Or so the plan was drawn.

Wolf packs and submarines on patrol rarely broke radio silence. At night while on the surface changing batteries, they "guarded" (or monitored) Pearl Harbor broadcast frequencies. If Voge had a message for a certain wolf pack or submarine, it was broadcast in code on those frequencies several times over several nights, until it was assumed it had been received, as it usually was. If these dispatches contained information derived from codebreaking, the first word of that encoded text was "Ultra" (from "Ultra Secret"). On seeing "Ultra," the junior officers assigned to breaking encoded texts were required to take the message at once to the captain. Because the codebreaking secret was so closely held, only he was authorized to break Ultra dispatches.

On the night of September 9/10, Voge broadcast an encoded Ultra message to Ben's Busters—*Growler, Pampanito* and *Sealion II*. It described the convoy in detail and gave its past and predicted noon positions. Because the three boats were then widely dispersed (especially *Sealion II*, en route from Saipan), Voge did the radio "talking" for them ordering all three to rendezvous at the point in the middle of the South China Sea he had selected, at 2200 hours, September 11. Thereafter the boats were to form a scouting line to intercept the convoy, which would probably come along in one or two hours. Later he broadcast a similar message—but with the different rendezvous—to the backstopping pack Ed's Eradicators, *Barb* and *Queenfish*.

The stage had now been set from Pearl Harbor, based directly on codebreaking information. What happened thereafter depended on the courage, skill and luck of the submarine skippers and their crews. If they did as well as Voge thought they would, it would be a dark time for the Japanese. The valuable oil, rubber, tin, copra and scrap metal in those nine big ships would never reach Japan's war production machine.

(2)

On the night of September 9/10, the fleet submarine *Growler* patrolled on the surface off the northwest coast of Luzon, the northernmost of the Philippine Islands. Her sinister gray-camouflaged silhouette blended into the mild, dark seas. She was alone. The other boats in her wolf pack—Ben's Busters—were to the east, *Pampanito* about 70 miles away near the Babuyan Islands, *Sealion II* much farther away in the Philippine Sea, returning to the patrol area from her torpedo reload in Saipan. Until now there had been little coordination within the pack and almost no communications.

Growler was a standard, assembly-line fleet submarine. Built by the Electric Boat Company in Groton, Connecticut, she had been launched in November 1941 and commissioned in March 1942. She was 311 feet long and had a beam of 27 feet and displaced about 1,500 tons. Her principal armament was ten torpedo tubes, six forward and four aft. She could carry twenty-four torpedoes, sixteen forward and eight aft. She also had a 4-inch-caliber deck gun for attacking smaller ships (sampans, trawlers) or for defensive purposes. She was powered by four diesel engines on the surface and a huge 250-cell battery submerged. She had a maximum surface speed of 20 knots and a maximum submerged speed of eight knots for one hour. (Much longer endurance submerged at slower speeds.) She could safely submerge to about 400 feet. She was originally designed to be manned by six officers and fifty-four enlisted men. But the addition of new equipment—and duties—had increased her complement to nine officers and seventy-five enlisted men.

While *Growler* cruised along on two of her diesel engines, charging batteries with the other two, the officers and lookouts on the bridge and a surface-search radar, known as the SJ, and sonar operators in the conning tower kept a sharp watch for enemy shipping and for Japanese antisubmarine aircraft and patrol vessels. Day or night, Convoy College was a dangerous place to operate. It was just the week before that *Tunny* had been caught on the surface by a Japanese plane. Only cool and skillful work by the sub's crew had saved her from total destruction. She was now limping back to Pearl Harbor for major battle-damage repairs.

Growler's skipper—and tactical commander of Ben's Busters—was Commander Thomas Benjamin "Ben" Oakley, Jr., thirty-two. Born on Staten Island, New York, Oakley was a graduate of the Naval Academy, class of 1934, where he had been more athlete than scholar. Injured in football, he had shifted to swimming and in his senior year had been named All-American water polo player. His roommate vividly caught his character in a sketch in the Academy yearbook, *Lucky Bag:* "Tall and rugged . . . Robust build and the boisterous, swashbuckling air of the pirates of the Spanish Main would have made him the hero of many a novel. . . . Rough and tough . . . in his studies he does not tend toward brilliancy but he has never had any worries over them, which is a happy condition; however, in common sense he is a match for any. . . . Will no doubt make a good leader of men. He's well-liked and a man who's readily followed through thick and thin. . . ." Oakley had married before the war and had a two-and-a-half-year-old son.

Thus far, by the quirks of assignment, swashbuckler Oakley had had a frustrating war. He had made four barren patrols as a junior officer on *Cachalot* and *Tinosa* before he had his own command, *Tarpon*, an older boat, which he took on a well-executed photo-reconnaissance mission to the Marshall Islands. In April 1944 he had been assigned to command of *Growler*, a famous boat within the submarine force. A previous skipper, Howard A. Gilmore, having earned the boat a reputation as a "destroyer killer," won the Congressional Medal of Honor on her when, mortally wounded on the bridge, he cried, "Take her down," sacrificing himself to save the boat. These were tough shoes to fill, but the brashly aggressive Oakley seemed the man to do it. However, on his first *Growler* patrol, Oakley had been assigned most of the time to unproductive "lifeguard" duty (rescuing downed Allied aviators) in the Marianas. He had found only one ship worth torpedoes, the 2,000-ton *Katori Maru*, which he sank with skill and daring. When he had set off from Pearl Harbor on this, his second *Growler* patrol, the youngest wolf pack commander yet, Oakley was out for blood.

The pack had arrived in Convoy College on August 29. Oakley noted the event in his log with a touch of humor and bravado: "Entered scheduled area—for doctor's degree." He was pleased the pack had drawn Convoy College. The Japanese were known to be feverishly reinforcing the Philippines against an expected invasion. The ships transporting these men and matériel would have to pass through his area, and the codebreakers were right on top of the traffic. Voge had warned of greatly intensified antisubmarine measures in Convoy College—radar-equipped aircraft, "hunter-killer" groups, jeep carriers, perhaps even submarines—but that was the kind of challenge that appealed to Ben Oakley.

The pack had not waited long for action. The very next night, August 30, Pearl Harbor vectored it to a Manila-bound convoy in Bashi Channel, backstopping Ed's Eradicators. This was the first time in the war that two wolf packs had been sent against a single convoy.

After the Eradicators' *Queenfish* made the initial attack, blowing up a tanker and scattering the ships, Oakley, unstintingly aggressive, moved in. Making the favored night surface attack, he fired six torpedoes, three each at a freighter and tanker, observing two hits in the freighter, three in the tanker.

Five hits on two targets out of six torpedoes was excellent shooting. But *Growler* had had no time to savor the victory. A destroyer peeled out and charged. Noting that it switched two yardarm lights from red to green, Oakley logged: "If that is the 'go' signal, we are doing it at emergency speed. He has a bone in his teeth and is firing everything at us. Many explosions from shells bursting in our vicinity. . . ."

There was no way *Growler* with a top speed of 20 knots could outrun the destroyer with a top speed of 40 knots. Most prudent submarine skippers would have dived, hoping to evade after a few depth charges. Perhaps mindful of *Growler*'s old reputation as a "destroyer killer," or perhaps simply recklessly courageous, Oakley cleared everybody off the bridge, let the destroyer draw to within 2,800 yards, then fired four stern torpedoes "down the throat." Luckily, one torpedo hit. Oakley: "His lights went out, sparks flew in all directions and a huge puff of black smoke shot up. Two explosions in rapid succession were heard at this time. . . . The destroyer disappeared from the radar." He added proudly: "We sure shoved that bone in his teeth down his throat." *Growler* was not able to mount another attack on the convoy remnants, but this was not a bad beginning. Headquarters later credited Oakley with sinking the tanker and the destroyer and damaging the freighter.

The second senior skipper in Ben's Busters was Commander Eli T. Reich, thirty-one, captain of *Sealion II*, a newer, deeper-diving boat. Like Oakley, Reich (pronounced "rich") was a New Yorker, son of a Manhattan policeman. At the Naval Academy, class of 1935, he too, had been an athlete: soccer, lacrosse, wrestling, water polo. But there the resemblance ended. Where Oakley was big, strongly built and zestful, Reich was slight and soft-spoken—and losing his hair at an alarming rate. He had ranked high academically at the Academy and had gained a reputation as an intellectual with a precise engineering turn of mind. He was married to Anne Jacqueline Hurley, who was an aide to

Secretary of the Navy James V. Forrestal. He had begun the war on the first *Sealion,* which was destroyed in a navy yard near Manila by Japanese bombs. Afterward, as a junior officer, he made four war patrols, three on *Stingray,* one on *Lapon.* None of these patrols had been very fruitful. However, Reich had been judged a comer, and when it was decided to name a new submarine in honor of the old *Sealion,* he was a natural choice to be her skipper.

Daniel P. Brooks, twenty-two, Annapolis class of 1944, the junior officer in the wardroom, recalled: "He was the only skipper I knew who subscribed to not one but *three* daily newspapers. New York *Mirror.* New York *Daily News.* The Washington *Post.* We'd pick these papers up in port, sixty days late, of course. Then, when we went on patrol, it was my job to 'deliver' three papers every morning to him at breakfast, as though they'd just arrived." The cook Fred "Mess Gear" Messecar, twenty-one, a genial six-foot three-inch veteran of six patrols on *Grayling:* "He loved fish and eggs for breakfast. Every morning the Filipino steward, Filemon Montierde, would go up on deck and collect the flying fish that had landed there and I'd fry 'em up for him." Joseph F. Ryan, twenty-three, a torpedo and gunnery officer who had served in destroyers before helping to commission *Sealion II:* "He was devoutly religious. Before leaving port, he'd have a Catholic chaplain come aboard, take the boat down to five hundred feet and hold Mass. Later, we got a Protestant chaplain to come aboard, too. During torpedo attacks, you could hear him at the periscope mumbling Catholic prayers."

The boat had made only one previous war patrol, but it had been a spectacular one. Cruising the waters of the East China Sea near Korea, Reich, in his quiet, methodical way, proved to be a cool and effective skipper. He sank a total of four big ships. Not many skippers had ever done that, let alone with a new crew on a maiden voyage. That performance had won Reich a Navy Cross Medal and high praise from Admiral Lockwood.

When the pack was vectored to the convoy in Bashi Channel on the night of August 30, Reich, like Oakley, had moved in unhesitatingly. Like Oakley, he set up on two ships, a tanker and a freighter, and fired six bow torpedoes, three at each ship. But *Sealion* was moving too fast when Reich fired. All six torpedoes ran erratic and missed. Undaunted, Reich swung around and fired his four stern tubes at the tanker. Two torpedoes slammed home, raising a tremendous billow of smoke. The ship apparently broke in half and sank. Later Reich was credited for this sinking. Now under fire from almost every ship in the convoy, Reich hauled off into the darkness and submerged while the crew reloaded the ten empty torpedo tubes.

Reich guessed correctly that the remnants of the convoy would turn south. After the torpedo reload, he surfaced and ran south, submerging before daylight. Later, when the convoy came along as predicted, Reich fired six bow torpedoes, three at a minelayer-escort, three at a freighter. The minelayer, the 1,300-ton *Shirataka,* caught fire and sank; three hits were heard in the freighter for damage. Later that day, Reich fired three more torpedoes at an escort, but lookouts spotted the torpedoes and the ship successfully evaded.

In these five aggressive attacks over a period of fourteen hours, Reich had expended nineteen of his twenty-four torpedoes. The five left were poorly distributed, one forward and four aft. Thus he decided to pull out of Convoy College and steam 1,300 miles to Saipan to get more torpedoes from the tender *Holland,* which had recently arrived there to establish an advance submarine base. He arrived at Saipan on the morning of September 5, reloaded and refueled, and departed for Convoy College early on the morning of September 7.

The third and most junior of the skippers in Ben's Busters was Commander Paul E. "Pete" Summers, who celebrated his thirty-first birthday in Convoy College on September 6. Born in Tennessee, one of seven children of a dentist, Summers was educated in rural schools. As a result, he had had to "work like hell at the Naval Academy," where, in 1936, he graduated in the lower quarter of his class. He, too, had been an athlete; among other accomplishments, star pitcher on the baseball team for four years. He, too, was married and had one son. In the first two years of the war, Summers had made seven consecutive war patrols under cautious and unproductive skippers on *Stingray.* Thereafter, he was sent back to fit out and help commission a new boat—*Pampanito*—as executive officer.

From the start, there was trouble in the wardroom on this boat. The all-volunteer crew had little confidence in the skipper; some refused to go to sea with him. When the boat reached Pearl Harbor, Lockwood's training officers decided the men were right, relieved the skipper and promoted Summers to command the boat. This was a heavy responsibility for Pete Summers to shoulder, and a difficult position. He became aloof, withdrawn, a man apart from his wardroom. He was a cold, demanding taskmaster who appeared to have small confidence in his officers and crew and showed reluctance to delegate authority.

This unhappy state of affairs placed a heavy burden on the exec, Landon L. "Jeff" Davis, Jr., twenty-seven, Naval Academy class of 1939. Davis had come to *Pampanito* from *Growler*. He had been officer of the deck when the mortally wounded skipper, Howard Gilmore, ordered him to "take her down" and it appeared to the wardroom and crew that he was still guilt-ridden over carrying out those orders. On *Pampanito* he was forced to serve as a buffer between Summers and the alienated wardroom, a touchy chore that Davis managed ably. One of the junior officers, Richard J. Sherlock, twenty-three, expressed the wardroom concerns: "Jeff was nervous and jumpy, a bit wild-eyed, always running all over the boat. But he was one of the finest men I ever met, in or out of the Navy. Without Jeff, life on *Pampanito* would have been unbearable."

Pampanito had a number of exceptional enlisted men in her crew. One was George E. "Molly" Moffett, radar technician first class. His primary job was to keep the SJ search radar finely tuned. He did not stand watches. But when a contact was made, he stood by in the conning tower to interpret it. Fire Controlman William E. Yagemann, twenty, who operated the radar at battle stations: "We called him Molly, but he was not effeminate. He was really an egghead, really an intellectual, one of the few in the fleet who really knew radar. Our radar was probably the best out there." Moffett's boss, Dick Sherlock, had this to say: "He was an extraordinary radar man. Not only that, he was more or less a spokesman for the crew, like the president of a local union." One of the quartermasters, John H. Greene, nineteen, added: "He could pick up a bird with our radar, it was that sensitive and finely tuned."

In two previous war patrols Summers had sunk no ships and had had two very close calls. On the first patrol in the Marianas, *Pampanito* was detected during a daylight submerged approach on a small convoy and depthcharged so severely the boat was nearly lost. On the second, off Japan, a Japanese submarine nearly hit the boat with two torpedoes that passed close down the port and starboard sides. By the end of the second patrol, many of the officers and crew had lost whatever confidence they had had in Summers, and the boat was known throughout the fleet as "The Peaceful Pamp." Many left the boat. Summers was probably also under the gun at submarine headquarters. The usual policy was to relieve a skipper—a professional disaster—if, after two patrols, he had sunk no ships. But Summers had been given another chance.

So far on this patrol, Summers had not done anything to inspire the officers and crew or rectify past failures. When the pack was vectored to the convoy on August 30, *Pampanito* did not close and engage the enemy. Instead, Summers went off in the wrong direction and flailed around aimlessly, later blaming this failure on a communications breakdown within the wolf pack. The wardroom was not pleased with this performance. The torpedo and gunnery officer, Ted N. Swain, twenty-five, a Naval Academy graduate, was particularly vehement. He believed Summers to be overly cautious.

Thereafter *Pampanito* was afflicted with a mechanical problem so severe it appeared Summers might have to abort the patrol. This was a squealing leak in the forward trim tank that, for several days, defied the finest engineering minds on *Pampanito*. It was finally isolated when two men, Lieutenant Howard T. Fulton and Motor Machinest Edmund W. Stockslader, twenty-two, courageously entered the tank while Summers took the boat deep. Later, while *Pampanito* lay doggo on the surface, another exceptional sailor, Gunner's Mate Anthony C. Hauptman, twenty-six, an amateur diver, repaired the leak from the outside by climbing down into the belowwater superstructure wearing a diving mask. But for this fine work, for which all three later received Letters of Commendation, *Pampanito* would have been heading home.

On the night of September 9/10, all three boats of

Ben's Busters received the Ultra from Pearl Harbor and the instructions to rendezvous in the middle of the South China Sea at 2200 hours on September 11. Ben Oakley in *Growler* was nearest the point and he proceeded westward at moderate speed. Summers in *Pampanito* had about 300 miles to go. He headed west at four-engine speed, making seventeen knots. During the day on the eleventh, he submerged so that he would not be detected and give away the game.

Eli Reich in *Sealion II,* still en route from Saipan, had farthest to go—about 600 miles. A less-aggressive skipper might well have concluded it was impossible to make the rendezvous, but Reich ordered four-engine speed. All day September 10, *Sealion* bore west at seventeen knots. That evening, after dark, the boat eased through heavily patrolled Balintang Channel without being detected. That night and all day the eleventh, *Sealion* remained on the surface. At 2030 that evening *Sealion* picked up another submarine. Assuming it to be friendly, Reich turned to close. This was *Pampanito,* which promptly dived. Both boats continued to the rendezvous without further contact.

Ben Oakley in *Growler* lay submerged at the rendezvous point that same evening. At about 2000, *Sealion* arrived. Oakley surfaced alongside her and, by megaphone, gave Reich his instructions for the next two days. This was the first direct contact Reich had had with Oakley since the pack had left Midway on August 17. An hour and a half later, at 2130, *Pampanito* joined the formation and Summers likewise received his instructions by megaphone.

The three boats would form a scouting line on the surface. *Growler* would be in the center, *Sealion* 8 nautical miles on the right, *Pampanito* 8 nautical miles to the left. With an effective radar range of about 8 nautical miles (16,000 yards) the three boats abreast would cover a swath of sea 32 nautical miles wide. The line would steer course 213 true (southwest), the reciprocal of the convoy's projected course of about 033 true (northeast). The speed of advance would be thirteen knots. The first boat to sight the convoy would break radio silence and make a contact report, for the benefit not only of Ben's Busters but also of the backstopping Ed's Eradicators. After the attack the Busters would rendezvous again the following night at a point roughly

180 miles to the northeast near Pratas Reef. If the remnants of the convoy held to the base course, that might give the Busters a chance for a second attack.

At 2230—an hour and a half before midnight—the Busters deployed into a scouting line, all hands tense and keenly alert. It was a good night for a submarine attack. The sky was about 50 percent overcast, with dark rain clouds for a background. The visibility was fair. The sea was State 2 or 3 on the Beaufort Scale, relatively calm. A quarter-moon would not rise until about 0230.

(3)

The backstopping pack of Ed's Eradicators, comprising *Barb* and *Queenfish*, was commanded by a senior captain from the Pearl Harbor submarine base, Edwin R. Swinburne, forty. A graduate of the Naval Academy in 1925, Swinburne, married with one son, had been a submariner for fifteen years. He had commanded a fleet boat in peacetime, but because of his seniority, he had been a "pencil pusher" in various staff positions since the beginning of the war. Admiral Lockwood was not yet certain whether wolf packs should be commanded by the senior submarine skipper, as in Ben Oakley's case, or by a separate senior officer, such as Swinburne. Thus, on this, his first war patrol, Swinburne was a guinea pig. He rode in *Barb*, skippered by Commander Eugene B. Fluckey, thirty-one.

Both *Barb* and Fluckey were relatively new to the Pacific war. Commissioned in the spring of 1942, *Barb* was one of seven fleet boats diverted to the United Kingdom, mostly as a political gesture. Based in Scotland, she had made five long, difficult and fruitless patrols in European waters and the North Atlantic, not once finding a target worth a torpedo. After a brief refit in the States, *Barb* had reported to Lockwood's command in September 1943. Her skipper, John R. Waterman, took her on two Pacific war patrols, during which he made two torpedo attacks and sank only one small ship. Thus, after seven war patrols, *Barb* ranked near the bottom of the ladder in damage inflicted on the enemy.

Gene Fluckey, a genial, soft-spoken officer with flaming red hair, had been caught in a career backwater since the beginning of the war. Born in Washington, D.C., Fluckey, like Reich, had graduated from the Naval Academy in 1935 and married thereafter. Following the usual big-ship duty and submarine school, he was an exec of an ancient boat, *Bonita,* patrolling the Pacific side of the Panama Canal to defend it from an expected Japanese attack that never materialized. After five monotonous and barren patrols, Fluckey was sent back to the Naval Academy for a postgraduate course in ship design. Finally, in February 1944, Fluckey had reported to Lockwood for combat duty. Assigned to *Barb* as a Prospective Commanding Officer, he was along on Waterman's seventh and final patrol. After that, Lockwood gave Fluckey command of the boat.

In a single patrol, Fluckey had lifted *Barb* from relative obscurity and set her on the road to fame and glory. Assigned to the icy waters of the Kuril Islands in company with *Herring* (which was lost), Fluckey made the finest maiden patrol of the war. He sank five big ships, winning a Navy Cross, unstinting praise from Lockwood and the steadfast loyalty and devotion of his wardroom and crew. To his men, Fluckey was a dream skipper: smart, innovative, unconventional, gutsy yet not reckless, a generous, unselfish officer who invariably placed the welfare of his men before all else. In violation of Navy regulations, he even carried beer on *Barb* to give to the enlisted men on special occasions.

First Lieutenant Max C. Duncan, twenty-three, Annapolis class of 1942, had just joined *Barb* after a tour on a cruiser. "He's the sharpest man I've ever known. He loved to match wits and loved to bet on things. He had a knack for turning a conversation into a bet. On *Barb,* the favorite bet was a quart of whiskey. I'm not sure the bets ever got paid off, but we kept all kinds of records. One time Gene had a huge number of bets on all kinds of wild things—such as what's the largest city west of the Rockies. Or some such trivia. The night before we got in, he decided it was time to settle all the bets. He'd won them all. Then he showed us how. He had a whole load of reference books in his cabin!"

The second skipper in Ed's Eradicators was Commander Charles Elliott Loughlin, thirty-four, making his first Pacific war patrol in the brand-new boat *Queenfish*. Born in North Carolina, son of a U.S. Army colonel who was killed in World War I by a German sniper only two days before the Armistice, Elliott Loughlin had followed his older brother Joseph to the Naval Academy, a member of the class of 1933. A superb athlete, Loughlin had been captain of the tennis team, All-American basketball player and, in his senior year, winner of the coveted Thompson Trophy for doing most for the promotion of athletics.

Loughlin was married and, like Fluckey, had wound up in submarines in the Panama backwater. In time he rose to command a creaky World War I-vintage boat, *S-14*, on which he made four war patrols in a fruitless search for German submarines. In the spring of 1944 he was assigned to commission and command *Queenfish*. When the boat reported to Lockwood, the Admiral was impressed with the high state of morale and training, but Loughlin, like any skipper new to the Pacific, was an unknown quantity. Some very impressive men had failed in the heat and tension of combat.

Loughlin was fortunate to have drawn a fine crew. Many were shipmates from his old boat, *S-14*. Others were veterans of war patrols on other boats. One of these was a motor machinist, Anthony J. A. "Tony" Alamia, twenty-one, who had made six patrols on *Drum*. Alamia and some of his hard-playing shipmates had provided the boat a unique "mascot"—a stuffed, antlered elk's head, mounted on a bulkhead in the crew's mess. The trophy had been "liberated" from the Elks' Lodge in Portsmouth, New Hampshire, following the commissioning party.

Ed's Eradicators had reached Convoy College on August 23, one week ahead of the Busters. They promptly encountered the intensified antisubmarine measures in the area. In the first six days, *Barb* was forced down nine times by aircraft. The antisubmarine activity, Fluckey logged, was "a bit terrific." *Queenfish* and the third boat, *Tunny*, were similarly harassed. Clearly the renewed enemy pressure foretold a dangerous time ahead for all submarines in Convoy College.

The first action of any consequence for the Eradicators came on August 30, when the pack was vectored along with the Busters to the convoy in Bashi Channel. One of

Loughlin's men, a sharp-eyed signalman, Douglas W. Coleman, twenty-nine, spotted smoke from the convoy, which was steaming along in bright moonlight. Loughlin maneuvered ahead, submerged and attacked, firing six bow torpedoes, three each at a freighter and a tanker. He scored four hits, sinking (as he thought) the freighter. The tanker, *Chiyoda Maru*, 4,700 tons, blew up with an awesome explosion, spewing flaming oil high into the sky, and then sank. In retaliation, escorts pounced on *Queenfish* and punished her severely. But she survived and Loughlin was off to a fine start.

Thereafter *Barb* and *Tunny* had pursued the convoy at flank speed, pulling around to dive ahead for a dawn attack. The skippers in both boats were on the point of firing when Reich, in *Sealion*, torpedoed the minelayer and freighter, again scattering the convoy. *Tunny* found herself in left field, unable to shoot, but Fluckey quickly shifted targets and let fly three torpedoes at a "brand new" freighter. All three hit and *Okuni Maru*, 5,600 tons, went to the bottom. Persistent escorts pounced on *Barb*, delivering a vicious depth charge attack. None of the submarines was able to mount another attack, but the riddled convoy turned around and went back to Takao.

During the week following, the Eradicators operated off the southern tip of Formosa. The pack had an extraordinarily busy and harrowing time. Late on the afternoon of August 31, Fluckey found a freighter—evidently a straggler from the convoy—and fired three bow tubes and watched through the periscope as the ship broke in half and sank. Escorts gave *Barb* another pasting. It was on the next day, September 1 that *Tunny* was bombed and forced to withdraw. Early the following morning *Barb* was also severely bombed by aircraft. (Fluckey found bomb fragments and tail vanes on the upper deck.) In the wee hours of September 4, Loughlin spotted a disabled seaplane on the water and charged with deck guns. Before Loughlin could score, however, it had hauled out of range, and not long afterward a Japanese submarine fired two torpedoes at *Queenfish*. Luckily they were seen and avoided. Later that same day, Fluckey mounted a gun attack on a sampan in broad daylight. The attack drew aircraft, which delivered another severe bombing attack on *Barb*. Early on the morning of September 5, *Queenfish* dodged two more submarine torpedoes. And so it went.

Several days later *Queenfish*, submerged in Bashi Channel, found another convoy. In the early hours of September 9, the pack closed and attacked. Loughlin shot first, firing all six bow tubes, three at an "old" destroyer, three at a tanker. The destroyer burst into flames and apparently sank. Loughlin put one more torpedo into the tanker for good measure. This ship, which sank, turned out to be a small freighter, *Manshu Maru*, 3,054 tons. Moments later, Loughlin fired three stern torpedoes at a big transport. All three hit, and the 7,097-ton *Toyooka Maru* blew up and went to the bottom. Loughlin was no longer a question mark. In two convoy attacks so far, he had fired sixteen torpedoes, scored at least ten hits and apparently sank four ships. For a tyro skipper on a maiden voyage, this was spectacular shooting.

Once again the relentlessly aggressive Gene Fluckey was frustrated. Aircraft drawn to the scene by Loughlin's attack had forced *Barb* down, denying Fluckey a shot at the big ships. Later, against his better judgment, he had fired three torpedoes at a shallow-draft escort. Two torpedoes ran under the escort harmlessly; the third ran erratic and circled back over *Barb*, another unnerving moment for all hands. After daylight, Fluckey had surfaced to chase the remnants of the convoy, but aircraft repeatedly forced *Barb* under. One dropped two bombs "very, very close," severely jolting the boat. After that, Fluckey had broken off the chase, a frustrated skipper. Out of the two convoys, he had sunk only two ships—and had wasted three torpedoes on the escort.

Early on the morning of September 11, while still in Bashi Channel, the Eradicators received Dick Voge's Ultra on the convoy from Singapore together with rendezvous instructions. By 0300 the two boats were headed west at four-engine speed. During daylight that day, aircraft forced *Barb* down five times. By nightfall the two boats had safely reached the rendezvous, seventy miles to the northeast of Ben's Busters. They patrolled on the surface, maintaining an alert radio watch, waiting for a contact report from the Busters.

(4)

Ben's Busters, deployed on a scouting line, continued on the southwesterly search course, all hands tensely alert. Before midnight the pack crossed the boundary and entered Douglas MacArthur's Seventh Fleet territory. No matter. There were no Seventh Fleet submarines in the vicinity. It was an infraction of small consequence, justifiable as "hot pursuit." Where was the Singapore convoy? Had the Japanese navigators strayed off course? Was it a false alarm?

No. At 0107, *Growler*, the center boat in the scouting line, got a radar contact dead ahead at the phenomenal range of 29,700 yards (almost 15 miles). At once, Oakley summoned the *Growler* tracking party. It was a small, skilled group that, utilizing frequent radar ranges and bearings, would determine the convoy's course, speed and zigzag plan, if any. They worked quickly. At a combined closing speed of 23 knots (13 for *Growler*, an assumed 10 for the convoy), in half an hour the two forces would be almost nose to nose. The tracking party reported a base course of northeast, speed 9 knots, which tallied with the Ultra prediction. Radar now showed "seven or eight ships" in three columns, with "various escorts ahead and on bows and quarters."

Shortly thereafter, *Sealion* and *Pampanito* made radar contact. At 0125 *Sealion,* on *Growler*'s right, logged the pips at range 23,000 yards (11.5 miles). At 0130 *Pampanito,* on *Growler*'s left, logged the pips at range 31,000 yards (15.5 miles). Both boats promptly manned tracking stations. Reich in *Sealion* counted "at least nine large vessels and an uncertain number of smaller escort vessels." Pete Summers merely noted "a large convoy."

Two of the three boats broke radio silence to make a contact report. Oakley was first. On a prearranged frequency, guarded by both his pack and the backstopping Eradicators, he reported seven or eight ships at 17° 45′

north latitude, 114° 50′ east longitude, course northeast, speed 9 knots (his navigation was in error). *Pampanito* picked up this report, but, as Summers logged, the code was "garbled" and his decoding officer could not break it. Summers broadcast his own contact report, which Oakley received. Apparently Reich did not feel compelled to clutter the air with further redundant messages. He maintained radio silence. Unfortunately neither of these contact reports was picked up by the Eradicators, now 85 miles to the northeast.

In *Growler*, Oakley, who would make the first attack, ordered battle stations. He would remain on the bridge for a night surface approach. His exec, Richard K. Mason, Jr., twenty-seven, Naval Academy class of 1940, took position in the conning tower directly below to supervise the fire control party. The other six officers and seventy-five enlisted men hurried to posts throughout the boat. Owing to a new personnel rotation policy, which had hit *Growler* especially hard, almost a third of the men were new to the boat, sixteen fresh from submarine school. However, Oakley had molded his crew into a coolly efficient fighting unit. There was no confusion or hesitancy on *Growler;* merely a compelling desire, inspired by Oakley, to inflict the greatest possible harm on the enemy.

Within a minute or two, Mason reported all hands at battle stations. On the bridge, Oakley manned the TBT (target bearing transmitter), a pair of binoculars mounted over a gyro compass repeater. There was a thumb-operated buzzer signal on the TBT. When Oakley lined up on a target and pressed the button, the target bearing was automatically transmitted to the conning tower and thence to the most complicated piece of equipment on the boat, the torpedo data computer (TDC). Operated by two officers, the TDC looked like a vertically mounted pinball machine. It absorbed all the input data (enemy course, range, speed, estimated angle on the bow), displaying it visually, and generated the firing solution, automatically and continuously setting the proper gyro angles on the torpedoes in the tubes.

Eyes glued to the TBT, Oakley maneuvered *Growler* to a position dead ahead of the oncoming convoy. The range was now closing very fast. At 0153, he picked out a big ship in the center column—probably a tanker— and began buzzing bearings to the conning tower. Radar supplied the ranges. In the forward torpedo room, torpedomen made ready the six bow tubes. Battle station telephone talkers relayed data being transmitted electronically by the TDC. Oakley was now ready to shoot. He buzzed one final bearing. Then, suddenly, he shouted: "Check fire!"

A radar-equipped escort on the starboard bow of the convoy had spotted *Growler*. It turned and bore directly at the submarine, making high speed. Again, a more cautious skipper would have aborted the attack and evaded the escort, diving deep and rigging for depth charges. Oakley unhesitatingly brought the TBT to bear on it, crying out: "New target. New setup." For the second time on this patrol, Oakley would fire "down the throat" at an escort. This shot, however, bow to bow would be infinitely more dangerous.

As the escort came closer, Oakley could make it out. It was a fleet destroyer. He could see two dome-shaped two-gun turrets forward and tripod masts. It had a "bedspring" search radar antenna on the foremast and what appeared to be a smaller fire-control radar atop the forward tower. At 0154, with *Growler*'s bow aimed directly at the oncoming ship, range 1,150 yards, Oakley fired three bow tubes. He logged: "Did not fire other bow tubes as range closed too rapidly for comfort." Instead, he swung hard left and speeded up to get out of the way and bring his stern tubes to bear. If the first salvo missed, he planned to dive and fire the stern tubes.

Forty-nine seconds after firing, Oakley watched with immense satisfaction as the first torpedo struck home. The destroyer "exploded violently—but beautifully—amidships," heeled 50° to port and turned hard right. The flash of the explosion was seen in *Growler*'s conning tower. Oakley logged: "Great sigh of relief from *Growler*."

Perhaps, but it was not yet over. Blazing furiously, the destroyer continued bearing down on *Growler*. The list to port increased to 70°. As it came closer and closer, Oakley could feel the intense heat of its flames, which lit up *Growler*'s conning tower. He saw "a horde of Japs" clambering up the crazily tilted deck to the bridge and foremast. At last, at a mere 200 yards' range, the destroyer plunged down and under. Seconds later there was nothing left except "a small fire burning on the water." So ended the largest escort of the Singapore convoy, the destroyer *Shikinami,* the vessel mistaken by the army POWs for a "cruiser."

This attack was unique in American submarine history and would never be duplicated. A "down-the-throat" shot against an enemy destroyer, bow to bow, was hazardous in the extreme. The theory—more hope than theory, actually—of the shot was that the oncoming destroyer would see the torpedoes and in panic turn, port or starboard, to avoid them, thus catching a torpedo broadside. But what if the destroyer, presenting the narrowest possible silhouette, did not panic and turn? The torpedoes were bound to miss. A few courageous skippers had attempted the tactic submerged, in position to go deep quickly if it failed, and several had fired stern tubes "down the throat" while running away, as Oakley had on his previous convoy attack. But no one had ever done it on the surface bow to bow. If Oakley had missed, the destroyer would have been on top of him in seconds. Oakley thought he could maneuver away, dive and fire his stern tubes, but almost certainly *Growler* would have been rammed and sunk.

When the details became known, the attack would generate heated and divided opinion among submariners. The high command, commenting on the patrol, would say it spoke "volumes for the courage and aggressiveness of the *Growler.*" Oakley would proudly log that "a small group . . . on board originated, to the approval of all hands, a new title for *Growler: Destroyer Buster.*" Others would consider the attack foolhardy in the extreme. They would point to another sentence in Oakley's log, considered closer to the true state of mind on *Growler:* "The officers and crew showed signs of nerve fatigue after the surface encounter with the enemy." A former shipmate from *Tinosa* days, C. Edwin Bell, summed up the majority reaction: "It's like playing Russian roulette."

Oakley had watched the death of *Shikinami* out of the corner of one eye. His main concern was the convoy itself, and the other escorts. The game had been given away, the element of surprise lost. He would now have to work quickly indeed. For his next targets he chose two freighters, now overlapping. These were probably two of the ships that had come from Manila to join the convoy. At 0159, he fired his four stern tubes, two torpedoes at each, range 1,900 to 2,500 yards. He saw and heard two hits in one freighter, one in the other. It's not likely that either of these ships was severely damaged.

Meanwhile, a second escort, one of the six flanking frigates, peeled out and charged *Growler*. It closed to 1,600 yards, firing its big bow gun (4- or 5-inch, Oakley estimated) and smaller 40 mm cannon. Oakley turned *Growler* away at flank speed, 19 knots. A shell fell 50 yards off the port beam. To confuse the gunners, Oakley "chased" the splashes, zigzagging wildly. A second frigate, far behind the other, joined the chase. Little by little *Growler* pulled away into the darkness, outrunning the slower ships. By 0222, *Growler* was safely out of range. In a burst of postbattle emotion, Oakley yelled down to the conning tower: "You're the best fire-control party ever seen." He secured, temporarily, from battle stations and commenced an "end around" to overtake the convoy and make another attack, hopefully before dawn. Torpedomen, meanwhile, reloaded the seven empty torpedo tubes.

When *Growler* had first attacked, the convoy turned to port, changing course from northeast to northwest. This maneuver had brought it directly toward *Sealion*. Reich, on the bridge, saw and heard the explosions of *Growler*'s torpedoes, then observed a bright red flare over the convoy, probably a general alarm. By 0210 the formation had closed to within 5 miles of *Sealion* and Reich ordered battle stations. By 0233 a quarter-moon was beginning to rise. The convoy had closed to 3.5 miles. Reich still counted nine big ships. At 0248 he commenced closing to attack. By then *Sealion* had achieved position on the port bow, dead ahead of a portside escort.

There were now four ships, irregularly spaced, in the port column. A big tanker led. Reich chose this ship for his first target. He eased in to 3,000 yards—displaying his full silhouette to the oncoming escort—and commenced firing bow tubes. The first torpedo swished out of the tube, then the second. But then a mechanical failure was discovered. The gyro setting gear had failed. The second torpedo went out with a wildly incorrect setting. Reich checked fire, hurriedly considering what to do. The best bet seemed to be to pull off, repair the faulty gear, then close for another attack.

As he gave the order to break off, the port escort, a frigate, saw *Sealion* and charged. Another frigate joined the chase. Reich turned away at flank speed. At 2,100 yards, the two escorts commenced firing large guns (4- or 5-inch, Reich estimated) and smaller cannons. The shells whistled overhead, falling into the water with big splashes. Reich turned *Sealion* slightly to port. The shell splashes drifted to starboard. Slowly, the faster *Sealion* outran the frigates. Reich was vastly relieved. He logged: "It was close and for a while too hot for comfort." Reich, too, temporarily secured from battle stations and commenced an end around. Torpedomen repaired the faulty gyro setter and reloaded the two empty forward tubes.

When Pete Summers in *Pampanito* received the initial radar contact on the convoy at 15 miles, he was 8 miles to *Growler*'s left. He bent on flank speed and steered northwest in order to "get ahead" of the convoy. By 0200, minutes after *Growler* had sunk *Shikinami*, Summers was "almost directly north of the convoy, in a good position for an attack," should the convoy maintain its base course. After *Growler*'s success, Summers noted a shift in the convoy disposition—ships milling around in confusion—and wrongly assumed that it would turn east. So he, as he logged, "headed east at full speed to get in position ahead of convoy if and when they headed in that direction."

Since the convoy turned not east but northwest, away from *Growler,* this was the wrong way to go. By 0300—after *Sealion*'s abortive attack and the chase—Summers discovered his error. He found himself in left field, far off the starboard quarter of the convoy and upmoon, not the most favorable position for an attack. He ordered an end around to the south and west of the convoy, to pull ahead on the dark side downmoon.

The wardroom was disappointed in this performance. For the second time on this patrol, both packmates had got in attacks while *Pampanito* flailed around in the wrong place without engaging. It was humiliating and demoralizing. Moreover, the advantage of surprise was now gone, and darkness was slipping away. If *Pampanito* did manage an attack, it might have to be in daylight against alerted escorts and perhaps even aircraft.

So ended the first phase of the attack on the Singapore convoy. With seven torpedoes, Oakley had sunk the destroyer *Shikinami* and probably slightly damaged two freighters. Reich had fired one torpedo before the gyro setter failed and one after for no hits and no damage. Both skippers would agree that the convoy was extremely well protected. The escorts had performed bravely and effectively, resolutely driving off both *Growler* and *Sealion*. In fact, so far, no real damage had been done to the convoy. The nine big ships, six with valuable cargos, were still afloat. Because of the communications failure on the contact report, the Eradicators, *Barb* and *Queenfish,* were still unaware that a battle was in progress.

(5)

When *Growler* had opened the attack on the convoy, there were probably six or seven hundred POWs topside on the forward deck of *Rakuyo Maru*. Most were sleeping, but a handful were awake. The cook, Bill Cunneen, guarding the sugar and rice back aft: "The destroyer charged around with lights blinking. He was the only ship with radar. Then we heard a loud bang. We jumped up to look." George F. Hinchy, thirty: "There was a flash of flame. The Japs said it was 'an island on fire.' Then there was an explosion and blackness again. We said to the Japs: 'Somebody's pulled the bottom out of that island. She's gone.'"

Harry Weigand recalled: "I was sleeping on top of Number Three hold by the bridge superstructure. There was a terrific explosion on our starboard side. I jumped up to look. I saw the mainstay of the escort burning like the devil and sinking fast." William R. Smith said: "I woke and looked to starboard and saw the huge flash of light that goes with an explosion, half a mile away." Arthur G. Wright's version was: "The destroyer was barely visible when there was a terrific explosion, a tremendous glare of light, and we saw the destroyer no more." William Emmett's: "There was a terrific explosion. A great big ball of fire lit up the whole blooming sky. It was a hell of a bang and a hell of a flash."

Soon everybody topside was wide awake. By then the Japanese crew were running to battle stations, manning the fore and aft guns. Paddy Dunne said that the Japs were in a big panic, "ringing bells and doing everything." Harry Weigand added: "The guards and the whole crew were really panicking. The forward gun on our ship fired a great flare. It landed on the other side of the sinking escort, but we couldn't see any subs. By then some of the Japs were actually sitting in the lifeboats."

Harry Pickett had an odd experience when he and his mate Ronald "Mac" McCracken were hiding under a pile of bags forward: "It was Mac's turn to be the spotter—to watch for the guards. I dozed off. Next thing I knew Mac kicked me in the face with his bare foot and said: 'Look over there.' The destroyer was on fire. We went to the rail, very excited. I thought, this is the big moment. The Allies are here! Then I felt two hands under my armpits. I looked around. It was a Jap guard from the railway we called 'Cat's Eye,' not a bad chap, one of the quieter ones. I thought, boy, if he gets twisty, he'll go right over the side, because the game's up. But he just tightened the straps on my life jacket and walked away. Wasn't that strange?"

The explosion woke men in the hold. There was no panic, no stampede topside; rather, anxious curiosity. The men topside, Ray Wheeler recalled, yelled down through the open hatch, giving a running account of the brief action: "They've hit one of the destroyers. . . . It's on fire. . . . It's listing. . . . Big explosion. . . . Ball of fire. . . . They must have got the magazine. . . . It's going under. . . . Gone."

These men had been out of direct touch with the war for a very long time. Now, face to face with its realities, the reaction was mixed. Some, like Sergeant Harry Jones, were downright exhilarated. He and a group rushed to the starboard rail and "cheered" the sinking. In the hold, Douglas A. Cresswell had a similar reaction: "It was a wonderful feeling knowing our Allies were out there." These men, and others, were happy to see the Japanese forces damaged. Some still entertained the fantasy that somehow the Allies could reach out and rescue them. Many were frightened. Sidney Johnson: "I was scared stiff. Terrified." Arthur Wright: "You can imagine our feelings. It seemed that the taunt that we'd be 'fish food' would come true." Others were unmoved. Ray Wheeler: "By that time you had a fatalistic outlook. I wasn't nervous being in the hold. If you got sunk and couldn't get out, that was it."

The guards and the ship's crew now sought to enforce the captain's rule that in the event of enemy attack all men (except the gravely ill) would return to the hold. Bill Cunneen: "The captain acted like he'd been drinking sake. Maybe his nerves were on edge. He ordered everybody into the hold." Harry Jones: "The crew and guards came to life with a will and drove us into the hold with rifles and fixed bayonets. Fear made them into near maniacs, ready to kill or be killed."

Quite soon the panic subsided. After the destroyer blew up and sank, the POWs saw no further signs of action. The convoy had reformed into orderly rows, the remaining escorts settled back into flanking positions. The *Rakuyo Maru* crew retired from battle stations and the guards gave up trying to force the men into the hold. Weigand noticed they were drifting away, hanging around "not too far away from the lifeboats." Most of the POWs would recall this as a period of "settling down." Jim Campbell, sleeping topside as his mate Roy Whitecross had advised him, was feverish. He woke up briefly, then fell back into a drugged sleep. So did most of the rest. *Rakuyo Maru* apparently had survived this night's onslaught.

On *Kachidoki Maru*, only a few men saw this sinking that night. Almost all the POWs were in the hold, in keeping with the captain's rule. Ernest Benford, whose father had died on the railway, was hiding topside with some mates, George R. "Robbie" Shaw, Joseph Anderson, Grapper Grapes and Harry Harding, and he saw it this way: "There was a tremendous explosion. She blew up before our eyes. When the smoke had cleared, she appeared to be in two parts and sank very quickly. There was immediate panic on our ship. Crew and guards were shouting at each other. By then we were down into the holds. We could hear them running about above our heads and shouting for ten minutes or so. We could sense and feel a lot more movement. She was zigzagging in very short legs for such a large vessel." Johnny Sherwood said: "Talk about panic! The bloody Japs were running all over the place shouting."

There was a near disaster on *Kachidoki Maru* at this time. She very nearly collided with another ship. This probably occurred after Oakley's attack on the two overlapping freighters threw the convoy into panic and forced the abrupt course change to the northwest. By this time, Benford and his mates had slipped back up on deck. Benford recalled that Joe spoke suddenly. "He was facing forward. 'Look at that ship ahead, we're catching it up fast.' We all looked. There was a moment of silence: then Robbie was first to speak. 'We're not catching it up,' he said, 'it's heading straight for us.' "

The POWs shouted a warning in a single voice. Pandemonium followed. The ship sounded a series of short blasts on the siren and turned hard to port. The oncoming ship, a large tanker, bore down. The POWs watched, mesmerized. The point of the bows struck *Kachidaki Maru* on the starboard curve of her bows. The ship shuddered and heeled over. The POWs were showered in burned paint and sparks as the tanker scraped along the full length of the ship. Benford: "We could have reached out and touched it. There appeared to be no one on deck and we wondered if they knew what had happened."

Kachidoke Maru heeled to an angle of 45°—or more. Benford went on: "There was lots of shouting. Everyone below wanted to know what was happening. We hung on whilst the ship rocked from side to side, gradually righting, until after what seemed an eternity, she was once again sailing on an even keel." As it turned out, the ship had received no serious damage, merely some deep dents. Two other POWs, Stanley Thompson, thirty-three, a dry cleaner's deliveryman, and Frederick J. King, forty, remembered that on the following day the Japanese mixed some concrete on deck and "plastered" the damage from inside the hull with cement and timbers.

After a time, the excitement quieted down. By 0300 the POWs on both vessels had settled back into fitful sleep. They knew nothing of radar: they had never heard of it. Nor did they know that three submarines were still stalking the convoy.

(6)

The three submarines pursued the convoy, each making its own end around. There had been no radio contact between them after 0219. By 0448, Ben Oakley in *Growler* had lost the convoy. Just why, is not clear. The radar sets were notoriously temperamental. Perhaps in the high-speed chase on the surface hers was jarred out of calibration. Eli Reich in *Sealion* and Pete Summers in

100

Pampanito maintained radar contact on the convoy, but since there was no communication between the boats, they did not know the pack leader had lost it. Had they known, they would not have cared much. Oakley had had his turn at bat.

By 0331, Reich had gained a position about five miles ahead of the convoy. His tracking party reported it was still holding a northwest course—toward the northeast coast of Hainan island. Reich wanted to move to the west of the convoy so that he could attack its port flank downmoon. Yet he hesitated to go west, fearing the convoy might at any moment turn right and resume its original northeast course. If Reich went west and the convoy turned east, *Sealion* would find herself far out of position. To recover, Reich would have to make another end around. But there would not be time for that before sunrise—at 0710. Playing the odds, Reich held position ahead of the convoy, while his tracking party watched sharply for any evidence of a course change.

At 0500 the convoy was still heading northwest, zigzagging radically at a speed of 10.5 knots. Reich was running out of time. In an hour and a half, morning twilight would be upon him. To be on the safe side, he would have to attack within thirty minutes. Accordingly, he maneuvered *Sealion* to a point off the starboard bow of the convoy, distance five miles. Here he was close enough to reach the convoy's present track. If it turned right to its original northeast course, he could also reach the new track.

At 0502, Reich submerged. His plan was to attack from "radar depth," where the boat's hull was submerged but the radar antenna remained above the water. The radar would provide more-precise ranges than the periscope stadimeter, which involved some guesswork. At the same time, Reich would man the periscope, in case the radar failed or the diving officer lost control and "dunked" the antenna. He also wanted to select the best targets and keep a human eye on the convoy for signs of trouble or change.

Periscope visibility was only "fair," but as *Sealion* closed the formation, Reich could begin to make out the ships. There had been no change in course. *Sealion* approached from the starboard bow. In the outboard starboard column, Reich saw there were four ships, led by an escort, a frigate. The first ship in the column was a "large" transport, the second a tanker, the third a freighter or transport, and the fourth a "large" transport, trailing behind the third ship about 1,500 yards (three-quarters of a mile). The fourth ship in line was *Rakuyo Maru*. Reich chose the second ship, the large tanker, for his first target, the fourth ship, *Rakuyo Maru*, for his second. Torpedomen made ready all six bow tubes.

Then, a near calamity! At 0514 the continuous automatically operating gyro setting gear failed again. There was no time now to haul off and repair it. Reich ordered gyros to be set by hand, a less-reliable method since it introduced a human factor, yet not at all unsatisfactory considering the good attack position *Sealion* had on the convoy. The switch-over was accomplished without missing a beat in the approach.

By 0520, Reich was very close to shooting position. In the conning tower, jammed with battle station personnel, there was a continuous flow of numbers. The radar operator, staring at the green scope of the screen, called off ranges and bearings, all the while watching the other ships for signs of change. At the periscope, Reich kept the cross hairs on the first target, the tanker, calling off the angle-on-the-bow estimates, while the quartermaster TDC turned cranks, pumping in the new data, maintaining a "solution" light. In the forward torpedo room, the small gyro angles were cranked into the torpedoes by hand.

By this time, Pete Summers in *Pampanito* had gained position dead ahead of the convoy. His crew was at battle stations; he was on the bridge at the TBT. Because of the bright moon, he, like Reich, planned to attack submerged at radar depth. His able battle station radar operator, Bill Yagemann, backed up by Molly Moffett, called off continuous ranges and bearings. It appeared that by dint of diligent tracking and maneuvering, *Pampanito* had the convoy all to herself. Summers gave orders to the officer of the deck to dive.

On *Sealion*, Reich called out a final periscope bearing and gave the order to shoot. At 0522, his exec, Henry C. Lauerman, twenty-seven, pressed the firing buttons for tubes one, two and three. The torpedo run to the tanker was 2,500 yards. When these torpedoes were away, Reich swung the boat left to aim on the second target, *Rakuyo Maru*. At 0525, Lauerman fired tubes four, five and six. The torpedo run to *Rakuyo Maru* was a mere 1,100 yards (slightly over one-half mile).

All three boats had set off on patrol with a full load (twenty-four) of "electric" torpedoes mounting a warhead of 668 pounds of "Torpex"—souped-up TNT. Copied from a German model earlier in the war, the US navy Mark XVIII electric was preferred by most skippers: while slower and shorter-ranged and more difficult to maintain, it left no telltale "wake" pointing back to the submarine. (Its propellers were turned by power from electric storage batteries.) When Reich had put into Saipan to reload from the tender *Holland,* he found she had no electrics. Thus he had been forced to take older Mark XIV "steam" torpedoes. Mounting the same size warhead and powered by a mixture of alcohol and water, the steam torpedo was faster and longer-ranged, but it made a wake as its propelling gases exhausted into the water.

Through the periscope, Reich watched the first three Mark XIV steam torpedoes streak toward the tanker. He heard three hits. He saw the tanker blow up and burst "immediately into flame." The fire was so intense and bright it clearly illuminated the second target, *Rakuyo Maru.* Reich watched as the second salvo of three steam torpedoes streaked toward the second target. At that distance he could see no sign of life on the ship.

On *Pampanito* the officer of the deck "had his hand on the diving alarm" when Reich's torpedoes slammed into the first ship. As Summers saw it, one or more torpedoes hit one ship, causing a "tremendous explosion." This was probably the lead ship in the starboard column, a transport. The explosion was followed almost immediately by "hits" in "another" ship which "burned brightly." This was no doubt the tanker. Thus if Summers had observed correctly, Reich had unwittingly hit two ships with the first salvo. But some confusion about that would always exist.

Immediately, the convoy radically changed course to the left. As it pulled away, Summers could see escorts turning on red truck lights and zipping everywhere, firing guns and dropping depth charges. *Pampanito*'s perfect attack position had been ruined and, once again, the element of surprise lost. Summers might have charged the fleeing—though very alert—convoy while it was still dark, but he chose a more cautious option, pulling out to make yet another end around.

In *Growler*, Ben Oakley saw the hits in the tanker, logging: "A large column of flame." To his surprise, it was an estimated 20 miles away, due west. Oakley immediately headed for the flame at flank speed. He soon made radar contact on the burning ship, range 12.75 miles. Heedless of the danger, he continued boring in at flank speed, all four engine throttles wide open.

PART FIVE

Abandon Ship

(1)

On *Rakuyo Maru* the POWs were almost instantly aware of *Sealion*'s attack on the ship—or ships—two miles ahead in the starboard column. In the darkness and confusion, they could not make out exactly what had happened—how many ships had been hit—and few of the accounts would match. However, most of them believed, and would later assert, that in this first salvo of three torpedoes, two ships had been hit and set afire, either two tankers or a tanker and a transport.

Four men—Terrence P. "Tobey" Johnson; Michael "Mickey" DeGaura, a well-known Australian jockey in civilian life; William H. "Sam" Fuller and Richard E. Laws—believed the ships destroyed were a tanker and a passenger-cargoman. They put it this way in an official consolidated statement: "A red flare went up and along the port side of the tanker which was right ahead of us. Then two torpedoes struck the tanker and it burst into flames, literally blew up, throwing flaming oil high in the air. Then we saw the ship which had been on the port bow of the tanker swerve in close to the tanker—almost collided, we'd say. . . . That ship was bigger than the *Rakuyo Maru;* she had a clipper bow and several decks. When she joined the convoy off Luzon, a sailor said she looked foreign—like a Scandinavian ship—and was supposed to be loaded with raw rubber. . . . It looked to us as if the other ship had been disabled, for they just seemed to drift into each other. Then the second ship caught fire aft and in a moment, there was a puff of smoke up around her bridge and she was ablaze forward. . . . Just after dawn, the ship which collided with the tanker went down stern first. Half an hour or so later, the tanker sank."

Others—indeed, a majority—would insist that the two ships that sank were both tankers. Blood Bancroft said: "At approximately five thirty A.M., the two tankers, only a few hundred yards off our port bow, blew up within a couple of minutes of each other." Another *Perth* sailor, Francis J. McGovern, twenty-four, saw it this way: "First, one of the tankers went. Just a ball of fire. The whole superstructure went up in flames. Then the other tanker was hit." While William H. Stones, twenty-four, gave a more picturesque description: "There were two tankers hit. Oil spilled all over the water. The ocean was ablaze. It was like Guy Fawkes night."

Later, when Reich returned to Pearl Harbor, Lockwood and his staff carefully evaluated the technical data in *Sealion*'s log. On the basis of that data and Pete Summers' assertion that two ships had been hit, and the testimony of dozens of POWs, Lockwood credited Reich with sinking a tanker of 10,000 tons and a transport of 10,000 tons in this initial three-torpedo salvo. Even if luck played a large hand, two 10,000-ton ships sunk with three torpedoes was an extraordinary achievement, and Reich and *Sealion* would receive high praise for the action.

After the war, when the Allies could consult Japanese records and properly assess damage to the maritime forces, an entirely different story emerged. An official body known as the Joint Army-Navy Assessment Committee (JANAC), assiduously examining all evidence available, concluded that Reich had sunk only one ship in that salvo. This was declared to be the 8,400-ton passenger-cargo vessel *Nankai Maru*. Built in Japan in the early 1920s, she was no larger than *Rakuyo Maru,* nor did she have a clipper bow or in any way resemble a Scandinavian ship. In fact, she looked like a slightly smaller version of *Rakuyo Maru*. The committee could find no record that a tanker had been sunk on this occasion, and that sinking was officially withdrawn.

The Assessment Committee's official sinking report was challenged by many skippers. They argued that Japanese records were incomplete, misleading, misunderstood or, in some cases, deliberately falsified. They provided many instances of unquestionably verified sinkings for which there were no official Japanese records. Although Reich did not officially challenge the Committee, his initial salvo almost certainly falls into this category. There seems no doubt that he sank not only the passenger-cargoman *Nankai Maru* but also a tanker for which no official record could be found.

The best guess, then, as to what happened on that first, three-torpedo salvo, was as follows. One of the three torpedoes hit an unidentified tanker, which instantly blew up and caught fire. The blazing tanker, maintaining some way, continued ahead and collided with the disabled and slowing *Nankai Maru*. The latter vessel might well have had a highly inflammable cargo (oil in drums on deck, for example) that burst into flames, leading some POWs to believe that she, too, was a tanker. In time, both vessels sank.

Whatever had happened, the POWs on *Rakuyo Maru* were electrified. Yet another sea battle had erupted within sight of those topside. This one was far more spectacular than the first. Over the years, the recollections of it would be embellished. Some would remember that "six or eight" or "every ship in the convoy" had been sunk. Few topside slept. Many watched the flames and gunfire in horrified fascination. Which ship would be next?

(2)

Sealion's second salvo of three steam torpedoes streaked toward *Rakuyo Maru*, now sharply silhouetted by the blazing tanker. One torpedo missed. Two others slammed into the vessel, ten seconds apart, one in the bow, one amidships in the engine room. Reich did not see the torpedoes hit. By that time, the starboard flanking frigate had charged and *Sealion* was going deep. However, he and others in the conning tower heard two solid hits, timed for the torpedo runs, and Reich was satisfied that his second salvo had bagged another big ship.

On *Rakuyo Maru* the Japanese crew, fully alert, saw the torpedoes coming. The POWs remembered they shouted: "Torpedoes on the right!" The bow gun crew manned the ancient artillery piece and fired three or four shots, apparently at random, or as a signal. Other Japanese on the bridge shouted orders and ran around, as Harry Weigand recalled, "like monkeys in the jungle." None of the shouts or orders did any good. This time there was no escape for *Rakuyo Maru*.

Some of the POWs, galvanized by the Japanese cries, also saw the torpedoes bearing down on the ship. The

Scotsman Mark Wheeler, thirty, recalls: "I was on deck. I saw a submarine periscope coming up. I whispered to the chap lying beside me, George W. Trafford, 'Hey! Look at that! Don't say nothing.' Then the torpedoes came flying for us. I said, 'Hold tight, now. There are two of them coming straight for us. They're going to sink us.' " The Britisher Thomas Carr recalls it much the same way: "I was on deck, looking over the side. I watched the torpedoes coming. I took a belly dive and told the lads to get down." Ed Starkey: "I was leaning over the side and saw two white trails coming. Everybody ran to the opposite [port] side."

When the torpedoes struck, ten seconds apart, the impact was severe but not cataclysmic. Most of the POWs topside recalled the explosions as "dull thuds." Both torpedoes, set to run at a depth of six feet, struck below the waterline. The one that hit amidships, some two hundred feet aft of Number 2 hold, blew straight into the engine room. The one that hit the bow probably blew into the cargo of rubber in Number 1 hold, or into the chain locker, or both. The impact of the bow hit—perhaps absorbed by the rubber—was so surprisingly mild that some POWs topside believed the torpedo had gone through one side of the ship and out the other without exploding. At impact, the ship shuddered and seemed to fall abruptly. Then the bow dug in, cascading a Niagara of water over the forward deck. It was the water—and the sudden drop —that would be most vividly remembered by those topside.

Harry Weigand recalled those moments of panic this way: "I was standing on Number Three hatch at the time and the impact and concussion of the torpedo threw me off the hatch and up against the winch. I received a nasty cut on the leg and shinbone. I was stunned for a few seconds and then everything was falling down on the ship: bits of steel and wood and rigging off the masts. A great wave of water came right over the fo'c'sle. We had to hang on for dear life to stop from being washed over the side. A great piece of steel just missed my head by inches."

The deluge of water was terrifying. Each man had his own way of describing it. Mark Wheeler: "I was gasping like a fish. My lungs nearly burst." Stan Manning: "I thought the ship had gone straight down. I grabbed some stays to hang on." Sydney C. Matsen, twenty-five, another *Perth* sailor: "It washed me all the way aft to the bridge

110

structure." Arthur Wright: "Hundreds of tons of water poured over us." Harry Pickett: "For a while, it was up around my chest." Bob Farrands: "It flattened us like a tidal wave." George Hinchy: "It was like being in heavy surf." Sidney Johnson: "It was like being hit with a fire hydrant." William R. Smith: "I was swimming, battling very hard, trying to surface, get air. It's a wonder I wasn't swept over the side." Harold Bunker: "It flattened us on deck." Roy Hudson: "I thought I was underneath a waterfall." Bill Cunneen: "I wasn't sure if I was in the sea or on the ship." Alf Allbury: "A solid wall of green pounded me flat on the deck. I lay there, flattened, helpless as the giant sea boiled and hissed about me. I thought for one terrible moment that we were plunging straight down into the boiling sea."

Those in the hold had a somewhat different, but no less terrifying, moment. The impact of the torpedo exploding into Number 1 hold, just forward of the steel bulkhead, was ear-shattering and mind-numbing. The water cascading over the forward deck drained into the hold, leading many to think the ship was on the way to the bottom. Ian MacDiarmid said: "When the water came pouring down the hold, I thought, 'Christ Almighty, we're sinking.'" MacDiarmid, Charles Armstrong, John R. Hocking, twenty-eight, and John R. Langley, thirty-three, remembered there was a strong odor of cordite. Andy Anderson recalled that the shock caused the old paint on the bulkhead to flake off and fall, "like a snowstorm." Ray Wheeler, who was leaning against the forward bulkhead, was injured: "The impact almost wrenched off my arm. My arms and legs bled profusely. There was some metal in them—fragments from I-know-not-where."

The shock of the explosion and the deluge of water caused instant hysteria in the hold. "There was a panic," said Dagger Ward. "Everybody started to get out straightaway. People were yelling and shouting and screaming and pulling each other down as fast as they got up." Harry Smethurst, twenty-three, added: "We knew instantly we'd been torpedoed. Everybody was shouting, 'Let me get out.' Everybody went for the stairway." Leslie Bambridge: "We couldn't all get up the ladder at once. There was a panic, a mad scramble to get out." However, when it was realized that the ship was not

111

sinking, the hysteria quickly subsided and the men commenced a more orderly evacuation.

The explosion of the torpedoes killed an undetermined
number of Japanese. The POWs gained the impression
that "many" had been instantly wiped out in the engine
room. Some topside were killed. Reg Harris, who was
far aft with a mate, Warrant Officer William G. Smith,
recalled that "when the torpedo hit amidships, it blew a
Jap through a door onto the deck. He was killed. We
had to kick him out of the way to get by." The bow hit
probably killed most of the gun crew. Harry Pickett's
words were: "The torpedo hit right under the artillery
piece. The impact knocked the crew over the side."

Within minutes—no more than three—the POWs had
shaken off the shock and made a quick assessment. They
concluded they were very, very lucky indeed. A few men
had been hurt by falling debris, some seriously; a few
had been roughed up by the deluge of water; but not
one POW had been killed and, so far as could be determined, none of them had been washed over the side.
Except for the two gaping holes in her starboard side,
Rakuyo Maru was essentially intact. She had settled
about ten to twelve feet deeper in the water with a slight
starboard list, but there was no indication she was on
the way to the bottom. She seemed to be hanging. There
was no sign of fire. The luckiest break of all was that
the bow torpedo had hit Number 1 hold and not Number
2. Had it struck a mere thirty feet farther aft, hundreds
of POWs would have died instantly.

(3)

The convoy was now in a chaotic state. The tanker and
Nankai Maru burned furiously, lighting up the area.
Rakuyo Maru drifted out of control, held afloat, apparently, by the buoyancy of her cargo of rubber. The six
remaining big ships fled willy-nilly in a westerly direction
—away from *Sealion*. The six frigates raced around firing
guns and dropping depth charges. One or two charged the
area where *Sealion* was detected.

Reich leveled off at 250 feet and rigged *Sealion* for
depth charge attack. He ran silently, evading to the south

112

and east. One escort dropped six depth charges. Fortunately, none was close. Reich eased *Sealion* deeper, to 350 feet, a standard evasive maneuver since the Japanese usually set the depth charges to explode at shallow depths. There were now screw noises on sonar all around the dial, the heavy *thump-thump* of the fleeing big ships, the fast *whir*ring of the escorts which were now "pinging."

One escort got *Sealion* on its sonar and six more charges fell. These were close, severely jarring the boat. Reich descended to 400 feet and changed course 90°, searching for a thermocline—a cold layer of water—which would deflect the *ping*s and give the Japanese a false bearing. Searching, evading, Reich planed down to 525 feet, below *Sealion*'s "test depth." Here, at last, he found safety. The depth charges continued, but now they were not so close.

No real damage had been done to *Sealion,* but the persistence of the escorts had denied Reich a chance to fire his four stern tubes. Had he been able to reach periscope depth and had he seen *Rakuyo Maru* still afloat and close by, he might well have fired one or two more torpedoes into her for good measure. Or he might have chased the fleeing six ships, obtaining their escape course and making a surface end around. Now those opportunities were lost. The escorts would keep *Sealion* pinned down for four hours. The remnants of the convoy would be safely out of *Sealion*'s reach. But she had done a superb job. With only six torpedoes expended, three big ships were headed for the bottom.

It was now up to the other two submarines. Pete Summers in *Pampanito* was heading north, maintaining radar contact on the main body of westbound ships. His tactical plan is not clear. Perhaps he was counting on the convoy to resume its original northeast course, but the range to the main body was steadily opening out. There was slight chance that *Pampanito* could achieve an attack position on a northerly course. Ben Oakley in *Growler* continued to close the smoke and radar pips on a direct course at flank speed.

(4)

On *Rakuyo Maru* the Japanese, without a word to the POWs, abandoned ship quickly and efficiently. They lowered away the ten lifeboats on the boat deck plus a smaller blue "rowboat," which the POWs believed to be the private property of the ship's captain, and a punt. The ten lifeboats and the rowboat, each filled with Japanese, reached the water within five minutes of the first torpedo hit. Two lifeboats on the poop were left behind.

Most of the Japanese abandoned ship in these boats, but many simply leaped over the side, with or without life preservers, probably intending to climb into a lifeboat from the water. William Emmett recalled that a Japanese guard rushed to the forward deck "firing his gun at I don't know what" and then jumped into the water. George Hinchy embellished the story with: "The Japs were screaming and jumping off the side of the bridge. I saw maybe eight or nine of them. They had their arms out when they hit the water; the life jackets came up and broke their necks. We didn't shed any tears." Bill Cunneen saw an officer on the bridge, decked out in Samurai sword and Wellington boots. He screamed and leaped into the water. Cunneen, happily: "He never came up again. One less."

Some POWs, responding to a survival instinct, ran aft to get in the lifeboats. They were rudely rebuffed. Thomas Carr: "The Japs took all the lifeboats. We weren't allowed near them. The Japs were standing there with tommy guns to keep us from the boats." Harold Ramsey said: "I went down the side of the ship where the Japs were getting into the lifeboats. They held us back with rifles and bayonets."

Despite these obstacles, quite a few POWs found a way into the boats. The most brazen case was that of Tommy Moxham, a streetwise Sydneyite who had vowed all along he would do so. The doctor Rowley Richards

114

would never forget Moxham's performance: "Tommy and his brother Harry were both on *Rakuyo Maru*. Tommy didn't worry about Harry, he just went. He got in the little blue rowboat with the ship's captain. He survived, Harry didn't." Russ Savage saw this, too: "There was a rope tying the rowboat to the ship. Tommy grabbed the captain's sword and cut them adrift. Tommy told me he threw the captain overboard and kept pushing him under the water and drowned him." Moxham returned to *Rakuyo Maru*, climbing a Jacob's ladder.

Raymond Burridge, thirty, whose younger brother Frank was in a Borneo POW camp, might also have entered this boat: "I saw a little dinghy and went into the water. There were two Japanese officers in it in full uniform, with swords three or four feet long. I swarmed over the side into the boat. Another POW came over the other side. The Japs said, 'You row.' So we started rowing. I said to the other bloke, 'When I count three, you get the one in front and I'll get the one in back.' So we tipped the boat over and drowned the Japs." Later, Burridge swam back and reboarded the *Rakuyo Maru*.

Harold Ramsey and William Mayne and a swarm of other POWs boarded another boat—with about the same results. The boat was a small punt. It had been lowered by two Japanese officers. Ramsey recalled what took place: "Before they could pull off, thirteen of us slid down ropes into the boat. One of our chaps said, 'Wait for me.' When we said we couldn't, he got very angry and threw a boat hook at us." It missed.

The eight-foot boat, now laden with fifteen men, sank until it had only a few inches of freeboard. The boat drifted toward the burning tanker, now aflame from stem to stern. Mayne: "We could hear the screams of men —either about to drown or those aboard the burning tanker. We could distinguish the Jap crew running about and some blown off by exploding drums of oil."

The Japanese were unnerved by the screams of their dying countrymen. One officer tied his sword to an oar and tried futilely to scull the overladen punt away from the flames. One officer stood up and stepped over the side, wearing full uniform and knee boots. This caused the boat to capsize. The officer never came to the surface, Mayne recalled. Leaving the other POWs clinging to the boat, Ramsey and Mayne swam back to *Rakuyo Maru* to begin again.

The Britisher Sidney Johnson and his mucker Lester Murrell ran aft, slid down a rope hanging from a davit and landed in a lifeboat occupied by two or three Japanese. Johnson said that the Japs weren't concerned about them. "They were trying to get the ropes untangled and get away from the ship. We pitched in and manned the oars. As quickly as we could, we pulled off about fifty yards from the ship. All the while people were climbing aboard from the water—both POWs and Japanese. In not very long, we were filled. We had about twenty Japs and fifteen-odd POWs." The POWs were not ejected from this boat.

Some Japanese did not escape the ship. They were waylaid by the POWs, who seized the moment to even old scores. The British recalled that these assaults were mostly the work of Australians. Harry Smethurst said this about it: "One big bloke picked up a sword and chopped up about six Japs. He just went berserk." William Stones saw that too: "An Australian—with a bush hat on—got a sword from a Japanese officer. I think he strangled him. Then he hacked up about a half-dozen Japs." Harry Jones remembered that "half a dozen or so POWs silenced the bow deck gun crew in no uncertain manner." He added: "At least they could say they had died for the emperor—even if it was a little bloody."

Later the Australians freely conceded these assaults. Vic Clifford recalled that his mate Frank McGrath (also of the luckless 2nd Pioneers) was one of the assailants: "Frank was a big, solid, strong guy who looked after me. He went berserk. I shouldn't say berserk. He probably just figured he was going to take some of them with him. We went aft. We saw some Japs coming up from the hold. Frank picked up a piece of timber—like a two-by-four—and as the Japs came up, he hit them in the head. I stood behind him. He wasn't killing them, just bashing them in the head. He got about three or four of these chaps." Bill Cunneen, who witnessed the massacre, applauded McGrath, recalling that a couple of other Australians tossed the stunned Japs over the side. "Real teamwork," Cunneen said.

Reginald S. Stewart, twenty-one, Harry Pickett and his mate Mac McCracken went aft in search of life preservers. Stewart told how they made out: "I and two mates, Jack ["Bags"] Baguley and Jock Ryan, were looking for life jackets. We saw these Jap girls running

116

and screaming. Three Jap soldiers grabbed them and threw them in the cabin and took their life jackets. The soldiers came out with the jackets in their hands. They never had time to put them on. I and my mates, Bags and Jock, grabbed some metal angle irons. We hit the soldiers with the bars and got the jackets." Pickett and McCracken watched approvingly.

Ron Miscamble ran into his mate, Reggie Harris. "I said, 'Reg what shall we do?' He said, 'Let's go throw the Storm Trooper over the side.' The Storm Trooper was one of our bad guards. I said, 'Bugger the Storm Trooper, let's worry about ourselves.' "

Within a very short time—perhaps no more than ten minutes—all but a handful of the Japanese had left the ship or been disposed of. The Japanese in the lifeboats nested well clear of *Rakuyo Maru*—and the POWs. The few Japanese who remained behind showed no inclination to exert authority over the POWs; on the contrary, they were friendly and helpful. Thus, for the first time in two and half years, the POWs found themselves unguarded. They were free men, technically no longer POWs. The freedom had come suddenly and bewilderingly. What each man would make of this gift would depend on his courage, will to live, survival instinct and luck.

(5)

All this time, the British and the Australians up forward had been leaving the *Rakuyo Maru* in droves. Fearing the ship would sink instantly and suck them down, or that another salvo of torpedoes might strike or that (as it seemed) the ship might drift into the flaming waters around the tanker and catch fire, many had jumped overboard immediately after the torpedoes hit. Twenty-five percent of the men still had no life preservers. David H. Clark, twenty-three, remembered that the blocks of rubber issued by the Japanese in Singapore as life preservers "sank on impact with the water." Only a few had canteens. Many were caught in strong currents and swept away from the ship toward the burning oil. Some who had no life preservers or other support and could not swim, panicked and drowned.

Others topside devoted their energies to helping the hundreds of men out of the hold. The chief petty officer from the *Perth,* Vic Duncan, assisted by many, executed the plan he had conceived for this emergency. They shoved the long hatch boards down into the hold and lowered cargo nets and ropes. The Australian, Francis A. "Titch" Lemin, who had turned twenty on August 6 and who was probably the youngest POW on the ship (he had lied about his age and joined the army at sixteen), remembered: "Vic Duncan—he was a terrific bloke." Many other Australians would echo that sentiment.

There was no longer raw panic in the hold, merely an ardent desire to evacuate as quickly as possible. John Langley climbed up a rope "hand over hand." Ian Mac-Diarmid went up the regular companionway amid a surging mass of bodies. Douglas G. Mayers, twenty-three, scaled one of the cargo nets. Harold Ramsey and scores of others came up a hatch board "like monkeys." John Wade and his older brother Ernest J. came up through a ventilator. By these means, in very short order the hold was evacuated without injury or noteworthy incident.

While the one group was helping evacuate the hold, other groups, some directed by officers, notably Captain Sumner, began throwing floatable objects over the side. These groups concentrated first on the stacks of life rafts lashed to the decks. The rafts came in various sizes and shapes. The majority were wooden floats, structures about 4 by 6 feet in surface and about 4 to 6 inches deep, with handhold ropes looped along the four sides. These floats were not designed to be sat upon but rather to support the weight of four to eight men in the water holding to the side ropes and supported additionally by life preservers. Optimally, the sixty rafts provided sufficient flotation for about one-third of the POWs.

Engaged in the heavy work of cutting the lashings and manhandling the rafts over the side, Paddy Dunne was astonished to find a Japanese, wearing a white sweater, pitching in to help. He might have been one of the civilians left behind; Dunne never found out because "one of the rafts hit him in the chest. He went down on deck, dead as a doornail. I don't know what came over me. I took his sweater and put it on. Then I defecated beside his body."

As they became available, the long hatch boards were tossed into the water. They would prove to be ideal rafts, superior in some respects to the floats. Each was large and sturdy enough to support three men out of the water, many more in the water. Each had a recessed handhold with a metal bar on both ends. This made them easy to lift over the side and provided a hold for those who used them as rafts.

Still others roamed the decks, tossing over anything that looked as though it would float. Tables and chairs from the dining saloon. Small hatch covers. The POW cookhouse on the aft deck and fowl coops. Oil drums. Pieces of bamboo. Wooden bits of timber lying on deck. Boxes of dried fish. Some even threw over the blocks of rubber issued by the Japanese, but no one had any faith in these.

The rain of falling debris imperiled some of those who had jumped. Denny Smith, twenty-four, recalled: "A lot of lads were killed because we were hitting them with the things we were chucking over." Ernest Fieldhouse saw a piece of debris fall "right on top of six heads." When he looked again, "the heads were gone." John Wade remembered that an Australian corporal, an orderly, broke his back when he jumped and landed on debris. Fortunately, however, these accidents were not common.

After a time, when it was realized that *Rakuyo Maru* would not instantly plunge to the bottom or drift into burning oil, the stampede on deck subsided. The officers managed to impose military discipline. The abandon ship procedure became more orderly. A raft would go over followed by six to eight men, then another raft and another contingent. In preparation, men pulled on life jackets and filled canteens. The men going over the side could see a string of heads bobbing in the water amid the floating debris. The line appeared to be strung out a mile, perhaps more. Clearly the currents here were strong, quickly taking the men far away from *Rakuyo Maru*.

Not everyone made haste to abandon ship. Some of the *Perth* group—Vic Duncan, Frank McGovern and his mate Jerry Parkes—judged the ship to be "on an even keel" and "not sinking too fast on account of the rubber cargo." When he heard about the two lifeboats left behind on the poop, Duncan suggested that these might be utilized by the POWs. When this word spread, some POWs—including many of the Australian and British officers—hung back. The doctor, Rowley Richards, joined this group. These men, and others, explored the ship, scrounging for food, water and survival aids.

McGovern and Parkes made straight for a ship's galley. This compartment was partially flooded, but they managed to collect some burnt rice from the sides of the cauldrons, a keg of *mizu* paste and two small kegs of water. Then they went up to the bridge to look for navigation gear. They found a small chart, which McGovern pocketed. He then took this opportunity to defecate, using some other charts for toilet paper.

Paddy Dunne, in his white sweater, and a mate conducted a similar exploration. In the Japanese passengers' cabins and a galley, they found bottles of sake, cigars and cigarettes, bread and cakes. They took swigs from the sake bottle and wolfed down the food. Returning to the forward deck, they offered the sake bottle to the British officers. It was gratefully received.

Russ Savage and his mates Ian MacDiarmid and James R. Mullens explored aft for goodies. They found drinking water and some rice in a cauldron. They drank and ate heartily and had a smoke. Savage: "The main thing was to always keep your stomach full when you had the opportunity. You never knew when the next time would be." Savage remembered there were men exploring all over the ship: "One chap went up to the radio room to try to send a message, but he couldn't. One chap went up to the bridge and did his business just to show what he thought of the Japanese. One chap came up with armloads of Jap money."

One man who tried to operate the radio was the British Sergeant Harry Jones. "I decided to look in the radio room to see if anything could be done. But the radio, such as it was, had been smashed to pieces by the Japs." Jones made his way to the captain's cabin, where he found POWs "calmly sitting down enjoying the captain's tinned food and cigarettes." They invited him to partake. One said, "Let the bloody ship sink. If I'm to die, at least I shall die with a full stomach."

Vic Clifford and the Jap-swatter Frank McGrath were joined by two other mates, Leslie Limbrick (Clifford's brother-in-law) and "Bluie" Dewsbery, so called because of his red hair. Limbrick and Dewsbery jumped over the side, but Clifford and McGrath decided to scrounge for food. "We went down a couple of flights and found the galley. We found stew and bread. We grabbed as much as we could eat. What the hell? If you're going to go, you're going to go. You might just as well go full as empty."

Ernest Fieldhouse and three mates also went up to the captain's cabin in search of food or anything else of use. There was a Japanese flag on one wall and several packs of English cigarettes on a table, stamped "Ajax—Duty Free for H.M. Ships Only." They found—and ate—some soya beans and sugar, then smoked. One man climbed into the captain's chair and said, commandingly: "Right, you men. Get the ship going. We'd better turn back for Singapore. No, the Japs are there. We'd better make for America. We'll see to the Japs later."

(6)

Probably 90 percent of the POWs left the ship in the first half-hour. It was a moment of highest drama. Fear of death—by drowning, fire, shark attack and other causes—commingled with the exhilaration of newfound freedom and a desire for revenge against the Japanese and Koreans.

Sam Fuller and his mucker George Prichard were among the very first to jump. They had been standing on a *benjo* when the torpedoes struck. They dived over instantly, without life preservers. Fuller wore a St. Anthony medal, a gift from Catholic missionaries in the Thailand jungle, but in his haste, he'd left behind his second most coveted possession: a chrome Ford hubcap that had served as his mess tin for two and a half years. A poor swimmer, he grabbed a floating board and looked around for Prichard. He was gone. Fuller never saw him again.

The cabinetmaker Charles Perry, a survivor of the sinking of the *Empress of Asia*, now abandoned ship for the second time. He recalled: "I was always pushy, always trying to be the first, so I was on the first raft." He left his $15,000 in Malayan money with his *kumicho*, Lieutenant Keyes. A Japanese tried to get on the raft. Perry shoved him away, but an Australian said: "Let him on." Whereupon the Australian choked him to death. Perry

121

concluded his story. "He threw him back in the water and said, with a bit of satisfaction: 'That's one less.'"

Eric C. Halfhide, thirty, a good swimmer, jumped without a life jacket. He found an oil drum and clung to its rim. Then he shifted to a raft, where there were four other men. Two Japanese attempted to cling to the raft, but "an ex-sailor and I pushed them under and drowned them."

Alf Allbury, having lost his mate Ted Jewell in the confusion on deck, jumped alone. He found the sea "surprisingly warm." He swam away from the ship and came upon a bearded nonswimmer holding a half-submerged spar. Allbury took the man in tow and made for a raft. But there were already eighteen men clinging to this raft. He left the nonswimmer and shifted to a less-crowded raft. There, to his utter amazement, he found Ted Jewell, a poor swimmer who had no life jacket. Allbury gave his life jacket to Jewell and hung on.

After filling their stomachs, Vic Clifford and Frank McGrath decided it was time to go over. They were still in the aft end of the ship. Spying some Japanese in the water, McGrath jumped first. Clifford hung back: "I just stood and watched him. He got this Nip around the neck and throttled him. *Gurgle*. Then he went on to another one. *Gurgle, gurgle*. Then to a third one and *gurgle, gurgle, gurgle*. They both disappeared. Either the Nip was strong and pulled him under or Frank ran out of steam. He was gone. He didn't even last an hour. He died within thirty or forty feet from the ship."

Clifford entered the water determined not to emulate McGrath's needless death. He saw a floating boom and swam to it. There were five other men hanging onto the spar, all Japanese. One of them said to Clifford: "No goodka, no goodka." Clifford thought, "Too right," and swam off because "I was afraid of those Japs. I thought I was swimming as fast as Boy Charlton [an Australian swimming champ], but every time I looked over my shoulder, I'd only gained about three inches or a foot." He finally made it to a piece of debris. Then he breathed easier.

Charles Armstrong teamed up with a half-dozen of his mates, seized a wooden staircase, threw it over the side and jumped in behind it. "We could not sit on the staircase, for our weight forced it underwater. So we just got a grip and hung on." Armstrong remembered the dream he had had in Singapore three nights in a row: that he would be torpedoed and then rescued. One part had come true, but would the second part?

Leslie Bolger, a poor swimmer, jumped with his mate William Scarpella. He grabbed a 4 by 4 foot raft with rope handholds on the side. Soon there were fifteen men clinging to this raft, including the Tasmanian doctor, Major Chalmers. Bolger's mate Scarpella was nowhere to be seen. Bolger, a devout Catholic, had a St. Dominic medal in his wallet, which was in the pocket of his jacket. It was the gift of a Sister Dominic, an Australian nun, who had told him: "This medal will bring you back." Bolger prayed.

Norman Ashworth, twenty-four, teamed with two mates, "Dabber" Hope and Jimmy Kershaw. They went amidships, found a raft, tied a line to it and threw it over. After Hope and Kershaw were in the water, Ashworth remembered his toothbrush and dentifrice. All along, he had been obsessive about the care of his teeth. He ran forward to the spot where he kept his things, got his toothbrush and dentifrice, put them in the pocket of his bush jacket and then jumped. The three men released the line and pushed the raft away from the burning oil. Ashworth felt no danger: "We were free for the first time in two and a half years. That's what really counted."

Phil Beilby, one of the last to leave the hold, threw over a hatch board and jumped with a life preserver and three full canteens. He had left behind his most coveted possession: his battered clarinet. When he hit the water, he lost one of the canteens. He climbed onto the hatch board and propelled himself along until he found the owner of one of the canteens, Victor Cross. They joined a big group on a raft, where there was a Japanese officer who displayed uncommon humanity. Beilby reported that he had a bottle of brandy and he passed it around until it was empty. His humanity probably saved his life.

When Alf Winter jumped over, he forgot to fold his arms over the kapok pocket on his chest. When he hit the water, the pocket flew up and cracked him in the chin and nearly knocked him out. He swam to a raft, already crowded with eight men. Then Winter said, "Gee, we'd better go back and get some drinking water." The others agreed. They paddled back to the *Rakuyo Maru*. Winter went up a Jacob's ladder that was hanging over the side. He found a "pile" of canteens brimming with water on the deck, but no corks. He gathered six and lowered them to the raft. "Immediately a wave came and tipped them over." They set the canteens upright again, but on the tippy raft, it was difficult to keep them from spilling. They paddled away from the ship as fast as possible, "deadly scared the ship would sink and drag us under."

Norman D. "Shorty" Calvert, twenty-three, a poor swimmer, and his mate William Jinks, an excellent swimmer, jumped together. Calvert explained that when he jumped, he went down and down. He thought he'd never come up. He had left behind a "little gold box" full of jewelry, the property of a friend who had died of dysentery in Burma. Calvert had promised "never to sell it" and to deliver it to the man's widow in Australia. Calvert and Jinks thrashed to a raft, already crowded. Jinks uncorked his canteen for a sip, but, Calvert ruefully remembered: "The bloody cork was no good. Salt water had seeped in." Most of the canteens were World War I vintage, with corks rather than screw tops. Like Jink's, most would become contaminated with salt water.

Ernest Hughes and two other Britishers, all nonswimmers, hesitated at the rail. "A Jap officer came up and asked why we weren't leaving the ship," Hughes said. "We told him we couldn't swim. So he told us to go up to the sun deck and get a raft." There they found four rafts, each with a hole cut in the center. They tossed one over, climbed down ropes into the water and paddled away, using a bamboo stick for a paddle. "Two Japs on a hatch board came by, talking nice, like, 'Hello, Tommy.' So we invited them to fasten their plank to our raft with a rope. We thought that when the Japs rescued them, we'd be rescued, too," said Hughes. Many others spared—or helped—Japanese with the same idea in mind.

Sergeant John J. Flynn, twenty-seven, was one of the few injured on the topside deck by the torpedo. He had been forward. The impact blew him into the air, and he landed back on deck on his head. He was still groggy when he slid down a rope into the water wearing a life preserver. A devout Catholic, he had a tortoise shell rosary around his neck. He joined two other men on a hatch board. "Then I vomited. It was caused by the hit on my head, I think. My head was ballooning a bit behind the ear. When I came around properly, I was on this board all alone. I was bleeding and had a chunk out of my left wrist. I joined a group of rafts."

A. Anthony "Tony" Clive, twenty-nine, threw over a hatch board and jumped. He, too, was in a bad way. He had malaria and had been blown up in the air by the torpedo impact, gashing his right elbow on the forward mast. He and another Australian—he never knew his name—crawled onto the hatch board and sat at either end, like two men on a seesaw. They paddled away from the ship. Clive: "I saw a medical orderly hanging on a raft. I swam over to him and asked him to have a look at my arm. It was badly bruised and bleeding. I wanted to find out if it was broken. It wasn't. But, of course, there was nothing he could do to help me, so I swam back to the hatch board."

After helping to evacuate the hold, the sailor Blood Bancroft and his mate, another *Perth* survivor, H. Lionel "Lofty" Nagle, jumped over the port side. Each had a life preserver. Bancroft also had a full, corked canteen of fresh water. A new diary he was keeping was wrapped in a cloth envelope and stuffed in the pocket of his tunic. They swam away from the burning oil to a group of rafts and wreckage, holding to ropes. In this group there was another Japanese officer. He, too, was spared to serve as "bait" for the rescue vessels.

The gardener Roy Hudson confessed that "many didn't jump immediately. I guess we were a little dumbfounded. We'd never had this order given us before. It takes a bit of doing. I had a life jacket. After twenty minutes, I jumped in with a chap named Frederick Carter. He didn't have a life jacket. We grabbed a raft and hung on." Left behind on *Rakuyo Maru* was the Ronald Searle sketch of Hudson, still in its bamboo tube.

Frank Coombes might well have asked himself what he'd done to deserve such a fate. He had been a member of the only unit that escaped intact from Singapore—the 3rd Motor Transport. They had embarked on a steamer and fled to Java, where they ran aground. As the Japanese closed in on them, Coombes had driven a truck containing all the luggage belonging to the outfit to a ship just getting underway for Australia. The ship's captain had urged Coombes to get aboard and escape with them, but Coombes had declined, thinking it would be desertion. That decision had landed him here, after two and a half years of hell as a prisoner of war.

Coombes jumped in and climbed on a hatch board. He lay flat on it "like a surfboard" and paddled around with his hands, looking for a place to light. He wore a leather money belt around his waist. It contained the remnants of a sizable collection of jewelry given him and his mate Ron Jones in Singapore, before they got away to Java, by a Chinese they had helped. What was left of Coombes's share was an earring adorned with nine small diamonds and a gold bracelet with thirty-two diamonds. He finally joined a group of rafts, and nearby "there was a Jap officer in the water with a couple of Samurai swords hanging around his neck and about four canteens. Very friendly. He asked if he could get on the raft. One of the blokes on the raft called him over and pushed him under and held him down."

The ex-merchant marine sailor Mac McKittrick also had a small store of jewelry he had collected in Singapore before the surrender. His was "a bundle of stones in a handkerchief." He kept these and a library book, *The Yearling*, and a Bible he had read "fifteen times" in his haversack. When he jumped from *Rakuyo Maru* in company with two mates, John Hunt (a lifeguard in civilian life) and John Skene, he left his treasures behind. McKittrick said: "Hunt and Skene were both very good swimmers. They were frolicking around like you would at the beach. I warned them not to waste energy. I never saw them again. They wore themselves out foolishly. A lot of good swimmers did the same."

In the confusion on deck, Harry Pickett's mate Mac McCracken was knocked out. When he got ready to go over the side, Pickett clamped the unconscious McCracken between his legs and went down a rope. Left behind in Pickett's haversack hanging on the ship was yet another sizable stash of jewelry. Pickett explained how he had got it: "In Burma, I discovered the Japs hid their illegal valuables in hollowed-out heels of their boots. They left their boots outside the huts at night and I stole as many as I could. I had three thousand Australian pounds' worth of uncut diamonds and a pair of jade earrings I had to leave behind." When they got into the water, Mac revived. They each mounted a hatch board. They saw some Japanese clinging to wreckage. "We put them out of their misery," Pickett said. "Pushed them under and held them. I drowned two."

Don McArdle threw a raft over and jumped after it. He plunged deep beneath the water. When he surfaced, lungs bursting, he could not find his raft, but another floated by and he grabbed it. He had a life preserver and, beneath it, his small haversack, which contained some papers, photographs and three wristwatches—his own and those of two friends killed in the fighting in Malaya. He was saving them to give to their parents when he got back to Australia. McArdle joined with four other Australians on the raft. "We had a few Japs amongst our group. A bunch of us took care of about four. We just held them underwater for a while, until they ran out of breath. and that was it."

After leaving the captain's cabin, Sergeant Harry Jones returned to the main deck to abandon ship. He was momentarily mesmerized by a small drama. The Japanese had left the "jig-a-jig" girls to go down with the ship. Four or five POWs took pity on them, outfitted them with life preservers and threw them over the side, shouting, "Over you bloody well go." Jones recalled they "appeared to be quite happy when they found themselves floating." Jones, leaving his valuable diary behind, jumped with an Australian and clung to a raft. He was fascinated by the murders taking place. "It was an amazing sight to see the Japs swimming over the water on huge timbers, using their hands as a means of propulsion, and ten or twenty POWs using the same means of travel, cutting them off in beautiful scissorlike movements—settling accounts for the last two and a half years."

Ray Wheeler, injured in the hold when the torpedo struck, returned to the hold to collect his personal effects before leaving. These consisted of a wallet, army pay book, photos, a personal diary and a bottle of pills he had been collecting for escape. (It contained mostly quinine.) He wore a sterling silver ring from the Middle East which, in Burma, "had been passed on by blokes that died." He was the fourth man to wear it. He had swapped a history of the Gordon Highlanders ("too heavy to carry") for it. Before jumping. Wheeler broke into one of the passenger cabins, found rice and biscuits (which he ate) and filled his canteen. He went over the side with Robert Dart and "Snowy" Walker. Dart, a weak swimmer, feared the water. Wheeler, still groggy and bleeding from his injuries, helped him into the water and shepherded him to a raft.

The Britisher Tommy Smith was also casual—and careful—in his departure. "Everybody was just diving off and swimming away. That wasn't for me. It was too dark. I wasn't keen to get in the water. I sat down on the deck and had a few smokes." He and two others, Jesse Harrison and Thomas Taylor, found a raft on the sun deck. They collected canteens left behind and filled their own. Smith found half a coconut and shoved that into the top of his life jacket. Then they launched the raft, jumped in and linked up with some other rafts, making a total of seventeen men in the group. Smith said: "I had a knife. I divided the half-coconut into seventeen parts, each about the size of a fingernail."

Harry Weigand was about to leap off the stern when he remembered that he had photographs of his wife Hilda (whom he called "Chickie") and son William in his haversack. He rushed forward to retrieve these personal effects. He said to himself: "Chickie, you and Bill will bring me luck." Then he ran aft again, pausing at the ship's galley for a "final drink of water," then went over the side. He swam out and joined a raft with eight other men, where, he said: "There were plenty of Japs on the rafts with our boys. One Jap officer really tickled my fancy. He had all his clothes on, boots with spurs, a little cap and his cheese-cutter sword strapped up his back." Weigand enjoyed the officer's misery: "There was fear of the water in his face. He really looked funny."

The Britisher Denny Smith had this memory of it: "I dived off a rail, twenty or thirty feet. I swam away fast. There were people all around in the water. Everywhere you looked there were men holding onto anything. Many nonswimmers were already dead. I and a couple of chaps, [William] Billy Bensley and [F. E.] Curly Wiles, an ex-prize fighter from London, made it to one of the *benjos* and hung on. We could partly get on it. Head and chest. We propped anything we could find under the toilet to make it float better."

Among the last to leave the ship were the Australian officers. Brigadier Varley, Captain Arthur Sumner, Lieutenants Lester Stupart, Laurie Phillips, James A. Burke and Campbell E. Smith, Phil Beilby, Bob Farrands, Harry Pickett, Bill Cunneen and Ray Wheeler all saw Brigadier Varley in the water. Wheeler remembers that "the men begged Brigadier Varley and the American Air Force Colonel [Melton] to take a lifeboat, but they said they'd take their chances in the water."

Those who saw Captain Sumner in the water had nothing but praise for his conduct. Neville Thams was one who told about it: "He was always on the move. He was instrumental in trying to keep everybody together in the water. He said not to stray too far because if a ship did come, it would be quicker and easier to rescue us if we were all together. And we had sick fellows. It was no good having the sick all over the place, so within reason, he tried to keep them together."

And so they jumped, by the dozens, scores, hundreds. By 0600 there were probably twelve hundred British and Australians in the water. They were strung out as far as the eye could see, clinging desperately to rafts and wreckage, calling out for mates and muckers, organizing into floating islands. Seldom had so many men abandoned a seagoing vessel with so little for survival. It was the hope —and expectation—of every man that before the day was over they would be picked up by the Japanese.

PART SIX

Rule Britannia

(1)

By 0615, about forty-five minutes after Reich had torpedoed *Rakuyo Maru*, Ben Oakley in *Growler*, still on the surface, had closed to the scene of *Sealion*'s attack. Oakley saw the tanker burning "fiercely" and logged that the "freighter" (actually *Nankai Maru*) "continues to burn." He was then tracking a radar pip (very likely *Rakuyo Maru*), but "the background of smoke and clouds" was so dark he could not see his target. The moon was bright; morning twilight was coming on. To avoid being seen, Oakley submerged to radar depth at 0624 and summoned his men to battle stations. He would shoot at whatever came his way.

The sonar operator reported "two ships" pinging. Oakley speculated correctly that they were escorts "standing by the ships in trouble." Five minutes later, at 0629, Oakley spotted a pinger through the periscope. It was one of the frigates. He incorrectly identified it as a 1,700-ton "Fubuki Class" destroyer of the "Amagiri Group." (Such misidentifications, usually for a larger ship, were commonplace among submarine skippers.) She had "two very broad well-raked stacks with wide base and typical Jap curved bow," Oakley logged. "Each stack had a black band at the top and the after one had a white band below the black." She was signaling another escort by yardarm blinker.

Oakley unhesitatingly made ready to attack this "destroyer," his third on this patrol. He descended to periscope depth and ordered *Growler* rigged for depth charge attack. At 0652 he fired six electric torpedoes from his bow tubes, range 1,650 yards. As the sixth left the tube, the diving officer momentarily lost control of the boat. *Growler*, bow down, plunged deeper. The periscope went under. Oakley decided then to "go deep" in case the torpedoes missed and the "destroyer" attacked. He ordered three hundred feet.

133

On the way down, Oakley heard two solid hits, timed for the torpedo runs of Number 1 and Number 3 tubes. "These hits were heard through the hull as well as on sound gear, and they were definitely not depth charges," Oakley wrote. Less than one minute after the first hit, the men on *Growler* heard five depth charges explode within the space of about three seconds—too fast to have been systematically launched. Thereafter, they heard no more pinging or screw noises from the escort. Then they heard loud crackling, one heavy explosion, a second heavy explosion, a distant depth charge, two more explosions, and finally, heavy "crackling, hissing, popping." These were indisputably "breaking-up noises" of the torpedoed and sinking frigate, intermixed with her exploding depth charges. The doomed vessel was the frigate *Hirado,* 860 tons.

Growler's attack took place not too far from the mass of men who had abandoned *Rakuyo Maru.* Blood Bancroft, Harold Bunker, Bob Farrands, William G. Smith, Ray Wheeler and Leslie Bambridge, among others, saw the frigate signaling the other escorts, then get hit. Bancroft, who also believed it to be a destroyer, said: "It blew up." Bunker said: "It just went *pffffffft.*" Farrands was more descriptive: "One half went one way, the other, the other." Smith described it this way: "There was a terrific explosion, a cloud of smoke and no sign of the ship." Wheeler saw it as: "The bridge part went up in the air and the two halves went down together. Within seconds there was virtually nothing there," and Bambridge remembered: "There was a bloody 'clang' and he was gone. He went straight down."

There was a mixed reaction to this awesome sight. Many were pleased to see the Japanese suffer another ship loss. Arthur Wright said: "We gave the sub a cheer and had a smoke on the strength of it—three puffs per man." Others—those who had been counting on the ship to rescue them from the sea—were not so ebullient. Frank Johnson recalled: "Here we were in the middle of the South China Sea, with nothing, and our stupid chaps are cheering."

Another frigate raced over to attack *Growler* with depth charges. She evidently did not have the submarine located by sonar, because the charges were wildly off the mark. But they fell very near the men in the water.

These continuing explosions, together with the terrific blast of *Hirado*'s instant disintegration, caused brutal and terrifying shock waves in the sea.

Barney Barnett described the sensation as "horrible— like it was squeezing your stomach into your throat." John Langley: "It was about the worst experience I ever had. First there was a slight tingling in the spine like an electric shock. Then the concussion. You vomited and moved your bowels at the same time." Alf Allbury: "The walls of my stomach collasped and my bowels emptied." Reg Harris: "It was like someone kicking you in the stomach." Jim Campbell: "I suddenly had a feeling as though someone was slamming me in the stomach with a sledgehammer." The ex-jockey Mickey DeGaura: "Each explosion nearly doubled us up with pain." Frank Coombes: "I saw many men vomiting blood." Leslie Bolger: "I was violently ill. I vomited."

Two men, Don McArdle and Ron Miscamble, were severely injured. McArdle: "I felt this *'whack'* in my gut. Then something trickling inside. I'd burst a blood vessel in the wall of my stomach. It swelled, getting bigger." Miscamble : "I came up vomiting and bleeding from one ear. I was in great pain and shock. I couldn't hang on. Reg Harris saved my life then. He held me up for at least an hour."

Some men might have been killed outright by the explosions, or mortally wounded; at any rate, Reginald H. "Jock" Hart, Jim Campbell, Harold Bunker and Doug Hampson were convinced of it. Hampson was sure his mate died the next day because of it.

Ernest Fieldhouse might have had the most terrifying experience of all the men who lived to tell about it. He was evidently very close to the exploding charges, one hundred yards or less. On the first, he was "half-stunned" and "lifted bodily out of the water and flung some distance." With each succeeding blast, he was again lifted and flung or driven deep beneath the water. He survived with no broken limbs, but he was "numbed and sick . . . too numb to feel any pain . . . completely overwhelmed."

On *Growler*, Ben Oakley was unaware of this suffering—or even that there were survivors from the *Rakuyo Maru* in the water. He heard depth charges, but they were not close enough for concern. Uppermost in his mind then was to get a periscope photograph of the sinking "destroyer" for verification purposes. He logged: "Very anxious to get a picture of this baby."

Growler thwarted this goal, however. She had become inordinately heavy, probably owing to some miscalculations on the part of the harassed diving officer. Instead of rising, as Oakley wished, the boat "settled to 350 feet," and Oakley had to put on speed to keep her from sinking deeper. It was a frustrating state of affairs. By the time the diving officer had the boat firmly under control, sonar reported the screws of another escort nearby. Since Oakley had only one torpedo left, another attack was out of the question, and a rise to periscope depth for a photograph would have been foolishly risky. So he lay doggo for the next hour and a half.

At this point, Oakley could well have been ecstatic. After a mere two weeks in Convoy College, he had earned his "doctor's degree," and *Growler*, reduced to one torpedo, was ready to head for the barn. He had sunk four ships and damaged three (or so he believed). Three of the ships sunk, he thought, were destroyers, well earning for *Growler* the proposed new title "Destroyer Buster." By existing policy, four ships sunk would mean a Navy Cross Medal for Oakley, his first, and a slew of lesser awards to give to his officers and men. No submarine skipper could ask for anything more.

Clearly it was time for the hard-charging Oakley to throttle back and relax. He did. For the rest of the morning, *Growler* remained submerged in the vicinity of the stricken ships, carefully observing and listening but making no more overt or provocative moves. Later, Oakley ran east, submerged, to clear the area. He would turn over command of the pack to the next senior skipper, Eli Reich, and head for whatever refit base Pearl Harbor ordered. With this successful patrol under his belt, Oakley hoped (as did the officers and crew) that *Growler* would be rewarded with that greatest of all South Pacific liberty ports, Australia.

(2)

At 0710 the sun rose on a dismal scene in the middle of the South China Sea. The unidentified tanker and *Nankai Maru* were still smoking. The *Rakuyo Maru* was still afloat but low in the water, drifting with the current. The tanker had leaked a vast thick coat of oil over the placid, slowly undulating water. Amid the oil floated wooden debris and oil drums, deck cargo blown from the two burning ships. In the oil, there were also many life-jacketed Japanese, survivors of the two burning ships and the frigate *Hirado*. Many had been badly injured or hide-eously burned. Other Japanese survivors—including those from *Rakuyo Maru*—crouched in lifeboats, nested here and there. Finally, there was a massive cluster of British and Australians, twelve hundred bobbing heads, clinging in forlorn knots to floats and debris, struggling to stay afloat and out of the burning oil.

Some British and Australians studied *Rakuyo Maru* by the light of day with considerable amazement. There was still no sign that she was sinking. With that great cargo of rubber, perhaps she would never sink. Had they been precipitous in abandoning ship? Why not go back and do the job properly? Build better rafts, stock them with food, water and whatever else could be scrounged from the ship. Perhaps the two lifeboats on the stern could be launched.

Scores of men began a backward trek to *Rakuyo Maru* with the hope of improving their lot. It was not easy. By that time, the swift currents had carried a majority of the survivors well away from the ship, perhaps a mile or more. The rafts and debris were difficult to propel, the men weakened by the shock of the depth charges, fear, exposure, seasickness, salt water, hunger and thirst. Bob Farrands and the group on his raft tried hard to return, but "we couldn't make it. She was broadside on the current and going too fast." Jack Flynn recalled that "the harder we tried, the farther she seemed to go away." However, eventually a small number managed to reboard *Rakuyo Maru*.

Wal Williams had abandoned ship with his mate Max Campbell. In the deluge of water on deck, Williams had lost his boots and glasses, stored in one boot. In the sea the two men clung to a raft and helped a fully uniformed Japanese climb aboard. After a time, they saw that *Rakuyo Maru* had not sunk and decided to return, as Williams remembered, "to get out of the water for a few hours." They swam back and climbed up a rope ladder. They were surprised to find that a large number of men had never left the ship: the doctor Rowley Richards, the *Perth* petty officer Vic Duncan, Frank McGovern, Russ Savage, Ian MacDiarmid, Frank Johnson and others, including "about thirty Pommies who couldn't swim." Some of the men were gathering materials to build rafts. The majority were aft, attempting, under the guidance of Vic Duncan, to launch the starboard poop lifeboat, one of the two boats left behind by the Japanese. Williams and Campbell joined this endeavor.

Bill Mayne was helping with the lifeboat. He noticed that one of the frigates was approaching *Rakuyo Maru* with all guns manned. Thinking they intended to open fire on the ship, Mayne and several others ran to the gun on the stern of *Rakuyo Maru*, because: "Perhaps we could at least die fighting." But the gun was not operable. "The Japs had jammed a shell in the breech." Fortunately, the frigate did not open fire.

The davit ropes to the lifeboat had been cut. It was sitting flat on the deck. It was too heavy to lift, so the *Perth* sailors rerigged the davit, tying ropes together. Meanwhile, Williams and others scrounged in the cabins for food, water and blankets and threw them in the boat. When all was ready, the men pulled on the ropes and swung the boat over. The launching was a near disaster. The knotted ropes would not feed through the pulleys: they had to be cut. One end of the boat got away. Williams said: "They couldn't hold it. The stern went right down, and she hung by the bow. All the stuff we'd collected fell into the sea. Somebody cut the other davit rope and away it went—everybody praying that all would be well with it. The boat crashed into the water and came out right side up. A great cheer rent the air." But the fall had sprung the planking, and the boat began to leak. The time was about 0730, twenty minutes after sunrise and about two hours after *Rakuyo Maru* had been torpedoed.

It was Russ Savage who had cut the davit rope: "I climbed out on the davit. I had a knife. I cut it free and then got my neck caught in a rope. The lifeboat dropped into the water. Then I got untangled and fell into the water. We plugged the leak with a blanket, but this was not too satisfactory."

There was one Japanese girl left alive on *Rakuyo Maru,* one of the "jig-a-jig" girls. She was sitting on the ladder to the poop deck, crying hysterically, and according to Williams: "A chap named [A. J.] Bert Harper, absolutely naked except for a slouch hat, was trying to comfort her. I said, 'Harper, take a look at yourself.' He did and nearly died. He placed his hat over his privates and blushed bright red." Ray Burridge remembered it well too. "She had a scarf around her head and a pack of cigarettes stuck into it. I told her that if she got them wet, I'd kill her."

English and Australians alike jumped into the water or slid down ropes to board the lifeboat. Duncan invited the Japanese girl to go along, but Harold Ramsey knew she couldn't on her own. "She was terrified. We tied a rope around her and lowered her to the boat. Then an English bloke turned to me and said: 'We don't have any hope, Aussie. Let's see if we can find some booze and go down with the ship.' I said: 'No, I'll get out of this.' The last I saw of him, he was standing on the deck waving a couple of bottles." Ramsey followed the Japanese girl into the lifeboat.

The boat was rapidly filling with water. Bill Mayne thought it must be more than sprung planking. He remembered that boats usually had bungholes in the bottom to drain out water. He felt around and, sure enough, found a bunghole with the plug missing. All hands not desperately bailing searched for the plug. Luckily, it was found. When inserted properly, the flow of water from the hole stopped, but the sprung planking continued to leak. Continuous, exhausting bailing was necessary to keep the boat afloat.

Vic Duncan took charge of the boat: "It had an engine, but I couldn't start it. There was burning fuel on the ocean and we were drifting toward it. There were no rowlocks for the oars, so we had to make some very fast and teach the guys how to row in short order. We got mobile and pulled away from the flames. We had some sick in this boat, including my mate [Thomas C.] Tommy Johnson, who had malaria, so we decided to return to *Rakuyo Maru* and try to find some medicine. Somebody reboarded and actually found some quinine tablets. Then we pulled away again."

Men in the water climbed—or were pulled—into the lifeboat. Soon it was dangerously overcrowded. "In the end, we had one hundred and thirty-five people in or hanging on to the lifeboat," said Duncan. "Probably sixty in the boat itself. We were no longer mobile." Paddy Dunne added: "We had to refuse quite a lot of those who were pleading with us to get in. We had to belt them, actually. We already had too many in the boat and couldn't take more. In fact, the Aussies in the boat told us English to dive overboard. He told them to jump over themselves. It was survival."

Eventually, Duncan worked his heavily laden boat into the vicinity of the nest of lifeboats filled with Japanese. His hope was that when the Japanese were rescued, his boatload would be, too. Duncan called one of the Japanese boats over and, as a gesture of good will, offered them the Japanese girl. The Japanese refused her, saying, *"Presento"*—indicating that she was a present for Duncan. However, Duncan insisted, and the Japanese, rather reluctantly, accepted her. Frank McGovern recalled they also demanded one of two 5-gallon kegs of water from Duncan's boat. It was hauled over at gunpoint. The men concealed the other keg with their legs.

Many men on rafts and pieces of debris tied onto Duncan's boat or floated close by. Two were Wal Williams and Max Campbell. They had decided the lifeboat was too crowded and climbed onto a floating *benjo*. (Rowley Richards recalled that one of them shouted: "Look at me, guys! I'm the captain of a floating shit house.") Another was Jim Mullens. Richards recalled that Mullens was a tremendous surfer. "In the water, he was having the time of his life, swimming from one raft to another. Having an absolute ball."

William R. Smith had left *Rakuyo Maru* alone. He found a hatch board and climbed on. "I rode it like a surfboard. I was very mobile. It kept me up out of the water when those damn depth charges were going off." He decided to return to *Rakuyo Maru* for food: "I paddled around the ship, found a line, tied up my board and clambered aboard. The ship was making noises like it was haunted. Hollow noises. Booming noises. A hold aft was flooded and full of debris. There were some dead Nips back there. I didn't feel happy on board her. I left and got back on my board."

He saw the nest of lifeboats and paddled toward it. When he got close, he was astonished to see that Vic Duncan commanded one of the boats. He thought: "Trust the navy!" Duncan could not take Smith aboard but ordered him to stay on the board and remain alongside the lifeboat. Smith: "Then they gave me a piece of chocolate!"

Herbert J. "Bert" Wall, twenty-one, had left the ship with a mate, Sergeant Ross Dunbar. Both had life preservers. In the water they met up with the youngest soldier on *Rakuyo Maru,* Frank "Titch" Lemin. "We called him Titch because he was so small," Wall recalled. "We'd taught him to swim in the rivers in Burma. I could hear his voice calling my name. I yelled, 'What?' and he said, 'Look, I'm swimming!' "

The three men helped onto a raft a man who had been injured by falling debris and hung on to the side ropes. The two Wade brothers, John and Ernest, who had left the ship together, were also hanging on to this raft.

Wall continued: "We hung around the ship for several hours. We got thirsty, so I swam back and reboarded. The stern was down. I looked into Number Two hold. Water was pouring in. The ship was creaking and groaning. I found a four-gallon tin of fresh water. I swam that back to the raft, but by the time I got back, it was almost empty. It had busted a seam. But at least we all got one drink of water out of it."

The men on this raft—Wall, Dunbar, the Wade brothers and others—also hoping to improve chances of rescue, decided to make for the cluster of Japanese lifeboats, and although it was very hard to paddle a raft with an injured man on top, they made it. They, too, were astonished to find Duncan presiding over a lifeboat. John Wade recounted how "they wouldn't take us, but they took the injured man. We tied on behind Duncan's boat, raft after raft."

Andy Anderson had teamed up with Francis E. "Frank" Farmer, thirty-one, a schoolteacher, in the water. They climbed onto two hatch boards, which Anderson had roped together. After daylight, Anderson, an excellent swimmer, decided to return to the ship and scrounge some food. He left Farmer on the hatch boards. "I swam back and climbed up a rope ladder. I found a canteen on the deck. I also found a tin of biscuits. I wrapped these in an oilcloth and tied it up. It was ghostly on the ship. You could hear the water sloshing around underneath and the ship creaking. I got back in the water." Now he could not find Frank Farmer. Seeing the cluster of Japanese lifeboats, Anderson, too, headed for it.

Later in the day, the Australian Lieutenant Campbell Smith led a party back to *Rakuyo Maru*. This party managed to launch the port poop lifeboat. Rowley Richards recalled: "We were still close enough to the ship to see Lieutenant Smith and his mob lower the boat." Smith was assisted by two *Perth* sailors. One of them, Leading Seaman Frank Johnson, a close mate of Vic Duncan's, had selflessly assisted many POWs that day, both on *Rakuyo Maru* and in the water. As the senior sailor on the lifeboat, and an able one, he, in effect, took command under Smith. This boat, too, picked up men from the water (though not so many) and hove to near Vic Duncan's lifeboat. All twelve of *Rakuyo Maru*'s lifeboats had now been launched.

Lieutenant Smith and Frank Johnson decided to move on—head east. The doctor Rowley Richards remembered that "they came over to tell us they were sailing east to the Philippines. At that point, I was so bloody seasick I couldn't get up to talk to them. Too sick to pull myself together and wish them luck. Dreadful." The Smith-Johnson boat sailed east until it was no longer visible to the others. There were perhaps thirty or thirty-five men in the boat, most names unrecorded. It was never heard from again. None of the men aboard her reached Allied lines. None was reported recaptured by the Japanese. All disappeared without a trace. The other survivors believed the boat was either sunk by a storm or by a passing Japanese vessel, most likely by a storm.

By midmorning the survivors had broken into two main groups. The larger mass, perhaps nine hundred men, had drifted far from the ship. These were the men who had left earliest with the bulk of the rafts and other debris. The second mass, perhaps three hundred and fifty men, were those who had kept close to the ship and Vic Duncan's lifeboat. The two groups were widely

142

separated, so much so that one could not see the other.

In both groups the men suffered. The sun was blazing hot. Since most had lost their head covering, their faces were soon burned red. Lips cracked from the sting of salt water. Life preserver straps shrank and cut. Many were still dazed from the depth charge concussions. Few had fresh water. Those who did, shared it, soon exhausting the canteens not already ruined by salt water leakage. Most of the men had left the ship weak from hunger. Few had scrounged food. Those who did, shared it, and it, too, was soon exhausted. The men, by now, were ravenous. By and large, those in the lifeboats fared better. They had a little food and water, which were very carefully rationed.

In spite of all, spirits remained astonishingly high. It was a painful new devil to cope with, but these were tough men who had already endured incredible hardship. Many were inured, even oblivious to pain and suffering. Lawrence W. "Laurie" Smith, twenty-five, described it this way: "I could tune right out, not think or feel anything for hours. I think this kept me sane." Most believed that this latest ordeal was merely temporary, that they would soon be rescued by the Japanese. A few, like Harry Jones, were still buoyed by the fantasy of rescue by the Allies. Some, like the surfer Jimmy Mullens, thought the whole thing was a big lark, a joke on the Japanese and a sweet diversion from the rigid confinement of captivity.

By this time, the tanker and *Nankai Maru* had sunk. The only ship in sight was *Rakuyo Maru,* still stubbornly clinging to life.

(3)

Pete Summers in *Pampanito* and Eli Reich in *Sealion* were unaware of what was taking place at the scene of *Sealion*'s attack. Various maneuvers had taken both boats too far away from *Rakuyo Maru* for visual observation. Both skippers were properly preoccupied with evading escorts and tracking the remnants of the convoy for yet another attack. They went about this task in quite different ways and without any communication or coordination.

At sunrise, Summers, who still had the main body of westward-fleeing ships on radar, submerged and continued tracking by periscope observation. His plan was to remain submerged until the range opened out enough for him to surface and make yet another end around. He tracked in this manner for three hours, until the convoy could no longer be seen through the periscope.

When *Pampanito* surfaced at 1122, the convoy could not be found by radar. Another touchy moment on *Pampanito*. Had they let the quarry get away without ever firing a shot? For thirty-eight agonizing minutes this seemed to be the case. But at 1200, exactly noon, the watch on the "high periscope" (periscope fully extended while the boat was surfaced, vastly extending visual range) picked up smoke on the horizon. Shortly afterward, the wizard technician, George Moffett, searching the bearings, got ships on radar. Summers and the tracking party breathed easier. The plan now was to hang off the convoy's starboard bow, out of sight, and attack after dark. When he had doped out the convoy's course and speed, Summers broke radio silence and got off a contact report on wolf pack frequency to *Growler* and *Sealion*.

After shaking the escorts, Eli Reich had worked *Sealion* about ten miles south of *Rakuyo Maru*. At 0926 he surfaced and set an easterly course to clear the area and get his bearings. Nine minutes later, high periscope reported a "corvette" escort almost dead ahead, range seven miles. Reich tracked and found it was headed northeast. He wrongly assumed that this corvette was part of the convoy and that the convoy had now resumed its original northeasterly course. This incorrect guess would dominate his thinking for the next twelve hours.

Reich decided to remain on the surface and end-around to the west of the convoy. Accordingly, he headed due north, well off the port flank of the "convoy." However, eleven minutes later, at 0946, high periscope reported a destroyer dead ahead, range eight miles. The road ahead was blocked. There could be no end around to the west. Reich promptly about-faced and headed south, thankful that *Sealion* had not been sighted. With that road blocked, there was only one way to end-around the "convoy." That was to go south, then east, then north,

144

overtaking the "convoy" from the starboard flank. At 0952, Reich ordered this plan executed.

Sealion circled to the south, then east, then north at full speed, 17 knots. Shortly after noon, Reich received *Pampanito*'s contact report. It puzzled Reich. The data improbably placed the convoy due west, range sixty-two miles, on a westerly heading. This ran counter to Reich's idea. He declined to act on the report, believing that the data might be inaccurate or obsolete; or that, even if true, the convoy would probably revert to its original northeasterly course for Formosa Strait. If so, *Sealion* would be in ideal attack position along its track. Reich stubbornly held to his original plan.

For some time *Sealion* had been bearing north toward the backstopping wolf pack Ed's Eradicators, *Barb* and *Queenfish*. They were still patrolling the assigned rendezvous, unaware of the sea battle that had been raging for ten hours. They had not received *Growler*'s original contact report, nor did they receive Pete Summers' follow-up report shortly after noon. The pack commander, Captain Swinburne, and the two skippers, Gene Fluckey and Elliott Loughlin, could only assume that the Ultra had been erroneous, as they sometimes were, or that for some reason the Japanese were not adhering to the prescribed noon positions or that something else had gone wrong.

Shortly after noon, both Fluckey and Loughlin were puzzled to see an American submarine booming along on the surface headed north. This was *Sealion*. Fluckey correctly guessed the boat's identity. However, unaware she had made the rendezvous the night before with the Busters and attacked the convoy (and was still pursuing), Fluckey assumed *Sealion* must have orders to patrol the convoy lane independently of both the Busters and the Eradicators. He was pleased to see her. He logged: "The setup looks good, if a convoy comes along, for a complete wipe-out with five subs in the area. All we need is a contact. . . . We are patrolling on surface all day so we can't possibly miss any contact report."

Reich, of course, did not see *Barb* or *Queenfish*. If he had, he surely would have closed them, brought Swinburne, Fluckey and Loughlin up to date and enlisted their assistance. He continued north at 17 knots. At 1329 high periscope reported "the tops of patrol vessel," bearing northwest, range ten miles. Reich logged: "This further strengthened our belief that the convoy was going to eventually head northeast." He doglegged east to avoid the patrol vessel, resuming his northward dash at 1440. He was still confident that he was engaged in a shrewd overtaking maneuver. If all went well, *Sealion* would be in a good position for a night surface attack after dark. Reich still had eighteen torpedoes, enough to destroy the remaining six big ships singlehandedly. But with each passing minute, Reich was drawing away from the real convoy.

Summers in *Pampanito,* now some eighty miles to the west of *Sealion,* doggedly hung on to the westbound remnants of the convoy. At 1508 the big ships made "a radical zig" to the north. A jolt of excitement swept *Pampanito.* This zig turned the convoy directly toward the boat. Summers thought it must be heading for Hong Kong, now due north. He dived and went to battle stations for a daylight submerged attack. But, once again, *Pampanito* was to be denied. The zig was only temporary. In a few moments the convoy returned to its westerly base course, toward Hainan island. Half an hour later, Summers surfaced and resumed tracking. He saw "clearly" through the high periscope "one large transport [no doubt *Kachidoki Maru*], two large freighters and one medium freighter." He continued tracking, now planning a night surface attack. Toward dusk, *Pampanito* had to dive to avoid being detected by an aircraft, probably a patrol from Hainan island.

In *Growler,* Ben Oakley, who had cruised east all day submerged, clearing the area, surfaced about dusk. His radiomen picked up a message from *Sealion* on the wolf pack frequency "inquiring about convoy." There was no word from *Pampanito.* For almost an hour Oakley tried to respond to Reich and raise Summers on radio, but he could not get through to either boat. He proceeded to the prearranged rendezvous on the surface, now trying to raise Pearl Harbor to report his success and torpedo expenditure, so that he could get orders to leave Convoy College.

(4)

By late afternoon *Rakuyo Maru* was clearly doomed. She had sunk deeper in the water. She listed sharply and her stern was nearly awash. She wallowed sluggishly and unsteadily as the rising seas broke over her bow. Even so, the men continued to return to her to see if they could improve their lot.

Arthur Wright, who had left the ship very late with his mate Frank W. Lawrence, found a raft and decided to stay close to *Rakuyo Maru* in order to salvage any useful items after she sank. They, too, were swept away by the current, so they commenced a long struggle to work their raft back in hope of getting more food. About two hours later, they made it. By then, *Rakuyo Maru* was very low in the water. Wright dived into the flooded saloons and galleys and found "bully beef, condensed milk and one or two tins of salmon." Lawrence searched the dry, upper staterooms for cigarettes.

Wright went up to the bridge, checked the ship's position in the chartroom, then scrounged for clothes. He found a suit and a pith helmet in what he believed to be the captain's cabin. He put on the clothes (storing cigarettes and matches under the hat) and together the two men relaunched the raft. By that time, "the decks were awash," and this time, they let the current take the raft well clear.

Stanley Manning and his mate A. A. "Ack-Ack" Robinson, riding a hatch board, decided to return to the ship and make a big raft. "We climbed up a rope on the low side and started throwing off everything we could find" was how Manning told about it: "The light was failing. The ship was making more and more noise. We could hear it creaking. Steel under stress has a sound all its own—sort of ominous. We decided we better leave. We got off and began tying our boards together, drifting in the current."

147

Doug Mayers had gone into the water with a mate named Bernie. Neither had a life preserver. A small wooden box floated by. They grabbed it and hung on, treading water. Mayers said: "Bernie wasn't a good swimmer. I was. He was frightened of his ability to keep afloat. He was only a little fellow. Everybody was weakened, weakened, weakened. Finally, he just couldn't hold on any longer. I couldn't hold him. He slid off and drowned. I paddled around trying to find him. But there was no hope."

Mayers then had an extraordinary mystical experience, a vision: "I'm not a religious person by any means. When Bernie fell off the box, I figured that was the end of me. What have I got now, on my own? Then I saw my mother, a perfectly clear image above me. That gave me a kick, kept me going."

Mayers met some other Australians and swam back to *Rakuyo Maru*. "She was listing on her port side. We just walked on her." They grabbed some drums, planks, cork mats and other material, lashed them together and made a raft. Then they ransacked the ship, found a bottle of Scotch whiskey, a box of dried fish, a big bottle of water and a big can of cooked rice. They put the goodies on the raft and pushed off. They drank some of the Scotch, but it made them violently ill and they threw it away.

David Clark had abandoned ship with two mates, Mervin Dorman and a man nicknamed "Cookie," a former merchant seaman. The three of them clung to a submerged raft they had found on an upper deck and tossed over. Dorman was ill with a severe attack of malaria. Later in the day they decided to return to *Rakuyo Maru*. After prodigious effort, paddling against currents, they reached her and tied up at the torpedo hole in the bow. Leaving Dorman on the raft, Clark and Cookie climbed through the hole and up on deck.

Clark recalled: "My job was to find water and, if possible food. I headed down to a ship's galley. The ship was hissing and groaning and giving a shudder now and then, and it was quite eerie. In the semidarkness below decks I found a storeroom full of rice bags. The water was waist deep. All kinds of objects were floating around. I was in near panic and anxious to get out. I filled a haversack full of rice, went back on deck, found some canteens of water and looked around for Cookie."

What Clark saw next he would never forget: "I couldn't believe my eyes. Cookie was climbing down from the bridge. He was dressed in a Jap officer's uniform. White jacket and braid. White shorts. White socks and shoes, and to top it off, an oversized pith helmet. It was too silly for words."

They reboarded the raft with Dorman. Then, Clark recalled, Cookie revealed his great finds. "He lifted the helmet off. It was crammed full of cigarettes and matches. He dived his hand inside the jacket and produced a huge wad of Jap currency. He assured us we would find the currency handy on the Chinese mainland."

The *Perth* sailor Syd Matsen had left the ship with another *Perth* sailor, Patrick W. Major, and a third man. All three jumped in holding hands. After a while Matsen and Major decided to return to the ship. "Pat wanted something to eat, I wanted a smoke," said Matsen, "and we climbed up a rope ladder. We could hear the water pouring in. All of a sudden, it gave a lurch. We jumped right over the side. But it didn't go down, so we went back on board again."

Matsen and Major decided to make a raft. When it was finished, they searched the ship for useful items. "We went scrounging for things we could sell to the natives when we got to China. Cups and plates, forks and spoons. Pat found some rice. I found some smokes and a couple of canteens. But when we got the raft into the water we had to ditch all this stuff. It was too heavy."

John Langley had gone over the side alone with a bundle of bamboo poles about 2 feet in diameter and 7 feet long. This, plus a life jacket, supported him fairly well. Later in the day a mate, William P. Webb, a man of about fifty and a veteran of World War I, swam up and asked Langley if he could take a rest on the bamboo. "I said sure. I was glad for the company. Webb said he was trying to get back to the ship, then about two miles away. So I decided to go back, too." They swam for hours and hours, reaching the ship about four in the afternoon.

They found several men on the ship. Among them were Bill Mayne, who had returned much earlier with Harold Ramsey, and Kitchener M. "Kitch" Loughnan, twenty-nine. Loughnan, a big, handsome, very popular grazier, had been one of a very large group of Australians who set off for *Rakuyo Maru* earlier in the day.

Kitch alone had made it. Now he and Mayne were getting hatch boards together to build a large raft. After scrounging some water, Langley and Webb pitched in to help.

Two Australian mates, Charles B. McKechnie and Cedric C. "Clarrie" Wilson, twenty-five, had found a bamboo raft and left the ship together. Wilson, too, had left a small treasure on the ship: two carved ivory statues of men fishing with herons, a "beautifully carved ivory balls-within-balls" and a wristwatch. McKechnie was in a bad way. The night before, he'd come down with a malarial seizure. When he jumped, he lost his canteen. He had a life preserver, but he couldn't swim. He and Wilson moved from raft to raft, finally settling on one with Reggie Harris, Harry L. Kinleyside, Frank Holcroft, Ron Miscamble and Bill Cunneen, among others. The longer Wilson studied the *Rakuyo Maru*, the more he believed he should return to it. Finally he made up his mind. He gave McKechnie his canteen, said goodbye and swam back. "It was a good mile away. I knew Charlie couldn't make it, so I went alone."

Left on the raft, McKechnie recalled: "I had no fear of drowning, no fear I wasn't going to get out of it. I just didn't accept the fact I was going to die." There was a *Perth* sailor on the raft, C. A. "Alec" Pethebridge. McKechnie was impressed by his resourcefulness and self-lessness: "Alec swam around and collected ropes and timber and rafts and lashed two rafts together. Eighteen of us got on the two rafts. Alec also gave his life jacket to another *Perth* sailor who couldn't swim."

When Wilson got back to *Rakuyo Maru*, he was exhausted. He found a rope ladder hanging over the side, but he had to rest twenty minutes before climbing the ladder. When he got to the deck, he encountered a British soldier. "To my surprise, this Pommie gave me a canteen and life preserver."

When Wilson arrived, Kitch Loughnan, Bill Webb, Bill Mayne and John Langley were about ready to launch the hatch-board raft. After searching the upper deck cabins for useful gear, where he found a canteen and a large tin of flaked fish, Wilson joined this group. They threw over about eight hatch boards and roped them together in the water. By now the seas were rising and work in the water was difficult. The hatch boards "went in all directions." Someone found a large piece of bamboo to use as a paddle and, finally, they set off.

The grazier Kitch Loughnan, the youngest of nine children, had been a butcher in various cookhouses on the railroad. Once he had had a chilling experience. "Eight of our chaps tried to escape in Burma. They were caught and condemned to die. The Japs assigned me and fifteen others to dig their graves. As we watched, they brought them to these graves. Brigadier Varley tried to intercede, but the Japs ignored him. He said to the eight, 'I'm afraid you're for it.' The chaps said, 'Cheerio.' The firing squad was, fortunately, good. They put two holes in the forehead of each man. Then we buried them."

Loughnan recalled that he was the last man to leave *Rakuyo Maru*. "Bill Webb had found a couple of dead Japs on the ship and from their bodies had gotten a bottle of brandy, a bottle of water and a tin of biscuits. I handed these down to the boys on the raft. Then I climbed down and got on, the last man to leave the ship."

Clarrie Wilson told what happened next. "We'd only got about one hundred yards from the ship when she went down. The bow went down, up, then down. She slid under, bow first. There was no suction, merely a bit of hissing noise—air being forced through openings. On the whole, it was fairly quiet. When she went down, it was just on dark."

The sight of *Rakuyo Maru* going down—long expected—evoked little response from the British and Australians, but the Japanese in the lifeboats were moved. Frank McGovern told of their reaction: "Towards dusk, we saw her go down. The Nips yelled, 'Banzai! Banzai!'" The time was about 1730—5:30 P.M., twelve hours after she was torpedoed.

The ship, by Reich's estimate, sank at 18° 22' north 114° 30' east longitude. This was south of the so-called submarine boundary by 8 miles. To avoid conflict with General MacArthur's submarine commander, Pearl Harbor would officially place the sinking exactly on the boundary: 18° 30' north. The water was about 6,000 feet deep. So far as is known, no POW went down with her, but she carried down most of their countless little valuables, including the $70,000 grubstake of Frank Johnson and his two mates.

While *Rakuyo Maru* was going under, an infinitely more compelling sight held the British and Australians transfixed. Two Japanese frigates and a merchant ship appeared, nosing slowly through the oil scum and wreckage. Spirits soared. After a long day of agony, everyone supposed, rescue was at hand.

The frigates hove to at the cluster of *Rakuyo Maru* lifeboats. Including the one boat manned exclusively by Duncan and the POWs, there were eleven altogether. The Duncan lifeboat was still jammed to the gunnels, so weighted down that there were only a few inches of freeboard. Dozens of men in the water clung to the lifeboat rope handholds. Scores more had tied on rafts, staircases, *benjos* and other debris. Still others were approaching the boats on rafts and hatch boards. The majority of these men in the lifeboats or heading for them were Australian.

All the lifeboats, and the men in the water, swimming or on debris, converged on the frigates. The Japanese survivors scrambled aboard, setting their lifeboats adrift. The POWs were denied. Wal Williams, who with his mate Mac Campbell, clung to a *benjo* tied to Duncan's boat: "We rowed to the frigate. We got pretty close. We could see Japs on deck and Japs being picked up from the boats. We shouted, 'What about us?' But they just waved us away." Paddy Dunne, in Duncan's boat, could see scores of Japanese injured lying on the deck of the frigate: "They shouted down at us to turn away. They had enough of their own people, couldn't take any more. Some of my mates shouted, 'Killers! Why don't you pick us up?'" The Australian soldier Frank Johnson in Duncan's boat: "There was a Jap standing by the ladder. If any of our blokes got up the ladder, he hit them with a pick handle." Arthur Wright, floating on a raft with Frank Lawrence, was bitter.

"The POWs were knocked back into the water with baseball bats." William R. Smith, in Duncan's boat, added: "A Jap officer came to the side and said, 'Don't come near the ship. We can't pick you up. If you come near the ship, the guns are on you and we'll have to open fire.' "

The Englishmen Sidney Johnson and his mate Les Murrell had spent the entire day in a lifeboat with about twenty Japanese and eight other POWs. They had not been ill-treated. Being in among a majority of Japanese, they thought their chances of rescue were excellent. But they, too, were denied. Johnson said: "The Japs ordered us to row to the side of the frigate. Quite a few boats converged there. The Japs scrambled aboard. But any POWs that climbed up were kicked off. Literally pushed off."

Within a very few minutes, the rescue of the Japanese survivors had been effected. Duncan said: "They were in such a hurry they weren't even trying to recover the lifeboats. Just their people." Frank McGovern recalled: "The captain of one frigate came to the rail with a megaphone, yelled, 'Goodbye,' and waved his hand. And then they left."

The POWs made haste to recover and occupy the abandoned lifeboats. In this effort, the Australians, who far outnumbered the British, took charge and thereafter dominated. Duncan took a leading part. "After they buzzed off, I dived over the side, swam over and got one of the empty lifeboats and brought it back to our boat. I then got a couple of guys to go get another one. We began to split our great mob of survivors amongst these boats."

Those in the boats rowed about collecting others from the water. It was getting dark, the seas were rising. John Langley, who was heading for the lifeboats on their hatch-board raft with Bill Webb, Bill Mayne, Kitch Loughnan and Clarrie Wilson: "Bill Webb said, 'Come on, lads, give it a great bush *Coooooee.*' So we all gave a *Coooooee* and paddled like mad. Then we heard a *Coooooooeee* in answer. The people in the lifeboats had heard us. It was Duncan's boat." Stanley Manning, who with his mate, Ack-Ack Robinson had got into a boat: "Darkness was falling. There were still a lot of men floating in the water or on hatch boards and rafts. They were calling out, 'Over here! Over here!'

We picked up all we could. But the voices were still there. I can still hear them today." Arthur Wright went on: "Then we heard a shout in the night, rowed over and picked up two chaps on an upturned table. They told us that before dark, others on rafts had been close, so we bellowed together, heard an answering cry, and picked up more of our mates." Some were left behind because they were too far away, as Bert Wall recalled: "The last thing I remember seeing that night was a bloke on the horizon, standing on a raft, all by himself."

In all, these lifeboats recovered about one-fourth of all the survivors, probably 350 men, a majority of whom were Australians. They were evenly distributed among the eleven boats, about thirty per boat. Among those picked up were the three senior officers: Brigadier Varley, the British Group Captain More and the lone American from *Rakuyo Maru*, Colonel Melton.

The men of the Duncan group redistributed themselves among three lifeboats, including the original leaky one with the useless engine. Duncan commanded the "lead" boat. He appointed two other *Perth* sailors, Syd Matsen and Pat Major, to command the second boat. The doctor, Rowley Richards, remained in the leaky boat with some sick, who did the bailing. All three boats were lashed together in a line, bow to stern. This group would remain apart from the other lifeboats commanded by Brigadier Varley, which had now drifted off about a mile—almost out of sight.

Duncan had a fair notion where they had been sunk. He believed the China coast lay about 300 miles to the northwest (actually, only 200 miles). He urged that they head for China in hopes of making contact with Chinese Allies. "It was a big coastline. I thought the winds and currents would take us there in no more than eight to ten days." No one disagreed with the plan. They were free men. All were determined to remain free, if humanly possible.

All boats rigged sails. Duncan's boat was grandly equipped with a mast and mainsail. Ably assisted by Jimmy Mullens, a skilled small-boat sailor, Duncan raised this, adding a "Viking-like spinnaker," which Mullens fashioned from a blanket and boat hook. On the Matsen-Major boat, Bill Mayne (an amateur sailor) rigged a sail, of sorts, with a blanket and oars. A stiff squall swept the group, forcing the men in the second and third boat to man oars to keep the boats from crashing together. Ultimately, the choppy seas forced the three boats to cut loose. Thereafter, they sailed or rowed along independently but within sight or hailing distance.

(6)

After recovering the Japanese from the lifeboats, the two frigates then proceeded to the mass of wreckage— by this time, several miles away—to recover individual Japanese survivors from rafts and debris. Many of these Japanese shared rafts with POWs who had spared them to use as bargaining chips. But it was all for naught. Here, too, the POWs were denied, fended off with small arms.

Blood Bancroft remembered one particular episode. "When we saw the frigate going about picking up Japs, we made this Jap officer we had on our raft stand up. There were four rafts in this group, and many POWs. We waved to the destroyer. The Japs lowered a boat and came over to get the officer. There was a Jap in the bow with a pistol pointing at us. They signaled the Jap to swim over. Then they took him back to the frigate. We thought the Jap officer might put in a good word for us, but we soon got the picture that they didn't intend to pick us up."

At every raft cluster, the story was about the same.

Doug Hampson's was a little bit different. "A small boat came up to us to collect a Nip officer we had on a raft. There was a Nip in the bow of the boat with a tommy gun. He motioned for the Nip officer to get in the boat. Then our Nip turned to us and said—and I admire him to this day for it—'Gentlemen, I'm sorry. This is the way of my people.' He gave us a little packet of dried fish and a little packet of rice. He said, 'May you be spared.' then he swam to the boat. The two frigates then got underway and cruised slowly up and down alongside our rafts. The Nips on the ship were lined up fore and aft at the rails, pointing their guns at us. We thought they were going to shoot us. We raised our thumbs at them, a signal meaning 'Up your ass!'"

Some of the Japanese were not recovered. Barney Barnett told of one reason why. "On one raft, there were a lot of POWs and one Jap. When the POWs realized they were picking up only Japs, they held his mouth shut so he couldn't call out and sat or lay on him so the Japs couldn't see him. He was really scared, alone among men who had been ill-treated by Japanese. Then the frigate left, passing us at fifty yards. The Japs were lining the rails and we thought they would shoot us, but they didn't. They just laughed at us. After it was gone, the POWs beat the Jap with their fists and killed him. He was bleeding heavily. Some of the men were already dying of thirst. They drank his blood. It was horrible."

When the last visible Japanese or Korean had been recovered, the frigates got underway. The skippers had one final diabolical trick up their sleeves, and three men told similar stories about it. Mark Wheeler: "The frigates swung around and rammed us. Went straight through us, split us in half. My mate and I went straight down and stayed until we couldn't stay any longer. When we came up, everything was scattered. I expect some got killed. I don't know." Harry Pickett: "A Japanese frigate tore through the middle of our blokes. There was wreckage and chaps all mixed up in the water, and he went right through the middle." Roy Hudson: "I'm sure they deliberately ploughed right through the groups floating around in the sea. They made no effort to avoid them. I can remember men being washed up high in the air on the bows and then going down again."

There was one last hope for this angry and forlorn group: the freighter that was in company with the frigates. It did not stop, either. Robert A. C. Collins, another *Perth* survivor, recalled: "Our hopes rose. 'About time that bloody ship got here to pick us up.' However to our dismay, it turned away. I watched it as long as it was visible, wishfully thinking that it was bound to turn back any minute. It did not, and my thoughts sent it to the bottom with an American torpedo in its guts."

The 900-odd men left behind in the water were stunned and outraged. Dagger Ward thought, "You lousy, rotten bastards!" Andy Anderson: "We hoped to be picked up by the dirty yellow devils, but no hope. They were only concerned about their own race of animals." Alf Allbury: "Our prayers, we thought, had been answered. Poor deluded fools. Even a year of . . . the

Burma railway had failed to teach us that there is no limit to man's inhumanity."

Despair set in. It was growing dark. They had been in the water fourteen hours or more. No one appeared to have any hope. Harry Weigand: "A lot of the boys dropped their bundles completely and, I know very well, died about an hour after the ships left us." Sam Fuller: "After that, we all knew that was the end. No one said it, but we all knew." Alf Allbury: "Men, almost at once, began to die . . . of broken hearts. Died knowing that cruelty has no frontier, and that though God wept for a fallen sparrow, the Japanese had in them so little of the milk of human kindness that they could leave a thousand men in the vastness of the China Sea to die a certain and terrible agony. . . . I laid my head on the raft and closed my eyes. After all that we had gone through, to be left to a death such as this . . ."

Then, a note of defiance. From a raft full of British. deep throaty voices could be heard singing:

> Rule Britannia, Britannia rules the waves,
> Britons never, never, never shall be slaves.

The mood caught and spread. Soon hundreds of British voices echoed across the dark sea. The Australian Jack Flynn: "I'll never forget that moment. I thought it was fantastic."

PART SEVEN

A Swift Sinking

(1)

Pete Summers in *Pampanito* continued tracking the westward-fleeing convoy. By 1930 hours it was a mere 52 miles from Hainan island. In the fourteen hours since Eli Reich's attack, the convoy—and *Pampanito*—had traveled 150 nautical miles. Now, with darkness coming on, Summers geared up for the favored night surface approach and attack.

The convoy now fell under the protection of land-based aircraft from Hainan. *Pampanito* had already dived once to avoid being detected by a plane. At 1936, one of the lookouts spotted another, very close: 4 miles. Again *Pampanito* crash-dived to avoid detection. She remained submerged for nineteen minutes. After a careful check of the darkening skies through the periscope, Summers decided the boat had not been seen and, at 1955, surfaced to resume the chase.

Summers and the tracking party received another rude shock. The convoy had again disappeared from the radar scope. Summers logged: "Felt very discouraged over possibility of losing convoy after long chase." It was yet another touchy moment on *Pampanito*. For what seemed the umpteenth time this patrol, she had lost—or thrown away—an opportunity to inflict damage on the enemy. The wardroom was again in an angry and disillusioned frame of mind.

What to do? Putting himself in place of the convoy commander, Pete Summers decided that at dark, when Japanese convoys usually made radical course changes, he would have turned and run for Hong Kong, some 200 nautical miles northeast. The convoy originally had been heading for Japan. Why shouldn't the convoy commander try his best to resume that direction? He might stop at Hong Kong, regroup, then continue northeast-ward toward Formosa Strait, hugging the coast of China under land-based protection, a common tactic for

161

Japanese convoys these days. What point was there in fleeing to Hainan island?

Thus convinced, Summers ordered *Pampanito* to a northeasterly heading—toward Hong Kong. One hour and eleven minutes later, the incomparable radar technician George Moffett reported a contact, almost dead ahead, at the astonishing range of 30,000 yards (fifteen miles). Summers logged happily: "Luck hasn't deserted us, this is the convoy." He was right. A quick plot showed it was still on a zigzagging westerly course, headed for Hainan, not Hong Kong. That Summers had stumbled across its track again was indeed sheer luck.

It was an ideal night for a submarine attack, dark with no moon, calm sea. Visibility was "good" with low-hanging clouds on the horizon. Closing rapidly on the surface, Summers made out the same four big ships he had seen that afternoon—large transport (*Kachidoki Maru*), two large freighters and a medium freighter—and "at least four escorts." The big ships were in two two-ship columns, *Kachidoki Maru* led the port column, the medium freighter the starboard column. One escort roved ahead and to starboard, one escort guarded the port flank, and two escorts brought up the rear. The tracking party reported the formation was on base course 280 true (west), speed 11-12 knots. It was zigzagging every eight minutes.

Summers approached the convoy from the port side, easing in cautiously. Forty-six minutes later, at 2152, one of the escorts fired a green flare over the convoy. It was a heart-stopping moment for *Pampanito*. What did it mean? Had they been detected? Summers changed to open out a bit. But there was "nothing further" from the convoy. No more flares or signals. No radical change in course or speed. No escorts charging. Apparently the luck was holding; they had not been seen.

At 2225, one hour and nineteen minutes after the initial radar contact, Summers ordered the crew to battle stations and commenced the run in to attack. His plan was a standard textbook solution: he would fire all ten torpedo tubes at the two ships in the near port column, four at *Kachidoki Maru*, two at the large freighter behind her. He would then swing the boat right and fire the four stern tubes at the two ships in the far starboard column, two at the leading medium freighter, two at the large freighter behind it.

Pampanito ran in at full speed. Summers manned the TBT on the bridge; the exec Jeff Davis supervised the tracking party in the conning tower. Francis M. Fives, Tony Hauptman, the gunners mate who had repaired the leak in the forward trim tank, and who was a special favorite of Summers', was on the bridge. He was delegated to keep an eye on the escorts, reporting their movements to Summers.

At 2235, in the final stages of the approach, calamity struck. While the torpedomen were making ready the six forward tubes, flooding them preparatory to opening the outer doors, the torpedo in number four tube made a "hot run." It moved forward in the tube, tripping the starting lever. Its propellers started turning in a high-pitched whine. The torpedo moved forward in the flooded tube (restrained by the closed outer doors), but the automatic gyro setter failed to disengage. It was jammed. Since this gear was linked to the other five tubes, none of the torpedo gyros could be set, even by hand.

This was a very dangerous situation. By deliberate design, a torpedo had to run several hundred yards through the water before its warhead was "armed" by an automatic water-turned device. But submarine torpedoes were complex and capricious. No one could predict with any accuracy what they would do. The hot run in number four tube could conceivably arm itself and explode, blowing off the bow of the boat and causing its instant destruction. Moreover, with all six bow tubes at least temporarily out of commission owing to the jammed gyro gear, *Pampanito* not only could not attack the convoy, she was highly vulnerable herself.

Ted Swain, the torpedo and gunnery officer, left his battle station and raced to the forward torpedo room. By the time he arrived, Torpedoman First Class James H. Behney, who was in charge of the compartment, had diagnosed the difficulty. He was a man of immense strength. Under Swain's supervision, Behney, employing brute force, broke the linkage to the rudder setter in number four tube. This freed the gyro controls in the other five tubes and by 2239, the TDC was once again automatically setting the gyros. That crisis passed, Swain raced back to his battle station.

One minute later, at 2240, Summers fired the five bow tubes. He shot three (one less than planned, owing

163

to the hot run) at *Kachidoki Maru,* two at the trailing large freighter in the port column. The range was exceedingly long: 3,800 yards (almost 2 miles), close to the limit of the Mark XVIII electric torpedoes. He swung the boat hard right and, at 2243, as planned, fired the four stern tubes, two each at the two freighters in the far column. Again the range was exceedingly long: 3,700 yards. So far, *Pampanito* had not been detected. The stopwatches in the conning tower timing these very long torpedo runs ticked away for what seemed an eternity.

Pampanito's shooting was excellent. Summers claimed seven hits out of the nine torpedoes. On the bridge, he logged, he and others saw all five bow torpedoes hit, three in *Kachidoki Maru,* two in the large freighter. One each of the two torpedoes fired at the two freighters in the far column hit, Summers logged. He saw one of these hits in the large freighter, but the hit in the lead freighter in the far column was obscured by *Kachidoki Maru.* However, it was "heard and timed" for that torpedo run, Summers reported.

During the next ten minutes, Summers hauled off and observed his handiwork. He logged that within that period, he and others saw the first two targets, *Kachidoki Maru* and the large freighter, sink. As for the third target, the large freighter in the far column, he logged that he "saw one hit just aft of amidships that blew part of deck house into the air." The ship "settled in the water" and "a faint glow was noted on board," indicating fire. The fourth target could not be distinctly observed with binoculars, even after *Kachidoki Maru* sank, owing to "much smoke and haze in that direction."

While they were thus absorbed, at 2253, *Pampanito* was severely jarred by a very close explosion. "Shook entire ship," Summers logged. He believed it was a depth charge "thrown" (rather than rolled off the stern) by an escort. But the escorts were much too far away for that, even in the unlikely event they had a "throw" capability. Most probably *Pampanito* had been attacked by a Hainan-based aircraft that in the excitement (and smoke and haze) had not been detected by sight or radar. Had the pilot's aim been more precise, *Pampanito* might well have ended her days right then.

Summers and the crew were euphoric. "Peaceful Pamp" was no longer an apt nickname for this boat. She had bared her teeth (at some remove) and snapped, inflicting her first damage on the enemy in six months of combat patrolling. At Pearl Harbor, Pete Summers would not only be off the hook but in line for a decoration. He was proud—and anxious to record this momentous occasion in *Pampanito*'s life. He asked Tony Hauptman, who was an amateur artist with considerable gifts, to lay below and sketch what he had witnessed on the bridge. Then he moved out to eject the hot run from number four tube and reload all tubes.

(2)

In keeping with the captain's orders, most of the 900 British POWs on *Kachidoki Maru* were in Number 2 hold at 2240 when Summers fired three torpedoes at the ship. Perhaps 100 or so were hiding topside, in violation of the captain's orders. Among these were Tom Pounder and his mucker Doug Spon-Smith. As they recalled, the Japanese escorts apparently detected *Pampanito* by sight or radar and gave the alarm before the torpedoes struck. Pounder said: "The blissful calm of the night was suddenly and ruthlessly broken by the frantic shouting of the Japs. . . . Louder and louder until it became a screech." Immediately afterward, there was a muffled explosion "somewhere near the stern." Without being told, Pounder and Spon-Smith both knew the ship had been torpedoed.

Roll Parvin had just left the *benjo* and had one foot on the ladder to the hold when the torpedo struck. "I heard a dull thudding crash from the stern. The ladder shuddered beneath my foot." Parvin, too, realized the ship had been torpedoed. His life preserver was below in the hold. He decided to continue below and fetch it. When he got down inside the hold, he discovered that no one in the hold knew the ship had been torpedoed. He informed the men, keeping his "voice low in order not to start one of those hysterical panics."

The news was greeted with monumental skepticism. "To my surprise, the issue was tossed from mouth to mouth around the hold and, despite the fact that by that time other men were descending the steep ladder into the gloom and bringing the same news as myself, a general debate was in progress as to whether we *had* been hit or not. Many dismissed the idea with contempt and settled down to talk or sleep again." Parvin found his life preserver and returned to the deck.

Ernest Benford, in the hold, recalled that "the ship seemed to slow and the bow rose to the accompaniment of a peculiar metallic clang, which seemed to come from the rear of the ship. We could only guess what had happened. The movement of the bow seemed consistent with the movements a ship might make if it ran aground. Then the metallic noise occurred again, this time louder and yet more muffled. Someone shouted up to those on deck. One of our officers called down to us to remain calm, stay where we were and await instructions."

Wally Mole decided to make for the stairway and get a few minutes on deck. It was dark, but he knew his way to the stairs as well as a blind man. To his surprise, there was no waiting, no queue. It seemed unbelievable. He felt his way step by step. When he got near the top, he bumped into a man who was so weak he could hardly make it. "I put my arms around his skinny waist and helped him along." When he got on deck, Mole realized the ship had been torpedoed: "The Japs were shouting and screaming like mad. I soon realized the terrible position. There were hundreds of our men down below, including sick and dying, and they had to be got out without a panic. Someone calmly called down and told them they could come up and get some fresh air. Slowly they started to come up, not realizing the danger."

Johnny Sherwood was topside. "Bang. We got it. The whole ship seemed to shudder all over. Then the engines stopped and the ship seemed to settle down quietly. Well, by now, there was a bit of panic in the hold, with all the men wanting to know what had happened. Our officer came over and shouted down that we had been torpedoed but to keep calm, as the ship was not sinking. Most of the men took that for granted, but others, not so sure, started to filter up through the hatch and hid themselves all over the place."

Thomas J. Grisbrook, thirty-two, was one of those in the hold. "There were several heavy thuds. We began to discuss amongst ourselves what could be happening. Some said we were being torpedoed. Others said, 'Shut your bloody row up; it is only depth charges.'" Grisbrook and his friends decided to make their way quietly to the ladder. They were about two-thirds up the ladder when they heard a great deal of shouting that the ship had been hit. Grisbrook: "Naturally all the men who could walk or move in some way rushed to the one ladder. We managed to scramble out at the top."

Tom Parrott was in the hold. He remembered a loud thud—not a bang. He lay there awhile, listening. The engines had stopped and it was deadly quiet. Then pandemonium broke out. There were sounds of things being dragged across the deck, banging, shouting. Parrott turned to a friend who lay alongside him and said, "I'm going up on deck to see what's happening." The friend stayed put; he was not concerned. As Parrott climbed the ladder, he found it more difficult than usual because the ladder was lying backward. When he reached the deck, that, too, was slanting. He thought to himself: "The ship has been torpedoed and I must get a life jacket." As he moved away from the hatch, a large gun lorry or box (it was too dark to see) fell into the hold he had just left. Parrott believed it killed his friend.

The misinformation from the POW officer that the ship was not sinking and that the men should remain calm and await instructions was unfortunate. *Kachidoki Maru* had been hit by two (not three, as Summers believed) torpedoes, one amidships, one farther aft. Both had been solid hits, tearing gaping holes in the hull plates, flooding the entire aft end of the vessel. For the men in the hold, five valuable minutes had been lost.

As on *Rakuyo Maru*, the Japanese feverishly launched lifeboats and rafts for their own personnel, leaving the POWs to fend for themselves. No word of any kind to abandon ship was passed. In fact, many of the POWs remembered that the captain shot himself on the bridge immediately after the torpedoes struck. Acting on their own, Pounder, Spon-Smith, Mole, Sherwood, Parvin and others topside cut loose life rafts and tossed them over the side, along with anything else that looked as though it would float.

Tom Parrott rushed aft on the main deck in search of a life preserver, passing several cabin doors. On passing one, he thought he heard the sound of revolver shots. A Japanese officer rushed out holding a revolver. Parrott: "I thought, this is my lot. But he wasn't interested in me. He was going around shooting the very badly wounded Japs—those who couldn't possibly have gotten off the ship." Roll Parvin also became aware of these extraordinary "mercy killings." A POW came running from the hatch of Number 3 hold, where many Japanese wounded were billeted, and shouted: "Two Jap officers are going round shooting the wounded Nips down there. The bastards!"

Ernest Benford recalled that "perhaps five minutes had lapsed since we first realized something was amiss." The bow had risen sharply; the deck was at an angle of perhaps 10°. His pal Robbie Shaw, who was on deck, came to the edge of the hatch opening and called down to him that the ship had been torpedoed and was sinking fast and that he should get on deck as quickly as he could. And make sure he had the water bottle and life jacket.

Johnny Sherwood: "Without warning, at exactly eleven P.M., the ship suddenly started to tip up with our end [the bow] going up in the air. That was it. Our officer shouted to us that the ship was sinking and that it was every man for himself. The next five minutes were the most terrifying experience I have ever had. The Japs were running and panicking all over the place. Our men were fighting to get out of the hold. The ship tipped right up. We were right up in the air at an oblique angle, with men shouting and screaming and jumping over the side."

In fact, the POWs in the hold were coming up at a leisurely pace, traditionally honoring the queue. Ernest Benford again: "By now, there was a queue of prisoners at each of the ladders in the hold. The angle of the deck had increased at an alarming rate. I joined a queue immediately behind two other pals, Harry Harding and Grapper Grapes, but I noticed that the gangway in the after end of the hold was not being used. There were at least thirty ahead of us in the queue. I suggested to Harry that we should use the after gangway. I was becoming worried at the rate we were sinking. But Grapper couldn't swim and preferred to use the forward ladder. Harry elected to stay with him to help him. Suddenly the bows lifted sharply. This must have set off some alarm bells in my head. I waited no longer. As quickly as I could, I made my way across the hold and up the gangway, which, by now, was parallel with the sea."

(3)

All who survived the *Kachidoki Maru* catastrophe jumped within the first ten minutes. After that, it was too late.

Stan Thompson told how "everybody was saying, 'Over the side, over the side.' I was petrified. But I wasn't going to go over the side and have somebody throw a raft on me. So I waited until I saw the last of the rafts disappear; then I went over the side. As I got up to make my move, the boat went. I went down with it. Everything that was on the forward deck where the gun was mounted just came whistling past my head. Fantastic noise. Stuff falling about everywhere. Once I was in the water, I thought I was seeing stars. But I was seeing phosphorescence. I could feel things falling around me. A chain, other things. Finally, my kapok life jacket forced me to the surface."

George Huitson added: "I was among the first up from the hold. The ship was already well down by the stern. The bow was up. The forward gun toppled back and fell into the hold. The deck was all gritty. While I was making up my mind where to jump—I had no life jacket—the ship just slid back and under. I went with it. I was sucked down. I remember turning over and over in the water. There were lights flashing in my mind. I can remember thinking, 'This is it. This is the end of the road.' But after a while, I popped to the surface, gasping for breath. I swam away from the area as fast as I could."

Raymond L. Stark, thirty, told his own story: "When I got on deck, the bridge was more or less going under. I shouted down the hatch: 'Any more of you lads who want to get out, get out quick. She's going under.' That caused a stampede, but I think many men were trapped in the hold. I crawled toward the bow on my hands and knees, it was so steep. I didn't have a life preserver.

169

When I got to the bow, I took a dive. The ship was on its way down. When I dived, I hit something in the water. I thanked God I could swim. I went hell for leather to get away from the ship."

Tom Pounder and Doug Spon-Smith planned to jump together, but Pounder went first. "The moment I hit the water I became submerged. I stretched out my arms and legs to swim, but neither limb could I move." Something had coiled around his body, and he felt himself being dragged down into the dark waters. Frantically he tried to free himself, but each time he failed. All around him the water brightened with phosphorescence, caused by the turbulence he created. His lungs were bursting for air. For a brief moment he was tempted to give up. In utmost desperation and despair he cried out for help: "Oh God!" Suddenly, as if by a miracle, the stranglehold on his body relaxed and he popped to the surface. Spon-Smith, a nonswimmer, leaped behind him.

Tom Parrott prepared to jump. " 'Right. Keep calm, Tom,' I thought. 'Jacket over head. Tapes around the back. Tie in front. Now climb over the rail.' I did this and looked down. The drop must have been forty to fifty feet. I froze. I couldn't move. Then a chap next to me jumped. This broke the spell." Parrott jumped, remembering to hold the top of the life jacket. Down and down. He thought he would never hit the water.

One of Wally Mole's pals suggested they slide down a rope that was tied on a rail and hanging over the side. They could not see the water below, but they knew that it was a long drop. Mole: "This poor chap began to lose his nerve. I was scared stiff myself, but time was running out. I climbed over the rail and told him to follow me. Unfortunately the rope was only about six feet long. As I hung there in midair, I could feel the other fellow climbing over the rail, so I let go." For Mole, the next seconds seemed like an "eternity." Then he hit the water. As he went down, he could see dozens of tiny lights. He felt that these were his last moments. But he was wrong. He came to the surface and swam like mad to get away from the sinking ship.

Johnny Sherwood and a mate fought their way to the side of the ship. Sherwood remembered that his mate shouted: "Jump well out or you will be sucked under." Sherwood could see heads bobbing up and down all over the ocean. Then he jumped—right on top of somebody's head! He felt a terrible blow on his bottom. "I killed him," Sherwood recalled. "He never came up." Sherwood surfaced, lungs nearly bursting, swam away from the ship and turned on his back.

When Ernest Benford reached the gangway entrance, he had to let go of his canteen and life jacket so that he could hang on with both hands. He looked down and saw the front wall of the ship's bridge disappearing under the waves. Unable to hold on longer, he fell. Fortunately, the bridge had disappeared, so he landed in the water. "I was sucked under I don't know how far. I began to take in water while still going down. Then I was coming up, struggling and fighting to breathe, my head jammed against something. At first I was pushing to get free instead of pulling. I began to rise again, turning over and over and striking other arms and legs. There were bodies everywhere. Then I became drowsy and I ceased the struggle to breathe. I began to enjoy the feeling. It was so quiet. I assume that I must have been near to losing consciousness. I don't remember coming to the surface. My next recollection was of sharp pains in the chest as I gasped for air and brought up water. I regained full consciousness and stopped spluttering. I was violently sick, vomiting a mixture of rice, oil and sea water."

Frederick A. Cooper, twenty-five, and his pal Sergeant Robert E. Pratton found two life jackets on deck and put them on. By then the bow had risen steeply. Cooper remembered: "This is when a lot of men panicked, in the hold and on deck both. They were jumping off the high part of the boat, smashing into things floating around in the water. I think a lot got killed." Cooper and Pratton waited until the water covered the bridge, then slid down the steep deck on their bottoms and moved off into the water. They submerged a fair way, but the life preservers brought them back to the surface quickly. Then they swam away from the ship.

Roll Parvin put his cracked and broken glasses in a pocket of his tunic and prepared to slide down a hawser hanging over the side. He kicked off his boots and leaped onto the rail, grabbing the hawser. For an instant he dangled over the side. Glancing down, he could see, far below, the scene of furious activity as man after man dropped from the end of the rope, splashed into the water and struck out to escape being jumped on by the next one down. Along the side of the ship, the sea was churned into a frothing mass by hundreds of thrashing arms and legs. "Then the hawser tore through my clenched hands, burning and scraping the skin from my palms. With my feet resting on the shoulders of the man beneath me, and the feet of the man above me dangling round my ears, I slid rapidly down. . . . I let go and dropped into the warm, enveloping softness of the tropical sea. . . . I struck out instantly to get clear of the next man to fall."

Then Parvin heard a cry: "She's going!" He looked back. "With a quick swing, the bows pointed directly upwards. An immense length of the ship struck vertically out of the water, in a seemingly impossible pose. . . . Then slowly, but with gathering speed, it started the long slide to the bottom. Again, for a fleeting second, it halted—as if undecided. Then a shattering roar from under the surface made it shudder and shake. And with this final gesture it slid rapidly out of sight, the eager waters rushing in to close greedily over the bows as they disappeared. Hardly had it gone than the sea directly above its grave gathered into a huge jetting spout that climbed silently up and up, to falter and then fall thunderously back into a boiling fury—further agitated by monstrous bubbles leaping up from below."

It was all over in fifteen minutes. By *Pampanito*'s estimate, *Kachidoki Maru* had sunk at 19° 18′ north latitude, 111° 53′ east longitude, in 360 feet of water. No one knew exactly how many POWs were trapped and drowned in the hold. Probably 300 of the 900. In addition, hundreds of Japanese, including most of the wounded soldiers, never got off. In all, probably 700 men, women and children drowned inside the ship.

(4)

Pampanito's attack had not been flawless. The damage inflicted might not have been as great as Summers would claim and be credited for at Pearl Harbor. The imperfect postwar Japanese records would credit him with *Kachidoki Maru* but not the "large freighter" Summers, Hauptman and others on the bridge claimed to have

172

seen go down. The one hit heard and timed in the "medium" freighter leading the starboard column might not have occurred, or, if it did, the damage was slight.

A second ship had been mortally damaged. This was Summers' third target, the "large freighter" in the starboard column at which he fired two stern tubes, claiming one hit that had blown off part of the deckhouse and caused a "faint glow." Japanese records would reveal this ship was actually a small old tanker, *Zuiho Maru*, 5,135 tons. From a distance, she could easily be confused for a freighter, with her boxy lines and amidships superstructure. She was fully laden with oil. *Pampanito's* single hit in her had touched off a fire in the oil tanks that would burn for days, but for now, she was still afloat.

Thus, according to Japanese records, *Pampanito* had positively sunk only one ship: *Kachidoki Maru. Zuiho Maru* was afire, though the gravity of the fire was not yet apparent to anyone on *Pampanito*. The other two big ships were afloat, possibly damaged. Counting the four escorts, then, there remained seven targets by Japanese accounting, or six by Summers' accounting. Either way, it was still a formidable segment of the convoy, well worth an aggressive follow-up attack.

But this was not to be. After pulling clear to eject the hot run in number four tube and reload all ten tubes, there was confusion and uncertainty in the *Pampanito* tracking party. Summers let the surviving big ships and two of the escorts get away. It was another touchy moment in *Pampanito's* wardroom. Frank Fives: "Everybody felt we should have done more than we did. We should not have broken off. Everybody was upset. The exec, Jeff Davis, spoke right up, saying, 'Let's go.' But by that time, Pete had had it. Everybody felt we should have done more. Everybody."

At ten minutes after midnight, radar reported two "possible" small pips near the spot where *Kachidoki Maru* had sunk. Summers tracked. He guessed correctly that the pips were two small escorts picking up survivors. One was stopped dead in the water, the other, well off (5 miles), was circling slowly. Summers approached cautiously. The bridge watch saw the stopped target by binoculars and reported it to be a "destroyer escort type." It was a sitting duck that could not be ignored.

At 0030, *Pampanito* commenced a run in. The target got underway, slowly. Summers logged: "Decided to attack as soon as possible and get clear." He set up and, at 0050, fired three bow tubes. Again the range was exceedingly long: 3,500 yards. None of the torpedoes hit. Summers logged that the torpedoes "apparently ran under target." Later, when the Pearl Harbor experts analyzed the attack data, they criticized Summers for firing from a position "that cannot be called the best" and from a range that was "nearly extreme" for the torpedo. All in all, it was a sloppy, halfhearted effort on the wrong target.

With that gesture, Summers gave up on the convoy and secured from battle stations. He ordered a south-easterly course to "pull clear and join up with the rest of the pack the following night." All hands on *Pampanito* were tired. They had been tracking the convoy for more than twenty-four hours. Many, including Summers, had not slept during that period. Some had been without sleep for up to forty-eight hours. Gratefully, men groped into the dark sleeping compartments and heaved themselves wearily into bunks.

While Summers had been attacking the convoy, Eli Reich in *Sealion,* 172 miles to the east, was patrolling back and forth in a futile effort to find it. His hunch, of course, had been wildly wrong. He found this out at about midnight when Summers sent off another contact report following the attack that sank *Kachidoki Maru.* No doubt chagrined, Reich logged: "The convoy evidently had remained on a westerly course throughout the day. Decided to continue on to westward to explore coast of Hainan and possibly regain contact with convoy should it change course to the eastward."

Ben Oakley in *Growler* was still circling around the rendezvous point, trying to get through on radio to Pearl Harbor and his wolf pack. Ultimately, he reached all. To his great joy, Pearl Harbor ordered *Growler* to Fremantle, Australia, for refit. As expected, Reich was designated to take command of the pack. He, in turn, informed Summers that he was closing Hainan to patrol there the following day and directed *Pampanito* to patrol "independently." Summers cancelled plans to pull out of the area, deciding to patrol off Hainan himself.

That same night Ed's Eradicators, still not having heard a single word about the convoy, gave up its backstopping mission. It set an easterly course to Bashi Channel. Later that night, Pearl Harbor passed along to the Eradicators incomplete reports on the convoy and the battle. Fluckey was so angry that *Barb* and *Queenfish* had never received a contact report that he took the extraordinary step of criticizing, by implication, a fellow skipper in his official patrol report: "Heard of *Growler*'s good work. Later heard *Pampanito* had hit convoy with the *Growler*. Glad two of the five subs made contact, but it is very disappointing for the other three to have wasted two days on this lane. Have no idea when *Growler* made contact." Had he known that *Sealion* had also attacked the convoy, Fluckey might have been furious.

(5)

At the site of the *Kachidoki Maru* sinking, some six hundred British POWs and numberless Japanese thrashed and flailed in the darkness to find rafts and debris. Many were badly injured and in shock and scarcely knew what they were doing. Only a few lifeboats and rafts had been launched, not nearly enough to support the survivors. British and Japanese alike shared whatever floated, sometimes fighting for space. Many survivors unwittingly swam or floated into thick oil, which had spilled from the ship's fuel tanks. Many survivors became violently seasick. For all, it was a ghastly time.

Roll Parvin, swimming toward a "large raftlike mass which was crowded with squatting figures," came upon a POW groaning in the water. He had injured his leg when he jumped. He thought it was broken. Parvin helped the man to the raft, but there was no room. One Britisher said, "Give him my place," and slid into the water. When the injured man had slithered onto the raft, Parvin saw that his leg was "gashed from knee to ankle and dangled oddly from a twisted and kinked thigh." Parvin left this raft and for the next hour swam from raft to raft, seeking a place for himself. None had any room.

Parvin recalled that while he was seeking a place to light, he heard the strains of "There'll Always Be an England" "swelling louder every moment as voice after voice, poised just above the level of the sea, took up the strain." Nearby, in a lifeboat, a group of "listless and dejected" Japanese, armed with rifles, came to life. Japanese officers ordered the soldiers to swing their rifles over the side of the boat threateningly. Parvin said: "Cries of *'braggero'* and *'canero'* and other Japanese exhortations, presumably meaning 'Shut up,' echoed across the sea." But for a long while, the singing went on.

Presently, Parvin found a small square wooden grating, to which three POWs were clinging. He joined these men. Soon they drifted into oil. "Talking was practically impossible. Every time a mouth was opened, oil lapped in with nauseating cloyness and burned its way down the stomach. . . . For the rest of that year-long night, we sped up shiny black slopes that glistened greasily in the moonlight, and slid into dark, mysterious valleys that melted into slopes again as soon as we reached them. With salt-clogged, sore and bleary eyes we watched the moon creep very, very slowly across the vast arch of the sky."

Ray Stark also saved an injured man. "I heard someone shouting, 'Help! Help!' I swam over to the man. He was a Scotsman, a corporal, Jock Kerr, who had smashed his leg. He'd more or less given up." Stark took him in tow. He saw a floating object and grabbed it. It was a wooden lavatory—a *benjo*. He pulled Kerr onto it. Kerr thought his ankle was broken. Stark now had a big bulge under his eye from the object he hit when he had dived off. They hung on.

Stark, an artilleryman and before that a coal miner for eleven years, was one of those Britishers who had first been assigned to work as a stevedore in Saigon. Later he and most of the men were sent to work on the railroad. In the ghastly British camps in Thailand, Stark had served on 323 burial parties. Now, riding the *benjo,* he wondered how many more of his mates had died, trapped in the hold, or how many more would die before rescue came. If it came.

Johnny Sherwood swam around for a while until he found a piece of hatch board. "This was just about the job," he thought. "Now I had something to lean on and rest." But as time went on, he collected six more men, including a Scottish sergeant. Only two men could lean on the hatch board at a time. The Scottish sergeant

176

and Sherwood took positions at each end of the board and allowed two men to rest every few minutes. But one man had swallowed a lot of oil and had almost passed out. Sherwood kept propping him across one end; he kept sliding off. "The other chaps were getting tired and wanting a rest. So at last we decided that it was better to let this poor sick fellow go and concentrate on saving the remaining six of us." They let him go.

Tom Pounder, who had separated from his mate Doug Spon-Smith, swam toward a lifeboat. As he got close, he saw it was full of Japanese. "Some of our chaps were trying desperately to climb into the lifeboat. But as their hands grasped the rim of the boat, the Japs beat them with the oars and slashed at them with knives." Just as Pounder reached the boat, one POW, more determined than the rest, had managed to climb aboard, and one of the Japs stabbed him in the back with a knife. "As the man collapsed, he was ruthlessly tossed overboard to disappear among the waves," Pounder recalled.

Pounder swam quickly away. He soon found a very large, partly occupied raft and crawled aboard. He peered into the dark, looking for Spon-Smith and repeatedly shouting his name, but there was no sign of him. Presently the half-dozen men on the raft began singing "Rule Britannia" and "Sons of the Sea." "The chorus was taken up by the others until everybody was singing at the top of his voice. . . . Once more we had triumphed over death and the Japs," said Pounder. But soon, the singing died off, and "the reaction after all the excitement was setting in now, and I felt absolutely worn out and sick. The tossing of the raft upset my guts, and I spewed up my evening meal of rice and seaweed into the China Sea."

Other survivors, Japanese and British alike, began to converge on this raft. The British magnanimously helped the Japanese onto the raft. One powerful British swimmer even jumped into the water to rescue a badly injured Japanese. Then a group of Japanese appeared, clinging to an overturned lifeboat. They left the boat and crowded onto the raft. Pounder had a shock: "One of the Japs now safely settled on the raft was the one with the knife, the very same Jap who had killed one of our lads in the lifeboat." Pounder gave him a wide berth. Then a smaller raft jammed with British and

177

Japanese tied onto the larger raft. The Japanese, who now outnumbered the British, repaid the kindness shown them by forcing the British off the larger raft. They were consigned to the smaller raft and the overturned lifeboat, which was also tied onto the larger raft. Pounder wound up on the smaller raft, sitting waist deep in water. "All we could do was sit, wait and hope. That night was the longest of my life."

Doug Spon-Smith had survived. "I came up and had oil in my eyes. My shorts had come off, but I didn't need those. Somehow I got to a raft. It was a very large one, with maybe thirty people on it, a half-dozen of them unarmed Japanese soldiers. There was very little conversation. We just hung on and hoped. I didn't think for one minute that I was going to die. I just wouldn't accept that. I just wouldn't give in. That, and a slice of luck, kept me going."

Fred Cooper swam to a lifeboat, yelling for help, but the boat was full of Japanese. He heard somebody shout: "Keep away from him, he's got a knife." Cooper: "I guess he panicked. He wouldn't let anybody else in the boat." Cooper swam on to a raft about three by six feet. There were six POWs on the raft, plus a Japanese officer who was moaning and groaning. Cooper: "He was disposed of. A bloke at the back of the raft sat on him and drowned him. That gave us more room."

Arthur R. Peddie, thirty, could swim, but his mate, Freddie Lacy, of London, could not. Lacy had nearly drowned in Thailand. He was afraid of water. The two men had jumped holding hands, but after they hit the water, Peddie never saw Lacy again. When Peddie came to the surface, the ship was gone. He heard shouts, struck out and swam to three men holding on to a couple of big spars. He joined them. Another two men came along holding a tabletop. They put the tabletop over the spars and all sat on the table. The rig sank down until they were chest-deep in the water. Peddie said: "We drifted near an overturned lifeboat. There were four Japanese sitting on the keel, dressed in white uniforms. They were nurses and orderlies. One of the men threw me a rope. I thought, 'That's good, they're going to tow us.' He told me to pull the rope. I did. There was a dead Jap on the end of the rope. So I flung the rope back at him, and we paddled away from them."

When Stan Thompson came to the surface, he found

a bamboo life raft right under his nose. As he started to climb on, somebody said, "Who's that?" He said, "Thomo," his nickname. A voice said, "Let him on." So Thompson said, "What's this 'Let him on'?" The voice explained that since the Japanese were kicking POWs off their rafts, they were not going to allow any Japanese on this one. Thompson said: "I was wearing a gold ring with a diamond star, my engagement ring. As I climbed on the raft, it came off my finger. When I realized it, I said, 'I've just lost something I could have flogged for fifty dollars back in Singapore.' A chap said, 'What's that?' I said, 'A gold ring.' He said, 'Oh, bad luck.' But a little later, another chap found it in a crevice between two of the bamboo poles. After I had described it, he returned it."

Tom Parrott remembered: "After swimming about two hundred yards, I saw a raft with about twelve or more people hanging on to it. After what seemed hours, we got ourselves organized. Two men would ride the raft for a spell, then change over with two more. This worked well at first; then, as we became tired, men wanted to stay on all the time and we had to push them off. About this time, we heard the sound of engines quite close. It may have been a submarine."

Parrott, a Londoner, was the son of a career army man, a sergeant major in the Royal Artillery. Tom had spent most of his school life at an army base in Ceylon, where—he was now thankful—he had learned to swim "really well." He had pleased his father when in 1938, at age eighteen, he, too, joined the Royal Artillery. After the war began, his outfit was posted to France to fight the Germans and evacuated from Dunkirk. The outfit survived the bombings of London and Coventry before being sent on to Singapore to face the Japanese. For a man of twenty-four, Parrott had experienced a great deal of suffering and pain. Now, incredibly, this. But he was optimistic: "Although things could not have looked worse, and I'm not a religious man, something inside me kept telling me I was going to be all right."

Frederick J. King had celebrated his fortieth birthday on July 30, in Singapore. He'd been a butcher before the war and because he was single, he'd been drafted in 1941. He went to Singapore as part of the 18th Division, arriving shortly before the surrender. He had survived the hell of the railway in comparatively good condition, and now he was faced with this. "I couldn't swim, but I had a life preserver. I was flung off the bow. I saw a piece of decking about seven feet square and crawled on it. It could have been a piece of ceiling. It had electric light bulbs and wires. There were two other men on the ceiling, a young POW and a Japanese soldier with a rifle. The soldier made us stay at one end, away from him. You could hear Japs in the water everywhere, hollering and shooting. We could see dozens of other people in the water. Lots of dead bodies, smothered in oil. Over the water, you could hear our chaps singing traditional songs, like 'Land of Hope and Glory.'"

Ralph Clifton had celebrated his thirty-seventh birthday on September 1, in Singapore. "When I went off the ship, I had a sergeant with me. He couldn't swim. He asked if he could stay with me. I told him I'd do my best. My pal Tosh Evans also wanted to stay by my side. This was something that one cannot explain. I am at a loss to say where *my* courage came from, but I never thought that I would drown. I just prayed that we would come out of it all right."

When Clifton had popped to the surface, he saw, to his utter amazement, a baby in the water all by itself. It was wrapped in swaddling clothes, floating along on its back, crying. By that time, Clifton's pal Evans had found a raft and climbed on. Evans heard the baby crying and thought it was Clifton. "I was something of a comedian and could imitate a baby crying. So Tosh called out to me. I had to explain that it was not an imitation, that I had a real baby."

Clifton swam to the raft with the baby. There was a female, a nurse, hanging on this raft. It turned out to be her baby! Clifton: "She was screaming. I told her the baby was okay. I handed the baby to a friend, [Arthur] Andy Devine, who held it for a long time. I helped the nurse get on the raft. When I started to get on, a Japanese officer cried, 'English white pig,' and tried to cut my hands off. He didn't want me on the raft; it was too crowded. There were two dozen people and it was half-submerged. But the nurse told him I had saved her baby. So then he let me on. The officer offered me a drop of whiskey, but I wouldn't have any truck with him. The nurse thanked me by stroking my head and saying, 'Thank you, English soldier.'"

Clifton and Devine were both Londoners, both married. Devine had no children, but Clifton's wife Doris had given birth to a daughter while he was at Changi—before he was sent to work on the railway. During the long night, thoughts of these loved ones at home sustained the two men. Then they saw a ship gliding along like a "ghost" among the rafts. Devine: "It could have been a submarine. We called out after it, but it didn't stop."

Wally Mole swam to a small raft, but unfortunately there were a couple of Japanese clinging to it and they strongly objected to his company. With his strength ebbing, he looked for refuge elsewhere. He heard English voices and swam toward them. He found three POWs clinging to a small raft. They gave him a hand. Mole was thankful for everything. "The sea all around was covered in thick oil. Actually, I think the oil was a blessing in disguise. It not only calmed the sea, but also helped to keep out the cold and gave us such buoyancy that it was almost impossible to sink."

This raft drifted into another, a larger, bamboo raft, crowded with POWs, including Clifton and Devine. By then, there were about two dozen people seated on it, half submerged. In the center was the Japanese nurse holding her baby. Two men on Mole's raft transferred to the larger raft, enabling Mole and the other man to get on the smaller raft. They tied the smaller raft to the larger one, and Mole just made it. "I was so exhausted by now that I must have passed out. When I regained my senses, the sea was no longer calm. I felt terribly seasick. My naked body was covered with oil and grease. My eyes were smarting. With each wave I was half drowned. But I held on with every ounce of strength I had in me."

George Huitson, a fair swimmer, found a square raft made of cork, with a wooden floor in the center, suspended on a net, about two feet down, to protect legs from sharks. He climbed on, joining several POWs and several Japanese soldiers, including an officer with a sword. "The Japs were very quiet," Huitson recalled. "Didn't say anything. The officer sat with his head in his hands all night long. Then we got another Jap, a young sailor still wearing his cap. He seemed to be enjoying himself. He quoted Lord Nelson: 'England expects every man to do his duty.' A big galvanized tank floated by. There was a Jap sitting on the tank, a friend of the

181

sailor's. The sailor jumped over and joined his pal on the tank."

Ernest Benford was weak, nauseated and very scared. "I had seen no one. It was so quiet. Not even the noise of waves breaking." He found a table with broken legs and hung on. He began to think he was the only survivor, when he heard a shout in English, then another, coming from opposite directions. Benford returned the shouts and started paddling toward one of them. As he paddled, a forlorn Japanese civilian flailed up and clutched the table. Fighting a strong current, Benford made a last, magnificent effort and reached a raft big enough to hold about twelve people. Benford and the Japanese, now moaning as if injured, climbed on the raft. Benford was vomiting continually. "Eventually I felt so weak and dispirited I could not even summon the strength to speak. I had lost interest completely and just wished I could die."

PART EIGHT

Oil and Madness

(1)

When dawn broke on September 13, the survivors of *Rakuyo Maru* were still divided into two distantly separated masses, those in the two groups of lifeboats and those clinging to rafts and wreckage. It was a fair, hot, tropical day. There was not a breath of breeze. The water was flat calm. There were no ships or aircraft in sight. The men were free of the Japanese but prisoners of the sea. For all too many, the sea would prove to be by far the harsher jailer.

In the early hours of the morning, the three lifeboats in the Duncan group were joined by two others. Bill Mayne recalled that at this time, the men were again redistributed among the four good boats and the fifth, leaky boat with the engine was set adrift. There were a total of 136 men in the four boats, 80 Australians and 56 British. Duncan continued to command the "lead" boat, Matsen and Major the second, into which the doctor, Rowley Richards, moved. Andy Anderson and Arthur Wright commanded the third and fourth boats. In the regrouping, the Matsen-Major boat was given a piece of canvas, which was used alternately as a sail (replacing the blanket) and as a device to catch rainwater.

These four boats were only scantily provisioned with food and water. Duncan knew that they had a fair supply of burned rice, scraped from the cookhouse woks, and two kegs of water, about six gallons. The food and water were strictly rationed, one billiard-ball-sized dollop of rice per man per day and a quarter of a pint of water per man per day. Russ Savage ladled out the water in a small cigarette tin twice a day. The other three boats also strictly rationed food (if any) and water.

The *Perth* sailors organized regular watch-standing groups on their boats. Bill Mayne recalled that on the Matsen-Major boat, the three watches were composed of sixteen men each and called "Red, White and Blue." Ma-

185

jor commanded the Red, Matsen the White, and Mayne the Blue. The men on watch sat on seats, manning the oars (there was no breeze all day). The watch commander held the tiller and the other men in the boat lay under the seats.

Nobody was overly keen to row. On all boats, tempers flared. Frank McGovern told about it: "There were two oars, and we put two men on each oar. Four Englishmen taking a turn on the oars packed up. Wouldn't row anymore. We kept trying to talk them into rowing, but they wouldn't. So we told Vic Duncan that anybody who didn't pull his weight was going over the side. The English settled down after that." The Australian J. Edward N. Porter went on: "Some of the other fellows were wanting to throw me overboard because I wasn't in a fit state to pull an oar, or help in any way since I had malaria, beriberi and pellagra. I found out then I had one true friend, Arthur Watson 'Blue' Kay. He defied anyone to lay a finger on me. Not a soul said another word." As a precaution, Vic Duncan collected all the knives on his boat.

Sometime during that day, Rowley Richards recalled, the four-boat Duncan group caught sight of the six-boat Varley group. They were too far away to hail, perhaps a mile or more, mere specks on the horizon. They appeared to be westward bound, as was the Duncan group. But later that same day, these boats, Richards remembered, "seemed to go about and sail in an easterly direction. We assumed that they had changed their minds about going to China and perhaps had decided to go to the Philippines instead."

Duncan, and others, believed the boats were making good headway. This is doubtful. More likely they were completely at the mercy of the swift currents in this part of the South China Sea, going in circles or milling around not far from the site of the sinking. Nor did the Varley group get far. No matter. Spirits were high. Clarrie Wilson: "We all thought we were free and heading for China. I don't think anybody gave any thought to what might happen if we got there. Our first aim was to get there."

(2)

The 900-odd *Rakuyo Maru* survivors clinging to rafts and wreckage had had a harrowing and wretched night. Many gave up. By dawn on September 13, after twenty-four hours in the water, others were on the point. Some, seeking to capitalize on their "freedom," exhorted the men to action, proposing and building elaborate islands of junk for the purpose of sailing or paddling to land, wherever it might be. They, too, had given up any hope of being rescued by a ship. If they were to live, it would be through their own ingenuity and resourcefulness.

This group of survivors confronted two new and severe problems those in the lifeboats were spared. The first was oil, probably spilled from the sunken tanker. During this second day, the currents swept almost all into a thick scum of it. It covered the men, splashing into eyes and ears. It coated the surfaces of the rafts and wreckage, making them slippery and difficult to hold on to.

The second problem was madness. These men had no food or water. On the railway they had survived long periods of hunger, but thirst was another matter. A great many had abandoned ship already thirsty and without canteens. One full day (twenty-four hours) in the water, enduring baking sun and salt-encrusted lips, had intensified thirst almost beyond tolerance. On the second day scores succumbed and gulped sea water. Probably because by now their frail and emaciated bodies had a very low tolerance for salt, these very quickly went stark raving—and often dangerously—mad. Thus these survivors, who had already endured unspeakable hardship and grief, had now to endure the unnerving sight of their own closest mates going crazy. In many instances the madmen had to be killed before they caused the deaths of others.

In many violent shipwrecks, sharks, apparently attracted initially by the great noise, have soon appeared on the scene. But in this instance, fortunately, sharks were few. Everyone lived in fear of shark attack but only a few survivors reported seeing sharks. In these cases the sharks were after Japanese survivors who were left behind. No instance of a shark attack on a British or Australian was reported. The sharks, usually prevalent in these waters, might have been repelled by the oil.

It was a time few cared to remember. Men saw—and did—things better left unsaid. In the years to come, some would block it from memory altogether. Some could not be sure that the things they "recollected" actually had happened or whether they had invented them. Few could recall, precisely, what they did, or who they were with on the rafts and wreckage. Most recollections, then, were surreal or impressionistic. But some men had vivid and specific recollections.

Charles Armstrong would never forget those days on his raft. "Very cold it was at night and burning our flesh black in the day. We had already split up from our party. They were all mad. We may have been, I suppose. We were on our own, anyway. The ocean, we thought, for us alone. We collected a lot of wreckage and worked in the water, and after a while we had a small raft on top of our ladder. Anybody far gone was put on it. Later we took turns resting on it. But it became full of oil and we could not keep on it. We slid off, took a firm grip and hung on. Men died fast from exposure and thirst. Some went the first day because of drinking salt water. I know of some who said, 'Good luck,' and just drifted off on their own. Many things took place in the water I could not tell you about."

Vic Clifford joined a group of eighteen Australians who were clinging to an oil-soaked island of debris. There was not another soul in sight. As far as they knew, they had the ocean to themselves. "Everyone was having hallucinations. The poor buggers were talking to their wives, their mothers, their kids. A couple drank sea water. They'd go delirious. One bloke said, 'Aren't you coming over to the island?' 'What island?' 'That island over there. My old man owns it. There's plenty of rice over there. Plenty of tucker.' I said, 'Pull your head in, Charlie.' He said, 'If you're not coming, I'm going on my own.' He swam about two yards and then just sank. Others would say, 'All right, Mum, you look after the kids.' Or, 'It'll be all right, son. Daddy will be home soon.' I mean, you'd cry to hear it."

Bob Farrands had left the *Rakuyo Maru* with most of his possessions: haversack, hat, shorts, shirt. In the haversack was his most valuable possession: the engraved silver cup for winning the Melbourne Cup "horse race" in Burma. When he jumped off the ship, he lost his hat. Soon after, he jettisoned his haversack and the cup. He took his shirt off to use as a hat and, on the first night, lost that. By the second day, he was down to only his shorts. His story was:

"On the first night, my mate and I decided our little bit of board was no good to us. We'd get on a raft. We went around and found these six Englishmen on a raft. There seemed to be room for two more. We asked if we could come aboard, but they refused. So it was going to be every man for himself. We waited until after dark and paddled in with fists flying. I had a set-to with an Englishman, [F. E.] Curley Wiles. He grabbed me by the throat. But when we finished up, I nearly drowned him. We kicked the six of them off. We said, 'Now it's ours. Do you wish to come back?' So there were eight of us on this raft. There was no further trouble."

Strachan White and his mate James H. Lansdowne lashed their raft to one supporting three Englishmen. White noted that a school of fish had collected beneath the rafts. "They came right up and bit our toes in the water." That gave White an idea. Using his toes as bait, he lured several fish over the half-submerged raft, then quickly tipped the raft. Two fish were trapped high and dry. They gave one fish to the Englishmen and shared the second. But the fish were a flop, according to White: "They were too salty. They made us thirsty."

Charles Perry, on a raft with several other Englishmen, saw what he was sure was a small fishing boat. He jumped off the raft and started swimming toward it. He swam about two miles, he thought; then he saw, to his dismay, that the fishing boat was only a ship's upturned cabin. He climbed on. "I looked around. The lads I'd been with were just a speck on the horizon. I started to cry. I did not like being alone. If you're with someone, you can talk, you feel safer. I spent the night on that cabin. It was the worst experience I had the whole time. I must have said my prayers three times that night."

Sergeant Harry Jones was still hell-bent to capitalize on the catastrophe and escape. He and eleven others (of whom only five could swim) built an elaborate raft and fitted it with a sail made of an oar and a scrap of canvas. When all was done and they were ready to set off to China, another group tried to take possession of the craft. Jones said: "It was necessary for me to instruct my little band to beat them off with any means at their command. As can be imagined, there was a terrific free-for-all. But we were determined and we came through intact." But it was all for naught. The raft would not sail. The Jones party drifted aimlessly, just like everyone else.

Doug Hampson: "People were doing strange things. An Australian warrant officer stood up on a raft and cried out, 'We're not going to be saved so we might as well all drown ourselves.' I got up on the raft and clobbered him. But it was too late. He killed any hope a lot of men had. From then on, we had lots of deaths. They dived down in the water to go get a drink or an imagined blanket. This one bloody captain kept saying he was going to his pub to get a drink. I pulled him back three times, but the fourth time I let him go. I drank salt water, but only one tiny sip at a time. It was bloody terrible."

Tony Clive: "The chaps got thirsty and started to drink salt water. It wasn't very long before they started to go off. The chap on the hatch board with me went. He started scooping up water. He got hallucinations. He thought he could see food and water. He was raving, babbling and waving his arms. I tried to restrain him. Hold him down, keep him from going. He started to get violent. Then it's a matter of survival for yourself. You're going to need all the energy you've got to last out yourself. So I had no other option but to let him go. He swam off into the darkness."

Joseph Bagnall, a nonswimmer, wound up on a raft with about twelve or fourteen men. Half were on top, half hanging on in the water. On the second morning, all hands were present. Later that day, unable to resist, the men began to drink salt water. Bagnall: "They were throwing their arms about and went into the water and just floated off. One fellow a few yards from our raft went mad and drank another man's blood. They were struggling in the water. The madman bit him in the neck and drank his blood."

Tug Wilson continued: "When daybreak came, the sun got hotter and hotter until it was almost unbearable. We had no water to drink. Our lips were dry and cracked. My tongue felt like a rasp. Our bodies were covered in oil.

Burned oily muck matted our hair. My mate Alf and I were both swimmers. We were constantly going to the assistance of nonswimmers that had slid off the greasy surface of the rafts. We found it an advantage to turn the raft over so the battens underneath gave some means of keeping one's body from slipping off. Men became desperate and short-tempered. Some broke down completely and sobbed. Not that they were soft or babyish. But it riled others that heard them into shouting at them. We prayed that help would soon come and joked to keep up our morale. All rather optimistic, trying not to believe that we were going to be left to perish in the sea after our miraculous escape."

Leslie Bambridge added other details: "You had to have will power not to drink salt water. I never drank it. But by the second day, some had and they went mad. One bloke who had been drinking salt water stood up on the raft and said he was going to milk the cows. He dived straight off into the water. That was the last we saw of him."

Alf Allbury and his mucker Ted Jewell clung to the same raft, in a cluster of rafts. There was a "vicious, lunatic struggle" on the next raft, and as Allbury saw it: "We sat watching it, listening to the curses and shrieks of four half-crazed men as they tore, hit and bit at one another. One of them had stood up, and in his hand was something that squirmed and shone like silver in the sunlight. It was a fish. There was a sudden splash, and two men tumbled still fighting into the water. But they were too weak to swim, and we saw the agony on their faces as first one and then the other threw up his hands and disappeared. They were less than ten yards away, and we sat there and watched, feeling nothing."

Roy Hudson was still teamed up in the water with Frederick Carter, an ambulance driver. They joined a raft supporting an Australian. Hudson confessed: "We saw two people in the water not far from us, smothered in oil. We waved to them. They waved back. We drew nearer to each other. Then we saw they were Japanese. We beckoned them to us. Then we did them in. We pushed them under and held them under. I can't say more than that. It was dreadful."

"A lot of guys just gave up immediately," said Barney Barnett. "I think most of the officers went the first day. We attributed that to the good, soft lives they had led. No working. I saw quite a few give up and drown the first twenty-four hours. Some drank sea water and went mad. They were screaming and shouting and raving. So what you did, you shoved them off the raft. You had to. I was right on the point of drinking sea water. It was very tempting. Thirst is the worst thing there is. But I didn't. I prayed. I never went to church, but I prayed."

Jack Flynn felt there was no hope. "On the second day, the big group started drifting apart and thinning out. That's when we got into the oil. That was terrible. It was a big black floating mass, like jelly, about three or four inches thick. It got all over you. Any part that was exposed. It blinded me in one eye. I couldn't get it out. I got a screw out of a raft and scratched the canvas of my kapok life jacket until I had a hole I could rip open to get at the kapok. I tried to wipe the oil off with the kapok, but it was all over me and I couldn't get rid of it. I thought that was the end of me. I felt completely helpless and hopeless. I didn't think we'd be getting out of it at all."

Tom Carr remembered that "we had about twelve rafts all tied together. The first night we lost three men off our raft. But it wasn't very good being tied together. With the rafts tied together, and the lads sitting with their legs in the water, they bashed together. It broke a lad's leg. The doctor came over to him. But you could see the doctor was going mad. He tried to mend the broken leg with nothing. He had no gear at all. He died later—just sank from sight."

Denny Smith was another in the group. "We began to thin out the second day. It was depressing because you knew the end was coming. One of the lads was crying out for water. He wanted water, he wanted water, he wanted water. We tried not to pay attention to him; we couldn't help him anyway. No one had any water. Quartermaster Boswell, our senior man, told us that you could wash your mouth out with sea water if you didn't swallow it and spit it back out. But on the second day, Boswell went mad. He started swimming like crazy. He could see his family. He was shouting to them, calling them by name. He got off a few yards and down he went. No man made any effort to help him. It was every man for himself."

Leslie Bolger shook his head ruefully as he remembered: "I hung on a raft with fourteen other men. It was about four feet square and had ropes on the side to hold to. We let two men at a time get on the raft to rest.

I had lost my mate, Bill Scarpella, but on the second day he reappeared. He was a very powerful chap, a very good swimmer. I said, 'Where have you been?' He said, 'Oh, I've just been and had a nice cup of coffee.' He'd been drinking sea water. And that was the last I saw of him. The doctor—Major Chalmers, the Tasmanian—came by wearing a life preserver. He was ill. Malaria. It had cycled on him while he was in the water. He was shivering and shaking. We invited him to get on our raft. He got on, but after two or three hours, he died. We pushed his body off into the sea."

Ernest Fieldhouse had latched on to a raft supporting twenty-four men. When dawn came, he counted only twenty-one. All were covered with oil. Fieldhouse was very thirsty. He inquired if anyone had water. Someone pointed out a man with a canteen. Fieldhouse swam to him and said, "Give us a drop of water, mate." The man unlooped the canteen and passed it to Fieldhouse, who took a swig. His face contorted. He spat the liquid out. It was salt water. Fieldhouse looked closely at the man who had so freely offered his canteen, then recoiled in horror. "The man's eyes were crazed and bloodshot, foam was oozing from his mouth and nostrils." The man lunged for the canteen, pushing Fieldhouse under, holding him there. Aware that he was in the "grip of a madman," Fieldhouse struggled wildly. Then, suddenly, the man relaxed his grip and Fieldhouse hurried back to the raft.

The *Perth* sailor Bob Collins, clinging to a raft with some Australian mates, sought a way to improve his lot. A man came paddling up on a rather magnificent "raft." It was a hatch board about 8 feet long and 2.5 feet wide. The man was Sergeant Noel C. Day of the Royal Australian Air Force. Collins and his friends thought riding this hatch board would be superior to hanging in the water. "There was a mild skirmish to get on his 'raft' but he held off everyone. Sergeant Noel Day calmly surveyed the bunch of hopeful faces pointed in his direction and out of his army and air force mates in the crowd, said, 'I'll take Bob Collins.'" Collins could not understand why Day had chosen him of all people, a navy man. Later, Day explained, "Do you remember the dollar you loaned me to buy those boots? I may not have been here if I hadn't bought those boots. I never forgot that, the day you loaned me that dollar. That's why I picked you." Later, Collins found a piece of a lifeboat and scratched a message on it with a pencil: "Left to perish by the Japs, September 12, 1944."

The cook Bill Cunneen, Reg Harris, Ron Miscamble and about sixteen other Australians built a floating Taj Mahal. They found a huge platform of timbers about 12 feet by 12 feet and 12 inches thick. They placed three rafts atop this platform and even tried—unsuccessfully—to buoy it further with oil drums. Miscamble: "Some of the fellows started drinking sea water within the first twenty-four hours. They would see an island and try to swim to it. Or they would go off to make tea or have a beer. At first we'd go after them and bring them back. They would struggle with you. So we reached an agreement. If anyone swam off, it was curtains. Good night. You just couldn't afford to do anything about it."

Reg Stewart told about having a couple of Pommies on the raft. "I had a bit of trouble with them. One Pom was unconscious, not dead, just out. So we tied him to the raft. But the other Pom thought his mate was a hindrance, and every time I turned my back, he kept untying this bloke and letting him go. He was going delirious. You couldn't talk to him. I picked up a bit of wood and hit him over the head and tied him to my back. He was all right after that."

There had been many sets of brothers on *Rakuyo Maru*. The Wades. The Moxhams. The Australian twins John and Burke Cobon. Some, such as the Wades, who got in the lifeboats, survived, but many died, including the Cobons. The most tragic family story was that of the Turnbull brothers of Brisbane, Australia. There had been three Turnbull brothers on *Rakuyo Maru*: John, thirty-two; William, twenty-seven; and Kenneth, twenty-three. They had all been born in England but emigrated to Australia. The eldest, Jack, was a professional sailor, having enlisted in the Royal Australian Navy in 1934. He was married and had four children. A survivor of the *Perth,* he had become a prisoner of war in Java. Bill and Ken were both in the same outfit in the Australian army, the 26th Battalion, and both were also taken prisoner in Java. All three brothers worked on the railway and survived. All three were selected for the first Australian Japan Party. All three boarded *Rakuyo Maru*.

Nothing is known about how Bill or Ken died, but one

survivor, Freddie Mills, at least remembered seeing Jack. "I saw him in the water and was with him when he quietly became unconscious."

(3)

One hundred and fifty miles to the west, dawn of September 13 came for the British survivors of *Kachidoki Maru*. These men, too, had spent a harrowing and wretched night. Clinging to half-submerged rafts and wreckage among a large number of Japanese soldiers, nurses and civilians, and still in shock, they were cold, thirsty and covered with black fuel oil.

When dawn broke, Tom Pounder was still on a small raft tied to a larger raft supporting many Japanese, among them the knife-wielder from the overturned lifeboat who had stabbed a POW to death. Pounder recalled: "With the light growing, the Japs livened up once more and carried on quite a long conversation among themselves. And then we knew the topic of this discussion, for their attention was suddenly directed at us. They told us all to get up from the raft. With what little English they had, they issued orders to us: 'Orll mei, orll mei help. Orrl mei pull. Orll mei help pull.'" They backed up these orders with "unsheathed bayonets and knives."

The Japanese wanted to refloat the overturned lifeboat, also still tied to the larger raft. They attached ropes to it and ordered the POWs to heave. After many tries, the boat turned over and remained upright. The body of a Japanese female nurse that had been caught beneath the boat floated away on a wave. The Japanese bailed out the boat, got in and pushed off, leaving the POWs behind. The POWs shifted from the small raft to the large one, which now became very low in the water.

Wally Mole, on the raft with Andy Devine, Ralph Clifton—the man who had saved the baby—and others, recalled a harrowing experience after dawn had broken. "Two Jap seamen that were on a raft similar to ours drifted close by, swearing and shouting at us. Each had a knife in his hands. Their intention was to board our raft and get the Japanese girl and baby. Each time they came close, I or somebody else near the edge managed to push

195

them away with our feet. This infuriated them more than ever. Eventually they succeeded in getting on our raft and started to strike out with the knives. I do not know how many they stabbed for I slid off and swam to a deserted lifeboat fifty yards away."

Soon after, the POWs were electrified to see two warships in the distance. All hands on the rafts immediately began kicking and paddling toward them. It was exhausting work for the survivors, among whom was Pounder. "After a dozen or so strokes my stomach heaved and for the second time I spewed into the sea. I became very weak and very faint, but I had to keep on and do my share. The others around me were also resting at intervals, all feeling the strain of the previous night's excitement."

They could see that the warships—frigates—were maneuvering about picking up survivors—Japanese, not British. By the time this operation had been concluded, the frigates were quite close to Pounder's raft. Would the POWs also be picked up? Pounder thought "this possibility seemed small." Then there was a startling development. Two Japanese officers appeared on the bridge of the frigate. They were talking at great length and pointing to the British on the raft. One officer was the frigate's skipper. The other was the notorious Lieutenant Tanaka, in charge of the *Kachidoki Maru* POW contingent.

Pounder went on: "Their conversation appeared to turn to an argument, their gesticulating becoming wilder and wilder and by their actions we could only assume they were talking about us. Tanaka was demanding while the skipper was refusing, violently, too. So our possible rescue was being debated and our fate hung in the balance. Obviously Tanaka was all for taking us on board; after all, we were still his charges. But the Jap skipper did not want us. . . . Then it was all over. A decision had been reached. Tanaka had won and we were to be picked up after all. This was the only time in all our association that we had anything to thank Tanaka for. But even now it was done only for his benefit. It was his job to get us to Japan, come what may."

Soon they could see a lifeboat, manned by POWs, moving from raft to raft. When it was full of POWs, it returned to one of the ships, unloaded and then set off again. Pounder continued: "The Japs had opened up their yellow hearts by allowing the survivors to board their ship, but they themselves had no intention of lifting a single hand to aid our rescue." Desperately kicking and paddling, Pounder and his mates propelled the big raft toward the rescue boat. They reached it and climbed aboard. The boat pulled to a frigate to unload. Pounder was saved, but he could not find his mucker, Doug Spon-Smith. "My heart sank and my eyes filled with tears. . . . Had Fate dealt me a further blow by robbing me of another of my close friends?"

Johnny Sherwood, Wally Mole, Ralph Clifton and Ernest Benford were among those picked up by the frigate. Sherwood said: "All of a sudden the alarm warning sounded and there was a panic aboard. They pulled up the ladder and were away in a matter of two minutes, but not before nearly all the men in our immediate group, including me, were safely aboard: about two hundred. I think about seven men were left behind. But they had a good chance of survival as those two empty lifeboats were also left."

Some of those left behind were picked up with another, larger group, in a second rescue operation later in the afternoon. One was Fred King. "A Japanese frigate came alongside of us picking up Japanese survivors. I tried to get on but was knocked off with a boat hook. So I was in the water again. I was depressed. I tried to take my life jacket off—to drown myself. But it was tied in the back and I couldn't get it unknotted. About five or six hours later, a small Jap fishing trawler came along and picked up everybody they could. About one hundred and sixty of us."

The trawler, now dangerously crowded, did what it could to help those still in the water, among them Stanley Thompson, who gave this account of it: "The trawler approached our raft. It was towing a line of five or six lifeboats. When she got near us, she wheeled and turned one lifeboat adrift. We paddled the raft to the boat and got in. There were twelve of us. Another raft came up and we took them aboard. Another twelve, making a total of twenty-four, including one officer. Everybody made suggestions as to what we should do. Whether or not we should row, or what. The general vote was that we were in no condition to row. Just drift."

Among the 200-odd left behind were Roll Parvin, Ray Stark, Tom Parrott, George Huitson and Doug Spon-Smith. Most of these men—and many others—managed to crowd into empty lifeboats left by the Japanese. Most of these boats had scant supplies of water and food—but enough, with strict rationing, to sustain life. George Huitson was glad he was left behind. "It was the first time we had been free in two and a half years. We began to formulate great ideas to get to somewhere or other, but we really didn't have an idea where we were or where we could go. We were just glad to be free men again."

The rescue frigates and the trawler headed west for Hainan island, some 50 miles distant. On the way there the POWs, who had no idea where they were being taken, were pleasantly surprised. The Japanese issued them food and water and hosed down their oily clothes. Johnny Sherwood was grateful for small favors. "After we had been traveling for about four hours, they gave us a ball of rice each and half a cup of water. That was at least better than nothing, as all our men were just lying practically on top of each other, completely exhausted. We were informed that we could urinate if we wanted to in an improvised lavatory built over the side of the ship, a wooden structure. It was getting dark now, and we had spent seventeen hours in the water with no food. Nearly all the men were asleep." Wally Mole said: "As the evening came on, we were so cold that we huddled together on the bow of the frigate like a load of monkeys to stay warm, wondering what the next episode for us would be."

Late that night the rescue vessels reached a small harbor on Hainan island. None of the POWs was ever certain exactly *what* harbor. (Many believed they were on the island of Amoy.) Johnny Sherwood and a group were put ashore in a barracks. Others, including Ernest Benford, were off-loaded onto a ship. Benford recalled: "As I went up the ladder, a voice called to me—Robbie Shaw, who'd been rescued by a trawler—and warned that the four Japs greeting us on the deck were hitting everyone with their rifles. We were told later that they were the only survivors from the sunken naval vessels in the convoy. It was like running the gauntlet. Being too weak to run, I was unable to avoid the blows from their rifles and almost went down. But I knew from previous experience in Thailand that it was fatal to go down. Survival depended upon taking everything standing up. To fall to the ground or complain was a stimulant which always sent the Japs right out of their tiny little minds."

Exactly how many British POWs were rescued in these two operations on September 13 is not known. Perhaps, as Sherwood and King believed, as many as 360. All of those

198

rescued remained coated in stinging oil. Many, such as Benford and Pounder, were seriously ill. Others were in even worse shape with terrible injuries and broken bones. The Japanese offered no medical assistance. Those who were conscious were grateful to find themselves still alive. They did what little they could to ease the pain of the sick and injured.

These survivors were lucky indeed. The worst had happened and they had lived through it. Ironically, it had been the unlovely beast Lieutenant Tanaka, apparently acting in his own best interest, who had been responsible for their rescue. Tanaka apparently also demanded that further rescue efforts be mounted for those left behind. Over the next few days, more yet would be saved, including Parvin, Stark, Parrott, Huitson and Spon-Smith.

(4)

At dawn on September 14, the 136 Australian and British survivors of *Rakuyo Maru* in the four lifeboats of the Duncan group prepared to face the third day on the water. Spirits were high. For two days they had been free men. They believed they were making good progress toward China. With luck and a fair breeze, they believed they might yet make good their escape.

The six lifeboats of the Varley group were still close by, perhaps several miles at the most. Occasionally those in the Duncan group caught a glimpse of them as the boats rose and fell amid the swells. Neither group had, in fact, made much progress. Both were probably still quite close to the site of the *Rakuyo Maru* sinking, though far beyond sight of the mass of survivors still clinging to rafts and wreckage.

In the early morning, the men in the Duncan boats saw smoke on the horizon to the north. A while later, they heard long and continuous machine gun fire. The majority of the men assumed—with sinking hearts—that a Japanese warship had come along and that it was machine-gunning the six lifeboats of the Varley group. A little while later three Japanese corvettes came into view, steaming in the general direction of the Duncan group. One peeled out of formation and headed for the boats. Fear swept the survivors.

Rowley Richards was fatalistic. "We decided that our turn had come. There was no panic. We merely bid our farewells to one another, shook hands, realizing that our short-lived period of freedom was to come to a rather sticky end after all. We hoped and discussed among ourselves that the end would be quick and merciful. We made mutual pacts that if any one of us was to be wounded, and not able to look after himself but wasn't dying, the survivors would make sure he was put out of his misery." Vic Duncan remembered saying: "If you believe in Christ, say your prayers now."

The frigate closed the boats, all guns manned, circling warily. Then a shout from the Japanese. Arthur Wright recalled that the Japanese wanted to know the nationality of the men in the lifeboats. Knowing that the Japanese liked Australians better than Americans or British, they fudged the answer. "Americans?" No. "British?" No. "Australian?" Yes. Whereupon the frigate hove to and Japanese sailors lowered scramble nets and made signs to indicate that the men should come aboard. They climbed aboard, still wondering, as Richards recalled, "what the trap was to be—whether we would be brought on board, interrogated and then be pushed overboard, or what."

In short order, the 136 men of the Duncan group were picked up and herded to a spot on the bow, beneath the forward gun. The Japanese posted guards. With vast relief, Richards concluded there was no "trap." They had had the good fortune to encounter a humane Japanese. The skipper (he seemed a mere "schoolboy" to Richards) asked many questions about what ship they were from and the circumstances of the sinking. Richards, in turn, asked in his fair Japanese if the skipper had seen the six boats of the Varley group, just to the north. The skipper pointed to the other two corvettes, giving the impression that they had rescued the Varley group.

Later, the men learned that this was not so. No trace was ever found of the Varley group. No records turned up to indicate they had been recaptured or had escaped to Allied lines. Richards, Duncan and most of the others in this group concluded that their earlier assumption had been correct: Varley, Group Captain More, Colonel Melton and the 200-odd other men in those boats had been massacred by the other two frigate skippers. But this was pure speculation. There was never any proof. The Varley group could have been wiped out later by a storm.

In any event, the Duncan group, jammed on the bow of the frigate under guard, was now glum. At daybreak they had been free men. Now, once again, they were captives. What lay in store? What new devil would they have to cope with? Where were they bound? What had happened to their friends?

The crew of the corvette provided for the survivors as best they could. John Langley said: "We were lucky enough to find a tenderhearted Japanese captain." Andy Anderson admitted that "the Japanese were quite nice—decent. They brought us out a cup of hot water with some kind of sweetener in it and a biscuit. And then an hour later the same again. And then again." William R. Smith confirmed it all: "They gave us some food, biscuits mixed in some sort of sop, with brandy in it. A half-mug each. Beautiful." Rowley Richards later reported, officially, the ration had been two biscuits and two-thirds of a pint of water.

The three corvettes steamed west toward Hainan island all that day and night. Sometime in the evening they passed through the area where *Pampanito* had sunk *Kachidoki Maru* and hit the tanker *Zuiho Maru,* blowing off the deckhouse and causing a "faint glow." *Zuiho Maru* was still afloat and burning, forty-eight hours after being torpedoed.

The POWs were awed—and frightened—by the spectacle. Wal Williams didn't like it at all. "We came upon the burning wreckage of a ship, no doubt recently torpedoed. We sort of circled around it, probably looking for survivors. I thought, 'What are we hanging around here for? We are sitting ducks for a submarine attack, silhouetted beautifully against the burning wreckage.'" Much to everyone's relief, the corvettes soon moved off and resumed the course to Hainan.

On the morning of the next day, September 15, the three corvettes entered a small harbor on the coast of Hainan, the same to which the British survivors of *Kachidoki Maru* had been taken. After the war, David Clark, on the basis of some research, concluded that the harbor was Sangai. By this time, the British survivors had been transferred from the ship and the shore to a loaded tanker anchored in the harbor, several hundred yards from shore.

The corvette with the *Rakuyo Maru* survivors pulled alongside the tanker at about 1100. The 136 Australian and British POWs from *Rakuyo Maru* were ordered aboard the tanker to join the hundreds of British POWs from *Kachidoki Maru*. Paddy Dunne remembered that "the steel platings were so hot you could fry an egg on them. We were in our bare feet, dancing around like Hawaiian girls."

Barefoot and in pain, Clarrie Wilson, from *Rakuyo Maru*, was helped by a most unusual turn of circumstances. He explained: "One of the Korean guards from *Rakuyo Maru*, whom I'd known on the railway, had been rescued. He was on the tanker. He brought me a pair of rubber shoes. There was a reason for this generosity. On the railway, I had been a truck driver. The Korean and Nip guards were not allowed to drive our trucks. This Korean was in my truck one day, drunk on sake. He insisted on taking the wheel—pushed me aside. He ran the truck off the road. I was able to grab the wheel and save the truck. I could have turned him in and he'd have been badly punished. But I didn't. So in this strange place and circumstance, he returned the favor."

When the survivors of *Rakuyo Maru* met the British survivors of *Kachidoki Maru*, they were appalled. Harold V. DeSailley, thirty-nine, said: "The condition of the British POWs on the tanker was shocking. Some were suffering from burns caused by the explosion of the ship. Others had been blinded by the oil and had to be led about." Frank McGovern: "The other survivors were in terrible shape. Broken arms and legs and black with oil. It reminded me of when the *Perth* sank." Harold Ramsey: "They were in terrible condition. Broken and smashed limbs and that." Russ Savage: "Hell of a mess. They were burned all over. They were blind." Andy Anderson: "Poor devils. Faces all full of oil. Moaning. Couldn't see. I felt bad. I thought they'd be blind for life." Ray Burridge: "I saw an English bloke with two broken arms and two broken legs. They had to set his arms and legs with no anesthetic."

Vic Duncan was stunned. "I've never seen people so demoralized as the British survivors of the *Kachidoki Maru*. Not all of them, but some. I was ashamed. Two Britishers stood at the bottom of the ladder crying for the Japs to give them water. Two Scotsmen came down. They were disgusted with their mob. They said, 'Hey, digger, mind if we toss in with your fellows?' I felt the British had really dropped their bundles. They just lay there in their filth and didn't try to do anything. A lot of them were cringing and scared. They'd had it. My fellows were still on their feet. Up and going."

Even Rowley Richards, who had faced appalling conditions on the railway, was shocked and nearly rendered helpless. "When we got to the tanker and saw the survivors of the *Kachidoki Maru,* it was a most ghastly time for me. They were lying about on the open deck or in some shade by the bridge. They were covered in oil and were in a dreadful state. They were burned. They were moaning and groaning. They were in excruciating pain from fractured limbs, sunburn and from the oil. It was horrible— equaled only by the worst 'death huts' on the railway.

"Burned human flesh is nasty looking at any time. The stench was awful. Burned flesh and the oil. I'll never forget it. My own human flesh weakness is what got me. I went to look at a few of these guys and had to throw up. It offended my own personal dignity that I couldn't cope with it. I reached my physical capacity, my limit. It was a very dramatic medical problem. How do you cope when you have nothing to give them?

"I finally got around to see everybody and did what little I could. Others in our *Rakuyo Maru* group helped me. What we did mainly was to try to wash them down with cool salt water. Our boys had to move them all on open deck to do this. That was murderous. They were in misery. So we waited until later in the day when the decks were cooler. When we tossed the salt water on them, it hurt like hell. They screamed in pain. Then our chaps bathed their eyes, trying to get the oil out. I made repeated requests to the Japs to transfer these men to land, but my pleas were ignored."

The Japanese on this tanker, unaccustomed to providing transport services for large numbers of men, were no doubt overwhelmed by the presence of these hundreds of POWs. They did little to provide the bare minimum for survival. Paddy Dunne remembered that they had no water. "We made little cups out of cardboard and held them under a tap where steam was coming out and waited for the steam to condense." William R. Smith: "They gave us a feed of rice. No containers of any kind. Just rice put on the deck." Frank McGovern: "The Nips gave us some rice. We had no utensils. So we took the ball of rice in our hands. It was hot and we were trying to juggle it and hold it. We'd take a mouthful, but we couldn't chew it. We were that dry. We went to the steam winches and got condensed water from that. Wet our mouth."

At first the POWs believed they had been put on the tanker only temporarily. Later in the day, to their horror, they perceived that it was to be permanent—that the Japanese intended to send them to Japan on the open deck of a loaded tanker. Both Sid Johnson and John Wade recalled that "they started to prepare for sea, rigging up wooden latrines over the sides." Ernest Benford's heart sank with fear. "Surely they wouldn't send us to Japan on *that!* But it was to be so."

The POWs were appalled. It was the last straw, the ultimate inhumanity. They rebelled. Ian MacDiarmid said: "When we were told we were going to Japan on this tanker, we said, 'No. We're not going to Japan on a tanker.' We'd seen what happens when a tanker is hit. We'd swim ashore. The Japs said they'd machine-gun us. We told them to go ahead. We'd rather be machine-gunned than roasted." Wal Williams added: "That was the closest I ever came to trying to escape. I thought that if we had to go to Japan on that oil tanker, we'd be history."

Later in the day, as if to underscore the hideous dangers, air raid warning sirens began to moan. Ever alert, ever considerate of the men in his charge, Vic Duncan made preparations. "We were right close to the fo'c'sle. An air raid alert came on. The wind was coming from the land. I told my men that if the tanker got hit, jump over the port side and swim to land. The fuel would spill and burn on the starboard side." But it was evidently a false alarm. There was no raid after all; no planes came.

The Japanese evidently had second thoughts about utilizing the tanker for POW transport. On the following day, September 16, all POWs on the tanker, including the seriously injured, were transferred by lighter to yet another ship. This was a huge, 20,000-ton "whale factory" vessel, the *Kibibi Maru*. The POWs did not know it, but its big whale-oil tanks had been converted to carry fuel oil. Potentially, it was as dangerous as a conventional tanker.

That day—four days after the first attack on the convoy—the Japanese suspended all formal rescue operations. Of the 1,318 POWs who had been on *Rakuyo*

Maru, only Duncan's group, 136 men, had been saved by the Japanese. Of the 900 POWs from *Kachidoki Maru,* the obsessive record-keeper Rowley Richards reported after a careful count that 520 had been saved. In all, 656 POWs out of 2,218 in the convoy had been rescued by the Japanese, leaving 1,562 unaccounted for from both vessels—1,182 from *Rakuyo Maru* alone.

(5)

Pampanito and *Sealion* remained off the east coast of Hainan for two days, September 13 and 14, patrolling independently. During the daylight hours they ran submerged. After dark they surfaced to charge batteries and to search by radar and binoculars. Both boats were looking for remnants of the convoy.

On the night of September 13, at 2100, the bridge watch on *Sealion* saw the glow of a burning ship on the horizon. The officer of the deck changed course to close it and notified Eli Reich. Two and a half hours later, at 2330, they were close to it—two and half miles. Reich logged: "The ship was listed 45° to starboard, screws and rudder well out of the water, and burning with a clear hot flame, generating a moderate amount of grayish-white smoke. Off the starboard side, for a distance of about 200 yards, the water was ablaze with weak flames just as if thick fluid had overflowed the starboard gunwhale, like molasses from a can. . . . The ship appeared a total loss, completely abandoned by the Japs, and not worth the torpedoes it would take to sink her."

This was the tanker *Zuiho Maru.* It had been about twenty-four hours since *Pampanito* had torpedoed her.

Reich turned north and, at dawn on September 14, submerged off the northeast coast of Hainan. All that day he patrolled the approaches to Hainan Strait. He saw only a small fishing trawler, probably one engaged in rescue operations. After dark, he surfaced and patrolled southward off the east coast of Hainan. He logged: "The glow of the burning Jap [ship] was still bright and remained visible throughout the night." This was the night that the survivors of *Rakuyo Maru,* rescued from the lifeboats by the frigates, passed and circled the burning remains of *Zuiho Maru*. Their worry that an American submarine was in the vicinity was not unjustified. They were lucky Reich was not close enough to pick them up on radar.

That same day, September 14, Pete Summers patrolled submerged not far from the scene of his attack on the convoy. At 1420 the periscope watch sighted a "large, heavy black column of smoke." He surfaced to close and investigate. At 1530 he logged: "Continued to close to about 10,000 yards, when we could see huge flames bubbling up from surface of water. Could not get a pip on radar. The position of this burning ship was within eight miles of our position on the night of 12/13 September. . . . In all probability, this is one of our two damaged ships." The ship, he wrote, was "a total loss."

That was true. It was not, however, a damaged freighter, as Summers thought, but the tanker *Zuiho Maru*. Summers was elated. This ship was clearly doomed and would soon sink. Counting *Kachidoki Maru* and the "large freighter" believed to have been sunk with the bow tube salvo (but not verified in Japanese records), this gave *Pampanito* three ships sunk and a fourth damaged. This surely would earn Summers a Navy Cross Medal and a slew of lesser medals to award his men.

Remaining on the surface, keeping a sharp watch for aircraft, *Pampanito* cruised the area. At 1540 the high periscope watch reported two small wisps of smoke on the western horizon. Believing these to be "two freighters proceeding toward Hainan," Summers ordered pursuit and called the tracking party to stations. *Pampanito* still had eleven torpedoes. Perhaps now she might add more scalps to her belt.

Heading southwest to close the "smokes," at 1630 the bridge watch reported seeing several life rafts and lifeboats. Summers logged: "All empty except for one about 8000 yards to the northeast which possibly had some men in it. Decided these were probably Japs who had been overlooked in the rescue of survivors, and since I did not wish to take the chance of losing the 'two smokes' while investigating this boat, continued to close the smokers."

If there were men in this lifeboat, in all probability they were British POWs, not Japanese. By now, the frigates had presumably rescued all Japanese from the lifeboats and set the boats adrift. All the *Kachidoki Maru* lifeboats were now occupied by the POWs left behind.

Had Summers investigated, he might have discovered the tragedy of *Kachidoki Maru* and effected the rescue of those British left behind. However, he quite properly continued pursuit of the smokes.

By 1700, *Pampanito* was close enough to the smokes that the high periscope could distinguish masts. Summers logged: "Appeared to be two small freighters although couldn't make out much except the masts and fairly high stacks." He ordered an end around, hoping he could "beat them to Hainan." At 1915, about thirty miles off Hainan, and a "little off the track of the two possible freighters," Summers dived to await darkness.

Thirty minutes after sunset, at 2013, Summers surfaced. There was nothing on radar. Finally, after much searching, Bill Yagemann picked up pips at 14,000 yards. They were disappointingly weak pips, not those characteristic of freighters. "Looked as though we had been fooled," Summers logged. They had been. On closing to 7,000 yards, Summers saw they were "two trawlers with high masts." Summers decided the targets were "too small" for torpedoes, and since "it was too dark to attempt a gun battle," he broke off the chase, reversed course and steamed away from the coast. "Very disheartened," he logged.

In all probability these two trawlers were involved in the *Kachidoki Maru* survivor rescue operations. Each one was probably loaded with British POWs. Had these been frigates rather than trawlers, Summers might very well have torpedoed them.

During that night, Reich decided his wolf pack had spent enough time looking for the convoy remnants. The hunting would probably be better back in Luzon Strait. He broke radio silence and ordered *Pampanito* to rendezvous with *Sealion* at dawn, 0700, September 15, about twenty miles southeast of the position of the burning *Zuiho Maru*. The two boats met as scheduled. Reich and Summers talked by megaphone. Summers was pleased to learn that Reich had seen the burning ship and declared it a "total loss." This outside confirmation from the wolf pack commander would assure *Pampanito* credit for sinking three ships.

Reich laid out the plan of action for that day and the next, September 15 and 16. They would go east, on the surface, some 400 miles back to the original patrol area in Luzon Strait. The due east course for that day would take them back through the area of the initial *Growler-Sealion* attack on the convoy. They might find some cripples, or some debris indicating exactly what ships Reich had sunk. This would help with his confirmations. At 0715—sunrise—the two boats formed a scouting line, twenty miles apart, *Pampanito* to the south of *Sealion*. They cruised due east at twelve knots, warily keeping watch on the bridge and by radar and high periscope.

PART NINE

"*Pick us up, please.*"

(1)

On the third and fourth days in the water, the survivors of *Rakuyo Maru,* clinging to rafts and wreckage, died by the hundreds. Thirst was the main killer. Men could hold out no longer. They drank sea water or urine or blood, went crazy and died—or were killed by others because they were too dangerous. Others lost the strength to hang on to rafts or wreckage. Still others died of despair. They gave up during the night and disappeared. Each day the rafts thinned out by one, two or three men. Those still clutching tenaciously to life were hideously burned by sun and oil; lips and tongues were swollen grotesquely. Some were blinded by oil. Nearly all had fallen into a trance-like mental state. Most hallucinated. Many prayed.

Alf Allbury and his mate Ted Jewell and one other Britisher awoke on their raft to find themselves almost alone on the sea. "Three days ago we had been a tiny fragment of a vast armada of flotsam that had blackened the sea around us. . . . There were only a few rafts within hailing distance now. One or two of them might have been no more than a few hundred yards distant, but others were little more than dark indistinguishable specks. Standing up, ranging the sea from horizon to horizon, I could count no more than thirty rafts. . . . Hundreds of us had died. Those left were now spread far and wide across the sea."

They missed being in company with others, so they began paddling and kicking toward a dark splotch in the sea. All day they propelled the clumsy raft toward it. In late afternoon they achieved their objective. They came upon two or three hundred men gathered on a huge pontoon of rafts. They had erected distress signals, colored shorts and other bits of clothing fixed to spars of wood. There was a large outer ring of rafts linked together with pieces of rope and the tapes of life jackets. Inside the circle were other rafts, unattached but safely harbored. Allbury: "They seemed organized compared with the disintegrated

211

rabble we had become during the last two days. They may have been drifting as aimlessly as we had, but at least they all drifted together. A lot of them still wore those familiar slouch hats. We had caught up with the Australian crowd. . . . We had found an oasis of life and hope in the wilderness of sea."

Under the leadership of an Australian officer, probably Captain Arthur Sumner, this group was preparing to paddle to a "small group of islands" said to be only two days away. Allbury was doubtful, but the officer was impressive. "He was courageous, tough; a man who could lead; a man I would be glad to follow. . . . Rather than sit and pray and wait for death to come, it was better, I thought, to clutch at any straw, however fantastic." Two-thirds of the group agreed to try it. The gravely ill and the skeptics were left behind on a cluster of rafts beneath the distress signals.

It came to naught. Sometime during the night all three men on Allbury's raft ceased to function. "When I sat up and looked around me the next morning, I had no distinct recollection of anything that had taken place during the night. I saw that Ted was still there beside me, but the other man had gone. We were no longer attached to the other rafts. They were not even visible. All I could see was a few scattered blobs spread far around us; they were lone drifters, too."

They drifted, only partially aware they were still living. Late that afternoon—it was September 15—one of the British doctors drifted by, lying delirious on a hatch board. Allbury and Jewell pulled him aboard the raft. They saw that he had dysentery, that he was dying. Allbury: "He kept asking for water. . . . I dipped my hand into the sea and let a few drops splash into his mouth. It would make little difference to him now, if he drank it or not. Once or twice we had to hold him down as he found a little strength in his ravings." A little while later the doctor died, and they shoved his body into the sea.

Doug Hampson tried drinking his own urine. "I've never tasted anything so horrible in my life. I went a bit silly, but I think I had enough sense to realize I was going silly. That afternoon the ocean seemed to be divided into paddies. You know, fences everywhere. In the corner of each paddy, there was a ship. I knew it wasn't possible, but I could see it clear as I can see anything. That night we picked up a bloke and put him on the raft with us. All of a sudden he said, 'I'm going to milk Strawberry.' He grabbed me by the throat and kept saying, 'You won't let me milk Strawberry.' So I gave him a poke in the guts and said, 'Go milk Strawberry.' And that was the end of him. It was either he or I, one of the two."

Laurie Smith recalled seeing what appeared to be a boat. "We all looked at it, peered at it as it slowly moved towards us. We speculated what sort of boat. It was small; no oars. As it got closer, we saw it was a swimmer. In an Australian accent he shouted, 'No good going that way—all sand.' Was he a comedian or bloody mad? Whatever! He was doing a great crawl and soon left us with an empty sea. The next day, Ted Rick said he had had enough. I watched Ted slide off the raft, still with his hat on. He swam a few strokes away, flung both arms up and disappeared into the water. I didn't see his hat come off and never again saw Ted Rick. The last thing I could imagine was Ted committing suicide, but that was what it was."

Leslie Bolger remembered that on the early morning of the fourth day, he "must have been going a bit off up here, because I imagined a beautiful island in the middle of the ocean. There were palm trees and it was green, lush green. On the island were these native women. I managed to get on this island and I asked them for a drink of water and they wouldn't give me any. I got really annoyed. I must have realized this would be my last day."

Ed Starkey: "The fourth day, we left the wreckage and started swimming about, from one thing to another, trying to find a better spot. We found some barrels that seemed to be riding well. The barrels were big. They were lying on the side. You could sit out of the water. By then, most of the wreckage had drifted away. There were just a few bits about. I don't remember seeing anybody else around at all. Then Bill Laverack said, 'Oh, I'm off.' And off he swam. He'd been ranting. I shouted for him to come back. Then I was all alone."

"If you come out of this," said his mate Alf to Tug Wilson, "promise me you will take this ring to my wife." And he told Tug his address. Tug went on: "Alf was an orphan who had been thrown out by his sisters from his home when he was quite young and brought up in an institution. He was a good pal to me while we were prisoners, and we shared everything we managed to get hold of. I asked him if he would also take word to my wife in Lewisham if he should get out okay. I had no ring to give him; the Japs had taken it. Alf slipped from the raft four times and was unable to help himself back, so we hung together for another hour. Then he died with a look in his eyes I will never forget, muttering, 'My wife.' "

Jim Campbell: "I was with twenty men, British and Australians, on two rafts. The rafts were so greasy that it was impossible to hold on. Eight men slipped off during the night. At dawn on the fourth day there were no other parties in sight. Horror filled the day. Six died before nightfall after what seemed like years of suffering. Most had gone mad. We all experienced mirages which took the form of fleets of vessels sailing across the horizon and the forests of masts of other ships whose hulls were beneath the horizon. Some of us knew them for what they were but found it quite hopeless to try and convince many of the others who insisted on swimming off to be rescued."

Jack Flynn recalled that "a bloke said, 'Hey look. A dragonfly.' I thought he was having hallucinations and had gone off. Then I looked with my one good eye and saw it too. I thought maybe I'd gone off my head. I nudged the bloke next to me and asked him if he could see it. He said yes. So I said to the first bloke, 'If that's a dragonfly, land can't be too far away.' And he said, 'No. About two or three miles.' And I thought, 'Gee, I could swim that.' I said, 'Which way?' And he said, 'Straight down.' You had to laugh at that. You really did."

Tom Carr also talked about that fourth day: "There were only three of us on the raft: myself, William Harrison—a strong lad who kept his senses right till the last—and another mate named Ross. During that day, I slipped off the raft. Harrison pulled me back on and tied my lifebelt tape to the raft. Later that day, a raft drifted past us. The dirty buggers were drinking their own urine. They were putting their penises in the other's mouth and peeing. It was ridiculous. That would send them mad. I couldn't do that. That night Ross slipped off the raft and drowned. We couldn't hold him any longer. We were only semiconscious ourselves."

Harold Bunker said: "Men were drinking their own urine. Those who did, I think, hastened their deaths. Two fellows had penknives. I saw them cut their veins and drink their own blood. They didn't last long. I think I was the strongest. I kept saying, 'We're going to get out of it.' "

214

George Hinchy continued: "People were raving mad. Dangerous. Grasping at everything. There were these two chaps who had put gloves on in Singapore and fought the Pommies. They were in good nick. They said, 'We're not going to go like that.' And they took off their jackets and deliberately drowned themselves. Nobody interfered with them."

The *Perth* sailor Blood Bancroft and four other Australians, fearing the raving lunatics in their group, decided to leave the main body of survivors. The five had been close mates since the railway. They collected five rafts and paddled off eastward, determined to make the Philippines. They tried stacking the rafts atop one another to get out of the oil. That didn't work. But eventually they were able to paddle away from the main body. Later they picked up a sixth man, Ray Wheeler, who was floating alone in the ocean in a life jacket, half-delirious.

Probably the best-organized, most highly disciplined of all the survivors was this group led by Bancroft. "We were compatible. When a decision had to be made, we were all in agreement. For example, drinking salt water. I knew from reading *Mutiny on the Bounty* that you shouldn't drink salt water. It was mutually agreed upon that we'd clobber anyone in this group who did. We had enough problems without that."

Roy Hudson recalled: "We did drink our own urine. Somebody had the idea because there's a passage in the Bible, Book of Isaiah 36:12. One of the fellows had some sort of cloth. We all peed onto the cloth in turn and pushed the cloth in our mouth and chomped on it. It was dreadfully salty. I didn't like it. One's mind did play tricks. One time someone raised the alarm that there was a ship over there picking people out of the water with a cargo net over the side. I could see this ship plainly. Looked like a fishing ship. I could see people climbing up the net. We left whatever we were holding on to and swam towards it. After we'd been swimming for what seemed like an eternity, one of the fellows, a little saner than us, shouted, 'You bloody fools, there's no ship.' That was my lowest ebb then. I thought it was the end now."

Harry Weigand: "Men were begging for water, saying, 'Oh God, give me water.' I said it, too, but in prayer. Men out of their minds would shout at me, 'Give me water.' All I could say was, 'Wait a little while.' Our mouths were burnt with the oil, and my tongue was swollen. I had great

215

difficulty in talking. I must have been beginning to go delirious. I saw ships wherever I looked. I still had my senses, but I could see ships, ships and ships. I knew I was just seeing things. I had Chickie's and Bill's photo in my pocket, so I got them out. They were wet and smothered in oil. I kissed Chickie and Bill goodbye and said goodbye to all my people, thinking that I wouldn't have my senses tomorrow. I said to Pat Smith, 'You are a young man, and I hope that you make it all right. If you do, will you go see my wife for me?' He said, 'Yes, Harry, but I think you are as strong as me, and if I make it, so will you.' "

Charlie Perry still sitting alone on the roof of the ship's cabin, had a vivid memory. "The next morning I saw something in the distance. It seemed to drift. I yelled, 'Ahoy!' They answered, 'Ahoy!' I dove off the cabin and swam to them. They were all Australian blokes on this wreckage, these rafts. When I got to them, they said, 'Get your own raft.' So I hung on to the side with my hand, and as a bit of wreckage came by, I grabbed it and managed to paddle to where they were. I took my shirt off and tied myself to them as best I could. By nighttime, they started going mad. Two of them jumped off and swam away. They were dangerous. There is only one thing to do with them; you have to push them over the side. To survive, you've got to be a bit cruel at times. The Aussies, after raving for a while, they calmed down and then just let themselves go over the side. They seemed to lose all power after screaming at you—you can't really describe it —and they seemed to calm down and then let themselves slip into the water and float away."

Two men in Bill Cunneen's cluster of rafts recalled they came very close to cannibalism—or at least to drinking the blood of another. Reg Stewart was one. "This one bloke on our raft was dead. This piece of packing case came by with a nail in it. We bent the nail and stuck it in his neck to try to get some blood, but he was dead and nothing came out at all." The other man, Don McArdle: "The thirst was awful. It's a dreadful feeling to die of thirst. Some tried to drink urine, but there wasn't much there. One of the boys on our raft, an Australian, was pretty far gone. In fact, he was dead, as far as I was concerned. We tried to cut a hole in his neck to drink some blood out of his neck. We scratched a hole in his neck with a piece of bamboo, but there was no blood."

Harry Jones was on another raft. He described the scene: "Some of our party, unable to bear the thirst any longer, drank sea water and their own urine. In a few hours they lost all resemblance of sane men. One of them wanted to hold a sick parade and demanded that we all swim past him in turn for examination. To this, our only answer could be to hold on as hard as we could to the ropes. When he became violent, which resulted in his slipping off the raft, we were forced for our own salvation to let him drift away. Even if we had wanted to help him, we were now far too weak. Two others whose eyes had now become pockets of pus through the action of the oil could not bear the pain any longer. With shouts of 'Goodbye and good luck,' they sank beneath the waves."

On the morning of the third day, there had been only four out of twenty-four men left on Ernest Fieldhouse's raft. He was in "a state bordering on delirium." The oil had blinded him. Yet the blinder he became, the more clearly he saw things: "Palm trees. Double-decker buses. Traffic lights. A fluorescent light that kept flashing on and off, spelling out a sign that he recognized: 'Fish and Chips, Fish and Chips.'" In one hallucination, he could actually smell the shop.

At dawn on September 15, Fieldhouse was aware of nothing except that his fingers were still curled round the rope of the raft and that he was safe for the moment. He shouted to the men on the raft, but there was no answer. The raft must be empty. He was alone. He reached up to grab the surface of the raft, but he could feel nothing. Nothing. He grabbed with both hands at the rope, but he could not feel or sense it. Slowly the truth dawned on him that there was no rope, and no raft either. The fingers that he had thought were locked round the rope were still clenched, but they were gripping nothing. In his delirium the night before, he had lost contact with the raft and drifted away from it. Alone, with no life jacket, Fieldhouse treaded water. His body was "surprisingly buoyant." Sometime later, he brushed against something in the water. It was a body supported by a life jacket. He removed the jacket and struggled into it, and "for the first time in many hours," he relaxed. He felt "ridiculously" safe.

Harry Pickett was another who tried drinking his own urine at one time, "but it was horrible. Mac McCracken drank salt water and died about the end of the third day.

217

After Mac went, I found three wooden steps that must have been blown off a ship. I remember thinking I wanted to go down in the hold and have a sleep. As soon as I'd get my face in the cold water, I'd come to and grab my plank again. I got these three wooden steps—they weren't very wide—and I got between the steps with a stringer under each arm. I remember talking to the water. I thought the waves going by were chaps with gas capes on going to the cookhouse. I tried to talk to them but got no reply, of course. I remember hitting the water with the back of my hand and saying, 'Well, if you don't want to talk, don't bloody talk.' "

(2)

Pampanito and *Sealion* surface-patrolled eastward on the scouting line, twenty miles apart. The *Pampanito* watch was tense. It was an absolutely clear day. The sea was almost flat calm. The visibility was thirty miles. The Japanese knew that submarines were in the vicinity. They would almost certainly have patrol planes in the air. *Pampanito* was a sitting duck.

Fleet submarines were equipped with a second radar set to detect aircraft, the SD. It was nondirectional and not very reliable. Many skippers, believing that the Japanese had developed gear to "home" on the SD, used it only sparingly. That day—September 15—*Pampanito* began by using the SD. It produced two nerve-jarring contacts, one at 0952, range thirteen miles; one at 1130, range twenty miles. *Pampanito* did not dive. However, at 1330 a bridge lookout spotted a plane close in—about four to six miles. It had not been reported on the SD. The officer of the deck dived at once. Fortunately, *Pampanito* had not been detected. Fifty minutes later, at 1420, she surfaced and resumed her eastward patrolling. At 1454, Pete Summers, "believing planes are using a radar detector to pick us up," ordered the SD secured.

About an hour later, at 1550, the four-to-eight watch began to relieve the twelve-to-four watch. Herman J. Bixler, twenty-one, a signalman third class, took his station on the bridge. Bixler came from a small rural community in Indiana—Geneva. He had earned his rating in quartermaster-signalman school at the University of Illinois. After further schooling, he had joined *Pampanito* at Midway, following her second patrol. This was his first war patrol. He had been on the bridge the night *Pampanito* attacked the convoy and had been "scared to death."

By now, Herm Bixler did not have to be told what to do. *Pampanito* was on the surface in very dangerous waters. There had already been three aircraft contacts. The SD had been secured. He focused his binoculars on his sector of the horizon. He started, looked again. He saw (as Summers officially logged it) "a lifeboat and a large quantity of debris floating on the surface of a calm sea." The officer of the deck, McMillan H. Johnson, notified the captain and began to close the lifeboat. Summers came to the bridge. He noted the position as latitude 18° 42′ north, longitude 114° 00′ east. He logged that this spot was "a little to the north" of the place *Growler* and *Sealion* had first attacked the convoy. I was about forty miles northwest of the position where *Sealion* had sunk *Rakuyo Maru*.

Summers approached the lifeboat warily. There was a belief in the U.S. submarine force that the Japanese often used lifeboats and debris as lures for American submarines. When the submarine stopped to inspect the lure, a Japanese submarine would torpedo it. There was no proof of this, no officially reported lure attack. However, all submariners viewed lifeboats and debris with skepticism and respect.

The inspection was carried out without stopping. *Pampanito* passed close at fast speed. The lifeboat was "abandoned," Summers logged. He noted no markings. It might have been one of the four lifeboats abandoned by the Vic Duncan group. Or it could have been one from the *Nankai Maru*, sunk by *Sealion* along with *Rakuyo Maru*. Or from the unidentified tanker sunk at the same time.

A few minutes later, at 1610, Quartermaster John Greene reported an even more startling discovery on the horizon: "Two rafts with men on them!" All hands on the bridge swung binoculars to the bearing. The men were waving "frantically."

Pete Summers logically assumed the men on the rafts to be Japanese, survivors of *Growler*'s and *Sealion*'s torpedoed ships. If he took one of them prisoner, he might gain some valuable intelligence on the ships that had been sunk. The rest could be disposed of by the boarding party, a special commando type of team trained to board smaller vessels for intelligence purposes or to sink them by lighting fires. Disposing of Japanese ship survivors was not officially condoned. Nor was it officially disapproved. There was simply no official policy. It was left up to the skipper.

Summers headed for the rafts and called away the boarding party. The torpedo and gunnery officer, Ted Swain, was its leader. The artist-gunner, Tony Hauptman, was the chief enlisted man. The big torpedoman Jim Behney was his main assistant. Swain, Hauptman, Behney and a half-dozen other members of the group rushed topside. Among them was another amateur artist, motor machinist Clarence G. "Mike" Carmody, twenty. They went out on the forward deck. Hauptman carried a 12-gauge double-barrel shotgun. He gave Behney a .45-caliber Thompson submachine gun.

There was no doubt that the boarding party was preparing to kill the men on the rafts. A reserve officer, John W. Red, Jr.: "We all thought they were Japs. Pete Summers passed the word to break out the small arms—we'll have some target practice." Dick Sherlock: "Pete passed the word below to break open the gun locker. Anyone who wanted to shoot a Jap, get a tommy gun. A whole lot of guys came up with guns, all set to have a ball." Tony Hauptman: "We thought they were Japs. We were not going to pick them up. The captain told me to do away with them. I was going to shoot them."

Again *Pampanito* closed the debris warily. It could be a Japanese trick, a human lure. Hauptman and Behney held the guns ready. As *Pampanito* swept by the debris for an inspection, they noted that the scantily clad men on the rafts were black. Some wore Japanese hats and caps.

The fire controlman, Bill Yagemann, had been on the bridge adjusting the aft TBT when the rafts were sighted. Now his attention was focused on the drama unfolding. As *Pampanito* turned and reapproached the debris he saw that there were about fifteen men on or clinging to the rafts, makeshift structures of hatch boards and timbers. He did not doubt they were Japs. Now he could hear a jumble of unintelligible shouts. Then suddenly—and startlingly—one clear, obviously Western, voice: "First you bloody Yanks sink us. Now you're bloody well going to shoot us."

Down on the forward deck, Tony Hauptman was stunned. "Who are you?" he called.

"Prisoners of war," came the reply. "Australians. British. Prisoners of war. Pick us up, *please.*"

Summers, Swain, Hauptman, Yagemann and others topside stared in disbelief and amazement, and with suspicion. Hauptman tossed a rope to one of the rafts, held up one finger and said, "One man. One man only." One man grabbed the rope, and they pulled him toward the boat. Other survivors jumped from the raft and started swimming toward the submarine. Hauptman shouted menacingly: "Stay on the raft!" Behney raised the submachine gun.

Frank Farmer, the Australian schoolteacher, had joined a large raft supporting many men. One was Harold D. "Curly" Martin, who had been in his outfit but with whom Farmer had had little contact on the railway or on *Rakuyo Maru.* Farmer: "The submarine was first sighted by a raftmate who earlier had been delirious. His claim to seeing two masts on the horizon at first went unheeded by his companions. However, he proved to be right. The submarine had two periscopes which at a distance did appear to be the masts of a small fishing vessel. I stood on the raft and waved my hat. The size of our group and height above the water caught the attention of the watch. As the submarine swept past, those on the deck appeared puzzled somewhat both by our appearance and actions. But the factor which undoubtedly brought her back was a report to the captain that Curly Martin had fair and curly hair, suggesting we were in fact European.

"It is difficult to describe our feelings as we saw that the sub was returning. But as it approached, they signaled for one man only to take the curling rope thrown from the foredeck. I grasped the rope and was hauled across the intervening water to the sub's side, up which I was assisted by two crewmen. When I thanked them in English, they were incredulous. I heard one call out to the bridge, 'They're English, sir.' I was escorted to the foot of the conning tower, where I met the submarine's second in command, Lieutenant Commander Davis. He was both distressed and dismayed that over two thousand Allied POWs were in the sunken convoy."

Frank Farmer thus became the first survivor of *Rakuyo Maru*—and of the Railway of Death—to return to Allied control.

Pete Summers' next order was decisive: "Take them aboard!"

The officers and men on *Pampanito* had never drilled for a contingency like this, or even dreamed of it. They responded to the challenge magnificently. When the incredible word spread through the boat, dozens rushed on deck and volunteered to help. Under Ted Swain's direction, they formed teams. Some swam out to the rafts with lines. Others crawled down on the bulging saddle tanks to pull the survivors aboard. Another team stripped the survivors of clothing and gave them a quick rubdown with diesel oil in an attempt to wash off the encrusted oil. Still others lowered the men down through the after battery compartment hatch into the small crew's mess, where Motor Machinist C. Boyd Markham and others gave the men another washing-down. Markham: "We started out using alcohol, but they screamed in pain. So we put that away."

The swimmers, of course, had the most dangerous job. They left the ship to enter what were known to be shark-infested waters. And if an aircraft forced the boat to crash-dive, they would have been left behind. The chief swimmers were Torpedoman Second Class Robert Bennett, twenty-four; Fireman Andrew L Currier; Seaman Gordon L. Hopper; Jim Behney; Bill Yagemann and Tony Hauptman. They were assisted on the saddle tanks by Mike Carmody, Edmund Stockslader, Electrician's Mate Third Class Donald I. Ferguson, Seaman Jack J. Evans, Motor Machinist Mate First Class John G. Madaras, Fireman Richard E. Elliott and others.

At first, some of those below failed to get the correct word. One of these was the ship's ebullient yeoman, Charles A. "Red" McGuire, Jr., twenty-four. The word he got was "stand by to take on prisoners." He thought this meant Japanese prisoners. When the first survivor was lowered into the crew's mess, McGuire was there waiting. McGuire: "I grabbed his head and smashed it into the ladder with all my strength. This guy says, 'Blimey!' I said, 'Who the hell are you?' He said, 'British prisoner of war of the Japanese.' I nearly died."

Topside, the men worked quickly and efficiently as *Pampanito* moved from raft to raft. All were shocked at the sight of these oil-encrusted, emaciated and foul-smelling survivors. For most of the crew—who lived and fought in an isolated, clean, bloodless environment—it was the first contact with the grim realities of war. Some were so revolted they could not carry on. Frank Fives: "I started to get involved, but my stomach couldn't take it. It was terrible. It was the first time most of us had seen the bloody side of war. I don't want to see that. That's why I chose submarines. I went back up to the bridge and took over as officer of the deck."

The survivors continued to be stunned, disbelieving, or overwhelmed with gratitude. Harry Pickett recalled: "I'd been on my own quite a while. It was darkish. I could feel the regular pulse of a motor through the water. Then I saw a sort of shape. Someone with a good old American accent shouted, 'Can you catch a rope, buddy?' My spirits went straight up. So I got the rope and they pulled me in. The exhaust of the sub blew spray in my face. The man pulling the rope was Jim Behney, from Florida, a big torpedoman, whose name I will never forget. He carried me below."

(3)

Summers' log starkly recorded the progress of the rescue:

1634—Took fifteen men off the raft. The survivors came tumbling aboard and then collapsed with strength almost gone. A pitiful sight none of us will ever forget.

1712—Picked up a second raft with about nine men aboard. This group was in a little better shape. They were cleaner and could give a little more intelligent story.

1721—Picked up another six men.

1730—Picked up another six men.

1753—Picked up about eleven men.

All hands on *Pampanito* began to feel a sense of history. Nothing like this had ever happened in the submarine force. It was unique. Electrician's Mate First Class Paul Pappas, Jr., twenty-three, rushed below to get his camera, a Rolleicord, to record the moment for posterity. Private cameras were strictly prohibited on American submarines, but Summers was happy Pappas had broken the rule. He not only encouraged Pappas to shoot all the film he had (three rolls), he gave him the ship's official 16 mm movie camera. Mike Carmody also broke out an unauthorized camera.

By this time, there were probably fifty men topside on *Pampanito's* decks, including both crewmen and survivors. At 1753, what Summers feared most happened. The Signalman, Herm Bixler, cried out: "Three planes in formation astern." Summers, in turn, shouted: "Clear the deck! Clear the deck!" It was a moment of sheer panic. Survivors and crewmen alike jumped or tumbled down the open hatches in a mad evacuation. But the crisis passed immediately. The "three planes" turned out to be birds. Later, Summers logged the discovery with strained humor: "Fortunately, one of the planes was seen to flap its wings, proving the formation to be large birds gliding in perfect order." Summers canceled the dive.

There seemed no end of survivors in sight. Summers broke radio silence, requesting immediate assistance from *Sealion.* Then *Pampanito* moved on to the next raft, while high periscope plotted the bearings on more distant ones. They saw many grisly sights in the water. Summers logged: "While heading for the next group, a small raft was passed close aboard. Its single occupant dead, with part of the head gone. Probably by a shark." This sight did not build confidence among the swimmers.

At 1840 a second panic swept the topside. High periscope reported what was believed to be the mast of a patrol boat. Again, Summers ordered the decks cleared and prepared to dive. The next report from high periscope was worse. The patrol boat turned out to be a submarine. It appeared to have a gun on the aft deck. That would not be *Sealion.* Some of the POWs had incorrectly cautioned that there was a German U-boat in the vicinity. The submarine *could* be German—or Japanese. Summers keyed the SJ radar—a method of communicating between American submarines and exchanging recognition signals or call signs—but got no response. At 1905, now "very suspicious," Summers dived and ordered his men to get *Pampanito* back in fighting trim.

Warily—very warily—Summers closed the submarine submerged and called the tracking party to stations. It was then noted that the other submarine "was practically dead in the water." That seemed odd. After a most careful periscope inspection at closer range, Summers decided it was *Sealion* after all. She was probably stopping to pick up survivors. The "gun" on the after deck proved to be a knot of rescuers. At 1940, Summers surfaced to resume the rescue mission. The light was fading rapidly.

Pampanito searched until it was dark. A lookout again startled the bridge with a report of a "light" on the horizon. On close inspection, John Red thought it not a light but someone waving a white flag or hat. Another raft. Summers closed the "hat" to find a single man on a raft. The hat turned out to have been his hand, bleached white from the immersion. He was brought aboard at 1957. Eight minutes later another raft was located in the pitch darkness. Twelve more men were brought aboard.

For the next ten minutes, Summers cruised back and forth over the area. No other rafts could be found. At 2015—after four hours of rescue operation—Summers ordered the search terminated. When an exact count could be obtained, it was learned that *Pampanito* had recovered seventy-three survivors, forty-seven Australians and twenty-six British. Among these were the Australians Alf Winter and Wally Winter. Alf Winter grinned wryly as he recalled: "I always thought it remarkable that *Pampanito* picked up two Winters and the captain's name was Summers."

Summers set a course for Saipan—the nearest Allied territory—at four-engine speed. He again broke radio silence and made his first transmission to Pearl Harbor. He reported his attack on the convoy, the sinking of the three ships and damage to one and the discovery of the POWs. He suggested that *Sealion* might not be able to accommodate all those remaining and that Pearl Harbor consider sending other submarines to the area.

Pampanito, like other United States fleet submarines, had only a single man trained in medical care. He was Maurice L. Demers, twenty-six, a pharmacist mate first class. Born in Manchester, New Hampshire, where he graduated from high school, Demers had worked as a bell captain on a Miami-based cruise ship before his military service. In 1940 he enlisted in the Army and became a dental assistant. Realizing he had made a "horrible mistake," Demers wrote to President Franklin D. Roosevelt, requesting a transfer to the Navy. When the immense paperwork this request generated was returned to his commanding officer—it was all a surprise to him—he angrily threw Demers out of the Army. Thirty days later, on Navy Day, October 27, 1941, Demers enlisted in the U.S. Navy.

After boot camp, Demers, on the basis of his brief Army dental apprenticeship, was assigned to a two-month Hospital Corpsman School. Then came very hazardous sea duty: medic on an old cargo ship, *U.S.S. Yukon,* engaged in Murmansk convoy duty. Demers: "We'd start out in Nova Scotia with a convoy of thirty or forty ships. Around Norway, the U-boats would attack. Bang. Bang. Bang. There went all the ships. We were picking up kids who'd been in the water only thirty minutes or so, and they had frozen arms and legs. So I said to myself, 'What am I doing here? Better to be in submarines.' Eventually, his request for a transfer was granted. After submarine school in New London, Connecticut, and a special eight-week cram course in medicine for submarine pharmacist mates, he was posted to the relief crew in the tender *Proteus* at Midway Island. By then he was married and his wife Rita was pregnant. In August 1944, Demers was assigned to *Pampanito,* following her second patrol. This was his first war patrol. He stood regular four-on eight-off watches as a radar operator. His battle station was sonar operator.

Because of space restrictions, Demers had very little medical equipment and only a small store of drugs. They were all contained, along with his medical books, in two small lockers in the after battery crew's sleeping area. In there he had gauze, tape, splints, water bags, intravenous feeding gear and the usual military medicines: morphine, plasma, adrenalin, sulfa powders and ointments, atabrine, quinine, tincture of benzoin, gentian violet, methiolate, sedatives (phenobarbital, sodium amytal), glucose, mineral oils, bismuth, belladonna, boric acid, vitamins, and so on. He also had a small quantity of amphetamines, supplied for submarine skippers to take during prolonged actions when extreme alertness was required.

Now, once again, Maurice Demers found himself treating men fished from the sea. Men who for two and a half years had survived on starvation rations in disease-infested jungles and prison camps. Seventy-three patients who might well have any number of exotic diseases difficult for a specialist to diagnose, let alone a pharmacist first class. Probably no enlisted Navy medic had ever faced such a challenging task alone.

When the men started coming down, Demers took up

station in the crew's mess, beneath the after battery hatch. He was assisted by the yeoman Red McGuire and the chief of the boat (the senior enlisted man), Clarence H. "Smitty" Smith, thirty-five. A regular Navy man, Smith had been in submarines since 1928. He was six feet tall and weighed 280 pounds. Demers said that they had a problem getting the survivors down the hatch. "It was too narrow to carry them down, and they were slimy with oil. So what we did was to put Smitty under the hatch. He had a big belly. They dropped the guys down the hatch onto Smitty's belly. And he'd grab them. Talk about makeshift rescue! But it worked. We got them down."

The first problem Demers faced was not simple. Where to put the survivors? There was barely a single inch of surplus space on *Pampanito*. Moreover, Demers believed they should be quarantined, in case they had infectious diseases. Conferring quickly with Summers and Ted Swain, it was decided that the best place for the survivors was the after torpedo room. There were a dozen crew bunks there. The torpedo stowage skids were empty: the four aft spare torpedoes had been loaded in the tubes after the attack on the convoy. The skids could be converted to bunks. There was room on the deck for more. No crewman would have to pass through that compartment for any reason. The survivors could be completely isolated. And, in case *Pampanito* had to fight her way out of Convoy College, the forward torpedo room was left in full military trim.

After the naked survivors received a second scrubdown in the crew's mess, Demers, McGuire, Smith, Markham and others led, or carried, them aft through the crew's sleeping quarters, the two engine rooms, the maneuvering room, to the after torpedo room. Torpedoman Peder A. "Grandpa" Granum, thirty-one, took over from there, helping to lift the men into the bunks. They were so skinny, Granum decided two of them could fit in each bunk. Once they were laid out and made comfortable, Granum, assisted by many other willing hands, bathed them with torpedo propellant alcohol, known as "pink lady." Other men began to convert the 21-foot torpedo stowage skids to bunks by crosshatching the open space with strong white line. Six of the worst cases—men Demers considered it dangerous to carry all the way aft—were put in bunks in the crew's quarters.

Demers went on: "They found more, found more,

found more. They kept coming and coming and coming. They were half-dead creatures. Few of them could speak. They were just looking at you like they were ready to pass out or die any minute. They were in shock. I had to give fifteen of them morphine shots. Once they got them in the torpedo room. I was able to start working on their eyes. Their eyes were real bad. Full of oil and dirt. After I cleaned the eyes, I started on the ears and mouths. Some of them had oil in their mouths and were so weak they couldn't spit it out or swallow it. Gobs and gobs of it, lying there, like chaws of tobacco. I'd get one looking halfway decent and I'd go to the next, and keep going around."

The quarantine was forgotten. Tough, grizzled, swashbuckling submariners were transformed into tender "nurses." "You didn't have to ask anybody to help. They just did it." All men not on watch volunteered. They helped Demers clean the men, resoaked the water rags the POWs were sucking. One of the ship's cooks, Daniel E. Hayes, thirty, who had worked in a drugstore before the war, became a full-time assistant to Demers. He prepared cocoa, tea, bouillon, toast. The volunteer nurses fed those men who seemed capable of taking food—but sparingly. The eating utensils for the survivors were washed and stored separately from the crew's—just in case. And so they worked, late into the night.

(4)

Eli Reich in *Sealion* received *Pampanito*'s request for assistance at about 1715. *Sealion* was then about twenty-eight miles to the northeast of the reported location of the survivors. At once, Reich swung to a southwesterly heading and bent on four engines. Forty-two minutes later, at 1757, the bridge reported "much debris" on the water stretching to the horizon in a southwesterly direction. Reich logged the position as 18° 44' north latitude, 114° 09' east longitude. This was about ten miles to the northeast of *Pampanito*'s reported position (barring navigational errors). The lookouts began to spot "many dead bodies" in the oily water, buoyed by life jackets. The first group of "living, shouting, beckoning survivors" was sighted at 1831, one hour before sunset. Reich logged: "The rescue became a race against darkness."

By the time the first rafts were sighted, Reich had organized teams for recovering the survivors. One team of four men was designated "swimmers." They would go into the water and tie lines to the rafts or singles. A second team was designated to help the survivors from the rafts to the deck. A third would strip the survivors of clothing and get them below as rapidly as possible.

The swimming team was headed by the junior officer on *Sealion*, Daniel Brooks. The other members were Boatswain's Mate First Class Henry A. Joyce, twenty-four, a onetime Maine fisherman; Seaman Norman C. Hunter, eighteen, and Seaman William F. Devitt, Jr. They were armed with submachine guns and pistols—just in case. The chief of the boat, Boatswain James L. Utz, twenty-seven, who had been in submarines since 1935 and had served on the original *Sealion* with Reich, took charge of the teams on deck. The exec, Hank Lauerman, conned the boat. As on *Pampanito*, two men, Joseph C. "Shorty" Bates and Harold D. Case, twenty-five, recorded the rescue with movie and still cameras.

Lauerman flooded the boat down—partially submerged it—so that the deck would be closer to the water. He then ordered the winglike bow diving planes rigged out flat on the surface of the water. Brooks, Joyce, Hunter and Devitt turned their weapons over to the others and got on the bowplanes with long lengths of line. At 1840 they began hauling the first of the "oil-coated, water-soaked, half-unconscious" survivors aboard.

The men on *Sealion* reacted much as the men on *Pampanito* had. They were shocked at the condition of the survivors and at this first contact with the harsh realities of war. And something more. The realization soon spread among them that the survivors came from one of the ships *Sealion* herself had sunk. Unwittingly, they themselves had caused the immense pain and suffering. There was no guilt or self-flagellation—*Sealion* had only been doing her job. But there was an awkwardness in facing the survivors, and rage at the Japanese for, in the words of the exec, Hank Lauerman, "the heart rending and useless slaughter."

The survivors were stunned and awed. Charles Armstrong was one of them. "That evening—the light was failing—one of the boys who could see (I could not open

229

my eyes for the pain) said he could see something picking up men. What it was, he could not say. Then, after a while, we could hear the engines in the water. We could all hear it. We gave a cheer—or sort of a croak it was. It came close by and then turned away. Well, that made us mad. We raised ourselves up and shouted and screamed and prayed. Then all of a sudden, it turned again and came towards us. I could hear voices shouting orders, and splashes. And the next minute, I felt hands clutch me and lift me up as though I were straw. I was carried along a deck of some sort. Then we stopped. I dared to open my eyes and saw a long knife pointed at my stomach. I felt a shiver and all sorts of things. Whoever he was pulled my Jap-happy string, cut it with one slice. It fell to the deck. And I did, too." His dream in Singapore, three nights in a row, that he would be sunk and rescued, had come true.

The sun set at 1931. Half an hour later, it was dark. In one hour and twenty-five minutes of efficient operations, *Sealion* had recovered fifty-four men, nineteen fewer than *Pampanito*. There were twenty-three Australians (including two *Perth* men and Noel Day of the Air Force) and thirty-one British. Even though there were still "many" survivors close aboard and calling out for help, Reich ordered the rescue terminated. He logged: "Even if daylight had lingered, only a very few more could have been taken aboard. The fortunate ones whom we had saved required nursing care, medicine and hospitalization. With a heavy heart, *Sealion* turned eastward and headed . . . for Saipan at full speed. It was heartbreaking to leave so many dying men behind."

Shorty Bates understood but was rueful. "I imagine that was one of the toughest decisions of Eli's life. The water was still full of people. He said, 'That's all.' When we got underway, I was still on deck. The guys in the water were shouting, 'Over here! Over here!' We just went on and left them. It was a bad scene. For years afterwards, at night, I could hear them calling out. 'Over here! Over here!' "

The rescue operations, now terminated, were wholly impromptu and without precedent or prior experience. They were carried out quickly in very dangerous waters six hundred miles behind "enemy lines." Had there been time to think the matter through, both Reich and Summers might well have picked up far more than 127 men.

Between them, they might have rescued all that could be found over the next day or so. True, the submarines would have been intolerably—and dangerously—crowded for a time. But after a day or so, a rendezvous could have been effected with other submarines patrolling the eastern sector of Convoy College—the five boats in Ed's Eradicators and Donc's Devils—and the most fit of the survivors transferred to those boats, thus relieving the dangerous crowding in *Sealion* and *Pampanito*. However, no criticism could be leveled at the two skippers. Confronted with an unparalleled challenge, their best judgment was to quickly pick up as many men as they believed they could reasonably accommodate and care for medically, without impairing the ability of the boats to fight, if need be, and thus endangering the lives of their own men.

Sealion, however, could be faulted on one point. In the rushed and emotional departure, it apparently did not occur to anyone on the boat that some provisions could be made for the survivors left behind. *Sealion* could have provided them water, food, quinine, clothing and hats, rope, Very pistol and flares—any number of desperately needed survival items. Especially water. Although *Sealion* had only a limited fresh water supply and distilling facilities, and these would be sorely taxed with the addition of fifty-four survivors, she could have left the others ten or twenty gallons of fresh water without imperiling those on the submarine. That water might have saved many more lives.

As *Sealion* sped eastward at full speed, Reich broke radio silence to inform Pearl Harbor of the rescue—and to report that many more survivors were still in the water.

The crew devoted its energies to caring for the survivors. As on *Pampanito*, an attempt was made to quarantine them. Since reloading with torpedoes in Saipan, Reich had fired only his bow tubes. The four spare torpedoes in the after torpedo room were still in the storage skids, so that space was far more crowded than on *Pampanito*. Some of the *Sealion* survivors were taken there, but the great majority (about thirty-six) were bunked down in the crew's sleeping compartment, which was, in effect, turned into an infirmary. Every one of the fifty-four survivors had a bunk. The *Sealion* crew shared the remaining bunks on a rotational basis called "hot bunking," or slept on the deck.

The pharmacist mate on *Sealion* was Roy J. Williams, Jr., twenty-one. Born in Floyd, Virginia, Williams had enlisted in the Navy in 1940, immediately after graduation from high school. Following boot camp, he attended Hospital Corpsman School and Dental School and was stationed at the University of Wisconsin. He requested submarine duty and after submarine school and the mandatory eight-week cram course for submarine pharmacist mates, he was assigned to, and helped commission, *Sealion*. This, then, was his second war patrol. Under ordinary circumstances, he stood four-on eight-off lookout watches on the bridge. Now, of course, he was relieved of watch standing to devote all his time to the survivors.

Reich designated eight men from the many volunteers in the crew to form a "nurse detail." Relieved of all other duties, they worked full time on the survivors under supervision of "Doc" Williams. These men were, in addition to the boatswain Joyce: Electrician's Mate William D. Hill, Chief Motor Machinist Stewart F. Kinzer, Motor Machinist Edward F. Pagel, Electrician's Mate Edward H. Schnoering, Motor Machinist Jack R. Smith, Seaman George E. Thornton and one of the ship's cooks, John C. Sweat. The nurses worked eight hours on, eight off. They were billeted in the chiefs' quarters in the forward battery compartment.

Williams, too, worked full time. "The physical condition of all survivors was poor. They were very weak, exhausted, malnourished—some shockingly so—and extremely dehydrated. Four were unconscious. Five had malaria—chills and fever, a yellow tint to their eyes. Fifty percent had rough, thickened and scaly skin. In many, the folds of the skin of the scrotum was particularly thickened, swollen and ofter cracked and sore. For these, we made scrotal supports. In some cases, there was swelling of the head of the penis. One man complained of pain in his chest. He was very emaciated and had a thick and tenacious sputum. I thought maybe he had tuberculosis.

"We gave each man a little water, gradually increasing the amount each time they took a drink. Then we wiped the oil from their eyes. To each of four men who seemed to be having some pain, I gave a Syrette of morphine. Then, after all were fairly comfortable, we started removing the fuel oil from their skin, using up two cans of mineral oil, which was all I had. Then we used hydraulic oil from a five-gallon can. Next, we gave each man who could stand a shower with warm water and soap. All had sores on their bodies—shallow skin ulcers. When we removed the oil, the sores looked very angry, so we put on a dry dressing. Later we dusted the sores with sulfa powder. Then after that, we cut off their hair, gave them a little bland food, and ten grains of quinine. Most of them fell into exhausted sleep."

The four unconscious men were suffering, Williams thought, from shock, exposure and perhaps malaria. One of them possibly had severe internal injuries from the depth-charging. Williams could see no external injuries. He gave them four units of plasma and 2,000 cc of glucose and saline (five percent dextrose). But for all his hard work, none of the four seemed to be responding.

The cook Fred Messecar: "I decided that since they were all Limeys, they'd want tea. So I made a lot of tea and we took it around. This one guy said, 'Make mine coffee, black. I'm a cowboy.' He was the guy in my bunk. I watched him real closely. When they first brought him down, he'd get this real scared look on his face. His eyes would get glassy and he'd shake. Like he was scared to death. Then he'd reach up real slowly and touch the hull. And then he'd settle back with a big smile. Then, a little later, he'd go through the same process all over again."

(5)

The heartbreak on *Sealion* at having to leave so many survivors behind was as nothing compared with the heartbreak those survivors experienced when *Sealion* steamed off. There were scores of men within sight of the boat. Those who could see and function were at first deliriously happy at the prospect of rescue. Then, when it failed to materialize, they were thrown into the depths of despair. Many gave up and committed suicide. But some were astonishingly stoical.

Blood Bancroft recalled: "We heard diesel engines. Then we saw a submarine on the horizon, zigzagging. We assumed she was picking up survivors, even though we couldn't see anybody, not another soul. It seemed to be starting and stopping and going this way and that. We *theorized* she was picking up survivors. We all got up on

233

our rafts and shouted and waved. Just as darkness settled, it came within two or three hundred yards of us. I don't think they saw us. Then it went off. Our hearts sank very low as we heard the engines fading in the distance. I think that all of us sent up a silent prayer."

Ray Wheeler: "On the fourth night, we saw the submarines. They were on the skyline to us. We could see them, but apparently we were hard to distinguish where we were. We hollered ourselves hoarse. Bill Smith, the warrant officer, grabbed an oar we'd fished out of the water and waved it. Then we heard these diesel engines start up, and they disappeared over the horizon. I wasn't angry, just disappointed. I remember one of our chaps shouted that if there was a God in heaven, he hadn't heard his prayers. I prayed."

PART TEN

A Race Against the Weather

PART TEN

A Race Against the Weather

(1)

At 0400 on September 16, while *Sealion* and *Pampanito* were speeding eastward toward Balingtang Channel, gateway to the Philippine Sea and safety, Ed Swinburne, pack commander of the Eradicators, received a high-priority message from Pearl Harbor. It informed the Eradicators that *Pampanito* and *Sealion* had found Australian and British POWs in the sea, survivors of a ship torpedoed and sunk the night of September 12/13. They had rescued a large number of men, but many more had been left behind. *Barb* and *Queenfish* were asked to render all assistance as quickly as possible.

Since relinquishing their backstopping role on the Singapore convoy, *Barb* and *Queenfish* had had a harrowing four days of patrolling in Luzon Strait. In the early hours of September 14, they had tangled with what they thought was a portion of a convoy but turned out to be a hunter-killer team of two shallow-draft patrol vessels. In close-in combat (1,580 yards), Gene Fluckey had fired two salvos of three torpedoes but missed with all, leaving him frustrated, unhappy and low on torpedoes (nine). For her pains, *Barb* had received a vicious depth-charging. In even closer combat (900 yards), Elliott Loughlin in *Queenfish* had fired four torpedoes into the group, missing with all, leaving him with only four torpedoes—all aft. *Queenfish*, too, had been severely depth-charged. Altogether the Eradicators had wasted ten precious torpedoes on this entrapment. Had American submarines not been so strongly built, both *Barb* and *Queenfish* surely would have been lost in the brutal depth-charging.

At the time the POW message arrived, Pearl Harbor had put the Eradicators on the trail of yet another convoy. Swinburne and Fluckey must have had mixed feelings about this message. It was immediately clear that if they were to divert to rescue survivors, the combat phase of the patrol was, for all intents and purposes, finished. *Barb*

237

had sunk only two big ships (as Fluckey thought; actually only one confirmed in Japanese records) and foolishly wasted nine torpedoes on shallow-draft patrol vessels. Compared with her first sensational patrol, it was not an impressive bag. Perhaps reflecting his disappointment, Fluckey again took the occasion to criticize Ben Oakley and the Busters by implication in his official patrol report: "We now have over 450 miles to go to reach this point [of the survivors] and must naturally give up the search on present convoy. The latter is not regretted, but the fact that the *Barb* and *Queenfish* were within seventy miles of the convoy on the night of 12/13, and are now 450 miles away is regretted." Translation: Had the Busters kept the Eradicators informed of the convoy attacks, they would not have withdrawn to Luzon Strait and would have been on hand, not only to help sink ships but also to rescue survivors.

Fluckey and Loughlin turned west, *Barb* at flank speed, 19 knots; *Queenfish,* already west of *Barb,* at full speed, 17 knots. Both boats remained on the surface all that day. Fluckey's crew turned the empty torpedo stowage skids into bunks "and organized ship to take one hundred survivors, if they are still alive." Fortunately, there was only one aircraft contact that day. Fluckey dived to avoid it. At about noon, *Barb* and *Pampanito* passed, going in opposite directions, without exchanging call or recognition signals. At about 1600, *Queenfish* and *Sealion* passed silently. Had *Sealion* and *Pampanito* loaded survivors to—or beyond—capacity, they might well have unloaded the excess to *Barb* and *Queenfish* at this time (or after dark), saving the Eradicators the long and dangerous journey west and, undoubtedly, saving more lives.

During the late afternoon, Fluckey detected an uneasy change in the weather. The barometer fell. The seas rose to Force 4. There were odd, wispy cirrus clouds high in the sky, with a strange, yellowish tint. His seaman's instinct told him a storm was brewing, perhaps a severe one. It was fall, the typhoon season.

Fluckey's exec, Robert W. McNitt, twenty-nine, an expert small-boat handler and superb navigator, was handed the responsibility of guiding the two submarines to the survivors. It was not an easy problem. The survivors had now been adrift in uncertain winds and currents for five days and four nights. By the time the Eradicators reached the general area, it would be six days and five nights. In making his calculations, McNitt consulted not only reports from *Sealion* and *Pampanito* but also an article he had fortuitously clipped from the technical journal "United States Naval Institute Proceedings." Written by a Coast Guard officer, the article propounded a set of rules for calculating the drift of rafts and lifeboats in the open ocean under various conditions. It was full of useful information.

That night at 2110 the radar operator on *Queenfish*, Charles M. Moore, twenty-nine, a superb technician fresh out of radar school, making his first patrol, hunched over the greenish display scope and did a double take. A strong pip had appeared at the unheard-of range of 34,000 yards —17 miles. At first he thought it must be a false echo of some kind. But soon a second pip appeared at 16 miles. Then several others. These were not false echoes. It was a convoy. To be picked up at such ranges, he surmised, the ships must be very large.

Loughlin hurried to the conning tower for a look. There was now no doubt about the contact. It was a convoy of seven large ships with five or six escorts, headed northeast on the Singapore-Formosa convoy lane at a speed of 12 knots. Loughlin sent off a contact report to Swinburne and Fluckey and immediately commenced an approach, making ready his last four torpedoes in the stern tubes.

Swinburne and Fluckey must have been astonished and delighted to receive Loughlin's report. It seemed hard to believe that the codebreakers had missed the sailing of a big convoy like this, but it was real, soon confirmed by *Barb*'s own radar operator. Working the bearing sent by *Queenfish*, he picked it up at the range of 15 miles. Fluckey wrote with mounting excitement: "This is by far the best our radar has ever done. Must be something bigger than usual in the convoy." It was an incredible stroke of luck, a great opportunity to redeem *Barb*'s middling bag and wasted torpedoes.

A fine moral point now arose on *Barb*, the boats were under orders to rescue survivors. Would they be justified in stretching those orders enough to attack the convoy? They still had 135 miles—about seven hours—to go to reach the place McNitt thought the survivors would be. McNitt had worked it out so that the submarines would arrive at daylight and have the full day to search. In view of the worsening weather, it might be the *only* day's search. If they attacked the convoy, one or both boats might be pinned down for hours by the escorts, perhaps all night, delaying the arrival until late afternoon. Inevitably, more survivors would die.

Swinburne made the decision: attack. He reasoned that the primary mission of the Eradicators was to sink ships. The rescue of survivors was secondary. So the delicate point was quickly disposed of.

Loughlin closed the oncoming formation on the surface. Although it was a dark, moonless night, at 2 miles' range he could clearly see that both of the two largest ships had bulky high superstructures "resembling large transports or escort carriers." Twenty-three minutes after the initial contact, Loughlin fired his four remaining stern torpedoes at one of these targets from long range—3,200 yards. Two minutes later he saw one hit. The flash of the explosion lit up the horizon.

Had any real damage been done? Seven minutes later the crew of *Queenfish* heard a "single terrific explosion" throughout the boat. It was "dissimilar to that of a depth charge or torpedo hit." Radar reported the target had stopped. Some of the ships—probably the escorts—had reversed course and were congregating near the target. Since *Barb* also heard this explosion, it was assumed the target sank. Later, headquarters credited Loughlin with sinking a 10,000-ton transport, but again Japanese records failed to sustain the sinking.

Queenfish, now out of torpedoes, could inflict no more serious damage on the enemy. She dropped back to trail the convoy; *Barb* moved up to attack. Fluckey approached the formation on the surface. He could now make out "several large, deeply laden tankers." Making ready all nine of his remaining tropedoes, he set up on two leading tankers. As he prepared to fire, these ships suddenly turned away. He looked aft for a better target. Fluckey's heart came to his mouth. He logged: "Ye Gods, a flattop! . . . This is undoubtedly the prettiest target I've ever seen." It had no funnels or superstructure above the flight deck. It was *Unyo,* the same escort carrier the POWs had seen coming into Singapore the day they left.

Working inside the escorts for a better shot, Fluckey closed to 2,000 yards and slowed to 10 knots. He wrote: "We now have a perfect overlap of the tanker and just beyond, the flattop. . . . About 1,000 feet of target." Radar reported an aircraft and an escort turning toward *Barb.*

At 2332, Fluckey fired all six bow tubes from a range of 1,820 yards, three at the carrier, three at the tanker. He saw one torpedo aimed at the tanker broach badly and run erratic. But the other five ran normal. Fluckey went ahead at emergency speed with full right rudder to bring his stern tubes to bear on the carrier. But the escort, only 750 yards away, was charging *Barb* at high speed. "Can't make it without being rammed," Fluckey logged.

Regretfully, he dived *Barb*, waiting for the inevitable rain of depth charges. Going down fast, Fluckey heard the five normal-running torpedoes hit exactly as he had aimed them: two in the tanker, three in the carrier. The escort passed directly overhead but, strangely enough, dropped no depth charges. Then *Barb*'s crew distinctly heard two ships breaking up and sinking.

The bridge watch on *Queenfish* saw *Barb*'s torpedoes hit the tanker. A huge ball of flame shot up into the black sky. Then the entire ship burst into flames. Less than half an hour later, the flames went out and the ship sank. Headquarters credited Fluckey with a 10,000-ton tanker. In fact, Japanese records showed her to be the 11,177-ton *Azusa*.

Although no one on *Barb* or *Queenfish* saw the carrier sink, the codebreakers picked up a report detailing her loss. When Fluckey returned to base, he was also credited with sinking a 22,500-ton Otaka-class carrier. *Unyo* was the fifth Japanese carrier lost to American submarines in the war. Fluckey's single salvo would become legendary in the submarine force. No one had ever sunk two ships of that size with a mere five torpedoes.

Fluckey had only three torpedoes left, and they were poorly distributed for an attack on major ships: one forward, two aft. He reluctantly decided against another go, logging: "Would like to chase the remains of this convoy to get rid of them. However, we would probably be held down during daylight when we must rescue survivors. The seas have been rising, and if we don't reach the survivors today . . . there will be none left alive. With a plum being dangled before my eyes, it is obvious after due consideration of all aspects that our primary mission now is to search for survivors."

At 0055 on September 17, *Barb* surfaced and rejoined *Queenfish*. The convoy had moved off to the northeast, but there were still two escorts at the scene of the attack, probably picking up survivors. Swinburne sent a contact report on the convoy for the benefit of the other wolf pack in Bashi Channel, Donc's Devils.

Barb and *Queenfish* now resumed the rescue mission at full speed. With the passing of each hour, the wind and seas mounted alarmingly. Beyond doubt, a heavy storm was bearing down on the area. It was beginning to feel and smell like a typhoon. Where in their rescue operations *Pampanito* and *Sealion* had raced against darkness, *Barb* and *Queenfish* would race against the weather.

(2)

That same day—September 16—the whale factory ship *Kibibi Maru*, with 656 POW survivors of *Rakuyo Maru* and *Kachidoki Maru*, left Hainan for Japan in a small convoy. She also carried about 1,000 Japanese survivors of *Rakuyo Maru*, *Kachidoki Maru*, *Nankai Maru*, the destroyer *Shikinami* and the frigate *Hirado*. The Japanese survivors were quartered topside. The POWs were quartered below decks in the cavernous whale butchering area, which, like the second deck of an aircraft carrier, ran the whole length of the ship. The POWs were allotted about one-half of this space. They were permitted to go topside in small groups to collect rations or use the *benjos*, rigged like those on *Rakuyo Maru* and *Kachidoki Maru*.

The POWs agonized over being battened below decks again, but the quarters, at least, were more spacious. Roll Parvin described it this way: "We filed forward and then descended another ladder to the deck below, the actual factory part of the ship. About twelve feet high, this huge iron cavern, which ran the whole breadth as well as length of the vessel, terminated in massive stern doors that could be lowered to form a ramp up which a whale's carcass could be hauled. The ship had obviously not been employed as a whaler for some time—Allied naval supremacy had precluded that—but all the machinery for rendering the blubber was still in place; the great boilers squatting like vast washtubs; winches standing like tombstones in a gloomy graveyard; and away up in the narrow bows, a row of miniature railway trucks perched forlornly idle on the tiny rails that snaked like rusty ropes across the floor between the machines. Here and there steel pillars sprouted roofward to support the unbroken sweep of the ceiling—which, in fact, was the main deck above. A string of dim blue lamps glowed eerily from high up along the sides. As we struggled in, their bluish haze reflected weirdly from our blackened skins, making us look like animated corpses."

The 520 British survivors of *Kachidoki Maru* were still a wretched and dispirited lot. They had washed off most of the oil, but nothing could be done for the many ill and injured. The Japanese supplied ample food (rice), by their POW standards, and a limited amount of drinking water, but no medical supplies of any kind. Most of the survivors had lost all their clothing and their personal possessions.

Johnny Sherwood had this memory: "We put our sick in one corner. The rest of us were just lying about all over the floor with not many clothes of any sort. A few men still had a shirt or an old pair of shorts. At this moment, I must admit, we were all rather down in the dumps. The men were again suffering from scabies and dysentery. I used to say to myself, 'God, I wonder just how much more we can take.' But take more we did. Those crafty guards knew we were suffering from various complaints. For fear of catching something, they kept away from us. When there was some rice and stew for us, or dried fish, they always shouted down in broken English, 'Two men *mishi!*,' Japanese for food. Two men only were allowed on deck to fetch our meager rations. Water was again our problem, as it was very hot in the hold and consequently our bodies needed more water. However, that was impossible to get. So we had to go without. After all, we thought, maybe if we do get to Japan they will treat us a bit better."

Ernest Benford described it as follows: "It seemed to me that all the threads with the past were snapping. There was no future. In fact, no intelligent person allowed himself to contemplate a future. I remember feeling very lonely and helpless and terribly frightened. My philosophy had been to ignore everything unpleasant that went on around me, the deaths of friends, of my father, the ugly diseases and the bestiality of our captors. I repeated to myself over and over, 'It doesn't matter, nothing matters anymore.' The sick and injured were placed near the gangway, the daylight filtering down the hatchway being the only light available to us. We sat or lay on the steel

243

deck with no covering and nothing to lie on. We were left alone to fend for ourselves, but there was nothing with which we could improve our quarters. The Japs supplied us with nothing—no medical supplies—no clothes and no bedding. We had the usual meals—rice and salt plums but no plates. We found a sheet of zinc, which was bent over and over into a crease and then torn into pieces. We ate off this with our fingers, and shared several mugs which survivors had been able to retain."

Wally Mole said: "My body was a mass of sores. My mouth was swollen and my lips parched. I hate to think of those poor chaps who had broken limbs as well. I know one chap who had two broken arms. There were two British doctors attending the sick, Captain [J. R.] Roulston and a Captain Taylor. The last named was only a small fellow, but that man worked himself to a standstill and gave comfort and hope to men who showed no will to live, and was an inspiration to all. We slept on straw that had been strewn on the floor, just like bleeding animals. They gave us food and water, but having no utensils, we had to put our mouths to the bucket of water to drink. We could not tell day from night in the hold because no light was let in and the lighting below was very dim."

The dysentery spread. Arthur Wright thought "half" the men got it. For many, the trip topside to the *benjo* was too difficult. John Langley told why. "In this great dark place, they tried to find their way to the toilet at night, and most of them couldn't contain themselves. It was all over the place." The stench in the hold was appalling. Many men died. Roll Parvin was one of those who became desperately ill. "Each day, now, we suffered the loss of one or two men, who died quietly and imperceptibly— to be carried on deck and rolled in mats of plaited rice-straw tied at head and foot like a man-sized Christmas cracker. . . . Death had lived with us for so long now that it no longer held any terrors. Several times before, when I had been at a very low ebb, men had quietly snuffed out all around me. But I had survived. I would this time, too. I felt sure." Rowley Richards kept doing his job. "I think eight people died on the trip. We wrapped the dead ones up and threw them over the side. We did the appropriate service. We'd been through this so many times before, we were pretty adept at conducting services."

The convoy set a course for an intermediate stop, Kee-lung, Formosa, hugging the coast of China. Once in the open sea, the POWs naturally lived in terror of another torpedo attack. The typhoon-whipped seas were building. The whaler wallowed and shook, making fearful noises. From time to time the Japanese dropped a depth charge off the stern, a measure designed to scare away submarines. The wave action, the depth charges, and other noises kept the men in a constant state of terror. Every noise was believed to be a torpedo.

Tom Parrott said: "After what we had been through, every wave which hit the side sounded just like the torpedo which hit the *Kachidoki Maru*." Tom Pounder added: "Whenever the ship lurched, these ladders and hawsers hung away from the steel plating. As the ship recovered and rolled in the opposite direction, they clanged back into position. This clanging boomed inside the hollow vessel like an explosion. At each sound everyone was jerked into nervous alertness and there was a mad rush for the hatch. I was as panicky as the rest. The first night was a hellish nightmare. It was impossible to sleep. I could only lie there and worry." Stanley Thompson remembered: "The word went round that if you had anything that rolled around and made noise, hold it, because everybody jumped out of their skin at any noise." Syd Matsen confessed: "I was so scared down in that hold that every night Pat Major and I held hands." Russ Savage: "Every time a depth charge went off, and they went off all the time, she used to ring like a bell. It would nearly send you mad."

There was apparently only one access ladder to the deck. It was guarded. All believed that in event of submarine attack, the door at the top of the ladder would be locked, denying the POWs an escape route. Vic Duncan, torpedoed twice now, took steps to circumvent that possibility. "I explored around and found another way up on deck. I told Frank McGovern and two or three other seamen the way out—if we got torpedoed again. I slept two nights on the upper deck among the Japs and they didn't even know it. The Jap survivors sat on the highest parts of the ship, all hunched over, watching for torpedoes."

The whaler did not encounter submarines on the Hainan-Keelung leg of the journey. The Busters had left. The Eradicators were now rushing to pick up survivors. Donc's Devils were busy in Bashi Channel with other convoys. There were no submarines in Formosa Strait. But she had to weather the full fury of the typhoon. The pitching and rolling caused a wave of seasickness, adding yet another appalling stench. William R. Smith was emphatic: "It was a hell of a storm, the roughest seas I've ever been on," and Rowley Richards agreed: "The trip was ghastly."

(3)

That day, *Pampanito* and *Sealion* sped eastward toward Balintang Channel on the surface. *Pampanito* now led by about four hours. Twice during the night, *Sealion* had stopped to conduct burials at sea for two of the four who had been gravely ill among her fifty-four survivors. These dead were never identified. An attempt was made to fingerprint the bodies, but the fingers were too mutilated to get a reliable print. The bodies were wrapped in mattress covers, weighted with heavy gun shells and dropped over the side while Reich read a brief, official prayer service.

On *Pampanito* all but one of the seventy-three survivors had begun to show improvement. That one was John "Jock" Campbell, a Scotsman with the Gordon Highlanders. Demers had diagnosed his case as "acute exhaustion, exposure, shock, dehydration and possible internal hemorrhage." There was a hole on the bottom of one foot which many survivors believed had been gnawed by a fish. Ever since he was pulled from the water, he had been in a "state of delirium." Demers had tried to give him an intravenous injection of dextrose and saline solution but he could not "locate a vein or even a drop of blood." Campbell, assigned to Ed Stockslader's bunk, thrashed continually, as though swimming, Dick Sherlock recalled. Clearly, he would not live long.

Demers had not yet slept, or even taken a moment to rest. He kept himself going with the amphetamine pills. He and the volunteer nurses continued to bathe and feed the survivors, and to dose them with vitamins, sedatives, quinine and sulfa powder and to treat the ulcers and water sores. The cook Danny Hayes also worked without respite, turning out soup, tea and other bland, mostly liquid, nourishment. All hands in the crew donated clothes for the naked survivors: skivvies and T-shirts, dungaree trousers and shirts. Some even gave white hats.

Those survivors on *Pampanito* who were conscious and registering were in emotional turmoil. They had difficulty believing it was true—that after the horrors they had experienced and seen for two and a half years, they were not only alive but also free men. Their wildest dreams had been realized. It seemed incredible, a miracle. Not only that. Having been brutalized for so long, they were deeply moved by the tenderness, concern and generosity of Ted Swain, Maurice Demers, Danny Hayes and the nurses.

Harry Jones, who had been so determined to escape, was almost overcome with emotion. "Almost at once a huge mug of boiling hot, thick vegetable soup was thrust into my hands, and on my first sip through my cracked and swollen lips, I was happy that my tongue, which in spite of its abnormal size, still had the power of taste, a taste of something good and wholesome, the like of which I had not partaken of for the last two and a half years. It was with difficulty that I held back tears of joy through at last being back among decent people who, though at war, could always spare a thought for, and give help to, those in distress. We fit ones from the raft sipped and looked at each other and I am certain my comrades' thoughts ran parallel with mine, namely, 'Thank God we made it and had escaped from the cruel sea and the barbarous Japanese military.' "

One of the many nurses on *Pampanito* was George W. Strother, twenty, a seaman making his first patrol. Earlier, a hatch had fallen on his big toe and almost severed it. Demers had wanted to snip it off, but Strother—in his Alabama drawl—had insisted on keeping it. Now it was healing rapidly. Assigned to "light" duty, Strother volunteered to help care for the six most seriously ill survivors —including Jock Campbell—billeted in the crew's sleeping quarters. He said: "Campbell came to once and talked to me. He had a beautiful personality. He'd been a cook on the Burma railway. He told me about his family. He had a wife and three kids. He had never seen the youngest child. I was just a kid then. I grew up pretty fast."

Other than heartfelt thanks, the survivors had little to give in return for all this care and attention. Among them, only Frank Coombes had anything of value: the diamond earring and diamond bracelet in his money belt. "To these three Yanks who looked after me so well—I'm sorry I can't remember their names—I gave the earring with the nine little diamonds." A. John Cocking of Western Australia promised Tony Hauptman a pair of kangaroo boots.

On *Sealion*, too, the pharmacist mate, Roy Williams, and the cooks, John Sweat and Fred Messecar, worked without rest, assisted by the eight rotating nurses. The survivors were no less overwhelmed.

Leslie Bolger said: "I'll never forget the Americans. Nobody runs down Americans to me. They couldn't do enough for us." Barney Barnett: "The guys on the submarine were wonderful. They did a fantastic job." Bob Collins, one of the *Perth* survivors, felt the same way. "I will never forget the compassion, generosity and selflessness of the *Sealion* crew, especially that tall red-haired character, Doc Williams, and another sailor in the after torpedo room, James E. Carr. Fine chap. He took a religious medal from around his neck and gave it to me. His mother had given it to him before he sailed. He said, 'You need this more than I do.' I still have the medal."

Approaching Balintang Channel in late afternoon, the bridge watch on *Pampanito* saw a heart-stopping sight: a four-engine Japanese patrol bomber on the port horizon, range three to four miles. The officer of the deck crash-dived, terrifying most of the survivors. *Pampanito* was now heavier by about 7,000 pounds, but the extra weight had already been compensated for, and she slipped under smoothly and quickly. No bombs fell; *Pampanito* had evidently not been sighted. Later, Summers came up for a careful periscope search and could find no sign of the plane. Forty-five minutes later, at 1700, *Pampanito* surfaced to transit the heavily guarded channel in darkness. Luckily, there was a heavy cloud cover.

While she was going through the channel, the survivor Jock Campbell died in George Strother's arms. It was a deeply moving moment on *Pampanito*, especially for Demers, who had worked so hard to save him. No one had ever died on *Pampanito* before. A burial party wrapped the body in a mattress cover and weighted it with a heavy spare engine connecting rod. The gunner Hauptman and others draped the cover with an American flag and took it topside through the after battery hatch. The photographer-electrician Paul Pappas was chosen to read a brief service "because they considered me clean-living." At 2023 the body was committed to the deep. Strother regretted one thing: "When he died, he was talking about his wife and children. I always meant to write and tell her, but I didn't." Mike Carmody, who was in the burial party, was moved to commemorate the burial ceremony with one of his paintings.

Coming up behind, *Sealion* had another death among the remaining two who had been severely ill. Again, no one could identify the man. This time, Williams was successful in obtaining fingerprints, but the man's identity was never determined by British or Australian authorities. At 2006 the body, wrapped and weighted, was carried topside. After Reich had read prayers, it was committed to the deep. The body went down slightly to the south of the spot where *Pampanito* had dived from the bomber earlier in the afternoon.

Shorty Bates remembered: "This guy had been swimming and swimming in his bunk. The pharmacist mate Williams was yelling at him. 'You've been saved! Take it easy. You've been saved.' He'd stop swimming. Then he started swimming again. Williams gave him a sedative to calm him down. He stopped. But then he started again. And then, finally, he died. Williams blamed himself, but there was nothing he could have done."

That night—while *Barb* and *Queenfish* were attacking the convoy—*Pampanito* and *Sealion* were racing through Balintang Channel on the surface. Neither boat was detected. By daylight, both were well clear of Luzon Strait and Convoy College. Saipan lay dead ahead across about 1,300 miles of open water only lightly and occasionally patrolled by Japanese planes. Word came from Pearl Harbor that a destroyer, the *U.S.S. Case*, would meet the boats halfway with doctors and medical supplies.

Both submarines were crowded to the gills. Designed originally to accommodate only 65 men, *Pampanito* now had 157 aboard, *Sealion* 136. It occurred to *Pampanito*'s Ted Swain that "we doubled our crew." On both boats the crewmen slept where they could find an infrequently used deck space; chiefs moved into officers' quarters; officers doubled up or slept on the wardroom table. *Sealion* had plenty of food—it had been only ten days since she had replenished in Saipan. But *Pampanito*, out from base thirty-one days and with more survivors, began to run out of food. The cook Danny Hayes: "Toward the end, the crew got hot dogs and beans, but they enjoyed it." Ed Stockslader remembered they finished up with "mustard bread." On both boats the cooks and bakers were so busy caring for the survivors that the crews got short shrift—mostly sandwiches. But there was, as always, no shortage of Navy coffee.

By this time, some of the fitter survivors had begun to talk about their war experiences. It was the first any of the submariners had ever heard of the Burma-Thailand railway. They were shocked speechless by the grim accounts of the survivors, the ghastly lives they had led in the hands of the Japanese, the atrocities and the death tolls. The *Pampanito* yeoman Red McGuire said: "This was the first time the war had truly come home to me. It really hurt." Dick Sherlock: "If there were any doubts that our cause was just, they were removed. If this is the treatment the other side give, God *had* to be on our side." *Sealion's* Harold Case: "You really knew you were in a war. The reality of it made me madder than hell at the Japs."

Realizing the value of this information to intelligence and war crimes agencies, Summers and Reich began to systematically interrogate the fitter survivors. Summers invited them to file a written report of experiences; Reich took down information on a wire recorder. Reich prepared an intelligence addendum to his patrol report. The two *Perth* men recovered by him, Bob Collins and John C. Houghton, provided the first information on the loss of the U. S. cruiser *Houston* (sunk with *Perth* in Sunda Strait over two years before) and the fate of her survivors—most consigned to the Railway of Death.

(4)

Barb and *Queenfish* reached the survivor search area at 0530 on September 17, about an hour and a half before sunrise. The sea was roiling—Force 4; wind blowing at twenty knots. Both sea and wind, Fluckey logged, were "on the increase." If the sea condition worsened, there would not be much time for searching. The only consolation was that the sky was overcast. This might discourage Japanese aircraft patrols and allow them to search on the surface unmolested.

Barb's chief of the boat, Gunner's Mate Paul G. "Swish" Saunders, twenty-six, a regular Navy man since

1935, organized the topside rescue party. Saunders had helped commission *Barb* and made all eight previous war patrols. His chief assistant was a second class motor machinist, Traville S. "Pig Eye" Houston, nineteen, who had made four Atlantic patrols on *Herring* and four previous patrols on *Barb*. Houston had grown up in Florida, where he became a strong swimmer and one of the earliest amateur skin divers. He was the unofficial ship's diver. On the previous patrol, when *Barb* had fouled her screws in a Japanese fishing net, Houston had braved chilly sub-Arctic waters to cut it away. Saunders and Houston were backed up by another half-dozen enlisted men. They had prepared heaving lines and knotted boarding lines.

Although *Barb* was not at battle stations, she was in an alert status. Her battle stations officer of the deck, Everett P. "Tuck" Weaver, twenty-six, took the conn. The bridge was crowded. Fluckey and McNitt were on hand, as well as eight or nine other men, keeping watch for Japanese planes, survivors and sharks. Some were armed, in case there were Japanese survivors among the British and Australians. Weaver, one of the few submarine officers never to attend submarine school, had come to *Barb* from five rugged and dangerous patrols on the old *S-30* in the Aleutians. Mindful of one near disaster on *S-30*, Weaver kept his lookouts on their toes.

On *Queenfish* the topside rescue party was organized by the first lieutenant and gunnery officer, John E. "Jack" Bennett, twenty-six, Naval Academy class of 1941. Bennett, making his first war patrol, had earlier seen much combat on the cruiser *San Francisco,* earning a Navy Cross medal for extraordinary heroism. His principal assistants were Ensign Edwin A. Desmond, Jr.; Quartermaster First Class Otto B. "Cowboy" Hendricks, a character from Onley, Texas, who wore a diamond-studded gold star in one earlobe; another Texan, Coxwain Robert J. Reed, a chunky body-building fanatic; Torpedoman Third Class Laurence F. Nadeau, Jr., a lanky Down Easterner who wore his grandfather's English-made hunting knife; Seaman Thurmond R. Milliren; and another seaman, Brooklynite Robert L. Dickinson. Below decks, the assistant engineering officer, John H. Epps, a "mustang" from patrols on *Finback;* and the chief of the boat, Electrician Paul Miller, also from *Finback,* assembled an enlisted group to assist *Queenfish's* pharmacist.

The two boats commenced the search for survivors

along what Bob McNitt judged to be the "farthest west position they could possibly be, considering tide and wind." *Queenfish*, completely out of torpedoes and thus unable to defend herself against enemy vessels, remained close (5 miles) to *Barb*, which had three torpedoes. Both boats maintained a continuous SJ and SD radar and high periscope watches. The bridge lookouts kept a sharp watch for enemy aircraft.

Four hours passed with no sign of wreckage or survivors. McNitt fretted, checking and rechecking his calculations. He need not have. At 0950 a report from *Barb*'s bridge proved he was right on the button: they had sighted wreckage and debris extending to the horizon. *Barb* and *Queenfish* changed course to go "down wreckage," all hands topside keenly sweeping binoculars on the oily mess for signs of life. About two hours later, at 1141, *Barb*'s lookouts spotted "several" floating bloated bodies sustained by life jackets. On inspection the bodies proved to be Japanese. McNitt: "The stench was unbearable. We wrapped cloth around our noses."

On they went, probing the repugnant debris. At 1227 they sighted "several" more "floaters," as Fluckey termed them. Some were Japanese, some were British and Australian. The bridge watch was discouraged. Could there possibly be anyone left alive after five nights and five and a half days in the water? The consensus was probably not, until at 1255, high periscope galvanized the bridge with a report that two rafts with live survivors had been spotted, one with three men, one with two.

Fluckey ordered full speed, turned to the bearing and broke radio silence to notify *Queenfish*. In a few moments the *Barb* bridge had the five survivors in view. Fluckey logged: "The at first dubious, then amazed, and finally hysterical thankful look on their faces, from the time they first sighted us approaching them, is one we shall never forget." *Barb* came alongside the raft with three men. McNitt recalled: "They were numb, almost insensitive. Just barely alive." After it proved impossible for the survivors to get aboard under their own steam, Bob McNitt put a line around his waist and dove over the side to help them. At 1303, *Barb* brought aboard her first three survivors.

Barb nosed from raft to raft, pitching in the heavy seas, sorting the dead from the live. When McNitt tired, the third officer, James G. Lanier, twenty-four, replaced him in the water. The enlisted men, Swish Saunders and Traville Houston, were constantly in and out of the water —and badly cut on *Barb's* barnacles and protrusions. The men were shocked at the sight of these survivors. McNitt: "They were in terrible shape. Haggard. Covered with oil. Sores all over them. Six days of baking in the sun. Dehydrated. No water. No food. Pitiful condition."

Queenfish found her first survivors at 1316. The first attempt at pickup was a tragedy. The radar technician Charles Moore, manning the high periscope, said: "The captain originally gave orders that we were not to stop. We were way, way out there and a sitting duck with no torpedoes. The idea was that Coxwain Reed, who was into physical fitness and quite stout, would reach over and strong-arm them aboard. It didn't work out too well. They reached for one fellow, missed, and he fell off his little raft or whatever he was on and sank. They couldn't catch him. Another fellow—maybe the next one—kind of slammed against the side as they tried to pull him up and he fell. Somebody disobeyed the captain's orders and dived in to get him. But he died." Thereafter, Loughlin approached the rafts at slow speed and stopped.

Queenfish, too, found that most of the survivors were unable to come aboard unaided. The two officers, Jack Bennett and Edwin Desmond, dived in with ropes. They were soon joined by the enlisted men Cowboy Hendricks, Bob Reed. Laurence Nadeau, Thurmond Milliren and Bob Dickinson. Others topside cut away the survivors' clothing and life jackets with Nadeau's hunting knife and lowered them down the forward torpedo room hatch. Torpedoman Eugene J. Wilson, twenty-four, in charge of the compartment, received the survivors down below. "I had a heavy reddish-brown beard. One of them who was semiconscious opened his eyes, looked at me and said in a feeble voice, 'Oh. It's God.' "

There were at this stage perhaps only thirty-five or forty survivors of *Rakuyo Maru* left alive. Most were indeed insensitive, numb, nearly dead. It had rained hard the night before; otherwise all might have been dead by now. None had eaten since the afternoon of September 11, and that meal had been the usual inadequate half-ration of watery rice. They were covered with caked oil. They were blistered by the sun. Their bodies were covered with salt water sores. Their lips were cracked and puffy-raw; tongues were thick. Their minds were going.

Alf Allbury's mate Ted Jewell had died on the fifth night, and Allbury felt his loss keenly. "I was almost past knowing or feeling anything. . . . I heard him calling me, calling out my name. And it came to me as though I were hearing it in a dream. And I realized he was not on the raft beside me and that he was floating somewhere near; but I could not see him. And I shouted and shouted, and his cries came back fainter and fainter, and more piteous, more urgent, as if he knew what was happening, until only the silence and the terrible loneliness of the water surrounded him. . . . And then, as I crouched there, fear crept slowly over me; the fear that comes with complete silence, limitless solitude, and the great loneliness of the night and sea. . . ."

On the sixth day, as *Barb* and *Queenfish* searched, Allbury, all alone on his raft, saw nobody. "Towards evening, the sea became even more boisterous. At times, the raft stood up almost vertically as angry waves pushed beneath it. I lay full length along the logs, clutching with both hands, and with the waves bursting and breaking round my head." His strength was gone; he kept blacking out: "And I knew each time I woke from the dream that it could not be very long now. This was the end; I was making my spiritual farewell to everything I had longed for and thought about these last few years. But I felt nothing. No emotion. I was past feeling anything at all. Mine, I knew, was the calmness, the gradual mental and physical negation of feeling, from which I could slip only into unconsciousness and death."

Barb found Allbury, alone on his raft. A crewman tossed a rope to him. "Then in a strange dream I fingered a rope that fell suddenly across my shoulders. And in the dream I sat looking at it, wondering what it was. And then I heard shouts that came to me faintly through a mist of darkness. And it disturbed me that this was a dream I did not understand. And I put the rope over my head and felt myself being pulled backward through the waves. And there was a huge wall of steel, all shiny and wet, and I was dragged up it and splayed out on something firm and cold, something that didn't heave and dip. And I could see a strange blur of faces—white faces with beards. And I could hear voices that were not Japanese. And I realized, disinterestedly, that I wasn't, after all, going to die. A hand nudged under my neck and something trickled down my throat and exploded into fire in my chest. And a voice, a deep, drawling voice, said softly, 'Relax, fella. Everything's gonna be all right.' And I whispered, 'Yanks,' and fell headlong into a wonderful unconsciousness."

Barb also rescued Doug Hampson, Neville Thams, Jim Campbell, Jack Flynn, Leo G. Cornelius, Tom Carr and others. Like Allbury, Campbell was alone. This is how he recalled his rescue: "On the sixth day, a typhoon started up. Water continually broke over me. I just managed to hold on. It was excruciating torture. My body was racked with an overwhelming numbness. The sun made my craving for water a searing agony. That afternoon I acknowledged the inevitable and resigned myself to death, which I felt was very near. I said goodbye to all my loved ones at home, my mother and father, brothers Tom and Leslie and my sisters Veronica and Gladys. In thinking of my sweetheart, Jean, I drained a bitter draught to the very dregs. Through all the suffering, her memory had kept me going. Now it was all but over. We had waited a long time to marry, and now I had to say goodbye. My stinging eyes were stung again as tears came suddenly.

"Towards evening, just when my resignation was about to collapse, I heard Jean's voice: 'Hang on, Jim. Hang on.' It came clearly across the water. I struggled to keep my mummified hands on the boards. Then a vision materialized one hundred yards away. All my partly blinded eyes could see was a vessel of some sort. I tried desperately to make myself seen or heard. I must have been sighted. I was far too weak to call out. The submarine came closer and closer till it ranged right alongside me. I remember no more."

Doug Hampson and Leo Cornelius had begun the ordeal on a raft with twelve other men. They were the last two men *Barb* rescued, and Hampson told about it: "On the sixth day, there was just Leo and me left. Then Leo said he was going to get a taxi and go home. At first I thought he was just kidding. Then I realized he was starting to see things. I said, 'There's no bloody taxis here, mate.' So I hit him just under the ear. Hard.

"In the afternoon, you could see this storm coming. There were black clouds, and the sea was starting to build and the wind was really blowing. We were sitting in water up to our waists. Leo was quite rational again then. He said, 'It's been nice knowing you.' I said, 'It's starting to look that way.' So we shook hands and said goodbye. Then Leo said he saw a boat. I said, 'Yeah, just like the taxi you saw this morning.' I stood up on the raft, and I couldn't see a thing. I told him not to worry about it, he'd be dead shortly. He kept insisting there was a boat, so I got up to look again. Then I saw it. I waved my arms like mad. We could see it getting closer. We didn't even care if it was a Jap. If they gave us a drink of water and a cigarette, they could shoot us. Then we saw it was a sub. The *Barb*. They dropped us a rope, and I went up.''

The well-organized six-man Blood Bancroft group was still intact. When it rained on the fifth night, they had filled their hats and a Japanese soya bean bucket, collecting about two pints of water. That kept them going. *Queenfish* found the group in this way, Bancroft reported: "The day wore on and the sea rose. By midday, the waves were ten to fifteen feet high. Most of us had to lash ourselves to the rafts as the seas were continually breaking over them. Early in the afternoon, we rose on a wave crest and someone shouted, 'There's a boat of some sort out there. It might be a submarine.' Naturally we went a little mad on it, waving, singing out and doing anything to attract attention. At first the submarine headed straight for our rafts, but she turned away and went in the opposite direction, causing much disappointment. But she was only picking up a few stray survivors. About fifteen hundred hours, she at last came directly at us through the sea was tossing her about like a cork. A line was thrown to us which I made fast to my raft. All our rafts were tied together, so everybody went through to the *Queenfish* on my raft.''

Blood Bancroft's rescue made a lasting impression on the *Queenfish*'s retrieval party and particularly on Jack Bennett. "Most of these poor critters in the water were too weak to even grab the lines we threw them. We had to swim for them. Then all of a sudden, here came Arthur Bancroft. He somehow had kept in remarkable physical condition. Here I am, reaching down to get him. I'm wearing shorts, shoulder holster, life jacket. And he somehow managed to stand up on this pitching raft and saluted me in that British-Australian way with the flat palm extended toward you, saying, '*H.M.A.S. Perth.* What ship, sailor?' I said, 'United States submarine.' When he got on deck, he almost bounded around. They led him toward the gun access hatch, under the bridge. He shook his fist at Loughlin and said, 'I knew you bloody Yanks would rescue me.' "

In the Bancroft group were Ray Wheeler, Eric J. Lihou, Ernest A. "Jack" Pearson, Lindsay V. Nunan and the senior enlisted man to survive *Rakuyo Maru*, Warrant Officer William G. Smith. *Queenfish* also saved Roy Hudson and his mate Frederick Carter, Phil Beilby, Stanley Bowhay, Harry Bunker, Vic Cross, George Hinchy, Freddie Mills and others.

Between them, *Barb* and *Queenfish* recovered a total of thirty-two survivors, twenty-two Australians and ten British, two of the latter recovered by *Queenfish* being unconscious and almost dead. Fluckey and Loughlin, consulting with Ed Swinburne, decided to continue the search through that day and the next—until the weather drove them off. Perhaps reflecting on the previous night's brief moral consideration of whether to attack the convoy or go after survivors, Fluckey logged: "Having seen the piteous plight of the fourteen survivors we rescued, I can say that I would forego the pleasure of an attack on a Jap task force to rescue any one of them. There is little room for sentiment in submarine warfare, but the measure of saving one Allied life against sinking a Jap ship is one which leaves no question, once experienced."

(5)

The pharmacist mate on *Barb* was William E. Donnelly, twenty-three. Born in Julesburg, Colorado, Donnelly had joined the Navy with his brother in December 1940. After boot camp, he attended hospital corpsman school and was in a convoy on his way to Manila when the war began. The convoy was directed to Australia, where for the next year and a half Donnelly served in medical detachments in Darwin and Perth. He volunteered for submarines, returned to the States for more schooling, got married and joined *Barb* for her second Pacific patrol. This was his third war patrol. He stood watches on the SJ radar and, during battle stations, was part of the conning tower fire control party. In preparation for the survivors, Donnelly had recruited enlisted assistants and converted a portion of the crew's sleeping quarters to a sick bay.

Below decks, Bill Donnelly received his fourteen patients in the crew's mess before bunking them down in the crew's sleeping quarters. There were six men assigned to help him, including the swimmer Traville Houston. Later this was increased to twenty. Donnelly: "The men were very weak. All of them had to be helped down the ladder. Only one of the fourteen could sit up. About eight were semiconscious. The other six were in a pretty good mental state. Many of them had multiple skin abrasions on their sides, arms and legs—from the rafts. Most had 'prickly heat,' which had gone on to 'salt burns'—enormous, superficial, tender ulcers. One had a deep tropical ulcer on his leg. About eight had edema of the ankles and feet. The scrotum of one man was swollen to the size of a large grapefruit. The shaft and head of the penis were swollen. Six men had penile sores. Three had ringworm. Most had very acute conjunctivitis. All were extremely dehydrated. Tongues were swollen, very red, dry, and were sore. Their teeth were generally bad. Three had mild gingivitis. All showed evidence of pellagra and some seemed to have beriberi. Several spoke of the underwater explosions which were great enough to cause abdominal pain and to force water through their anal canal. Some said that following this, for a couple of days, they were very sick and vomited many times. Practically all had fever from ninety-nine to a hundred and three degrees."

Donnelly and his medical posse treated the patients, as they arrived, on a sort of assembly line. After settling the survivors in the bunks, they gave them three tablespoons of sweetened water and chipped ice cubes, repeating this "in small nips at short intervals." Then brandy in coffee. Meanwhile, teams went from man to man, cleaning oil from the eyes with boric acid solution. This bathing was repeated every three or four hours. In the worst cases, they applied yellow oxide of mercury. Then they removed the oil from the skin with warm water and soap and cut off the matted hair. It took about forty-five minutes per man to remove the bulk of the oil. When this was done, Donnelly treated the abrasions and ulcers with sulfa powder and dressed them with gauze. He treated the man with the swollen scrotum with ice bags and sulfadiazine orally. He gave all of them APCs and vitamin tablets.

By 0200 the following morning, they were "all squared away."

Next day, while *Barb* looked for more survivors in the pitching seas, Donnelly continued the water treatment and added very bland food: soft-boiled eggs, crisp toast, eggnog and ice cream. (Most fleet submarines had ice cream machines.) "Some of them had trouble tolerating the soft diet," Donnelly logged. "Some had indigestion. One man vomited and four had diarrhea, which was cleared up with bismuth." That day, most of the men began to have bowel movements, using one of two of the crew heads, reserved only for survivors. *Barb* was rolling heavily. Some survivors might have been seasick.

The survivors on *Barb*, like those on *Pampanito* and *Sealion*, were deeply moved by the rescue and by the thorough and tender medical care. Fluckey logged some of their early comments: "I take back all I ever said about you Yanks." "Three bloody years without a drink of brandy, please give me another." "Turn me loose and I'll run to that bunk." "Be sure to wake me up for chow." "Matey, we're in safe hands at last." "As soon as I can, I'm going to write my wife to kick the Yankee out."

The *Barb* crewmen were generous not only with their time but also with their personal possessions. They rained dungarees, shirts and trousers, skivvies, hats, toothbrushes, razors, combs and cigarettes on the naked survivors. In addition, they passed the hat and collected $300, which was divided among the survivors, about $21 per man. Fluckey was sure that "this included practically every cent aboard ship." The pack commander, Ed Swinburne, confirmed it. "I made a personal survey. The *Barb* fellows had only twenty dollars left—all in loose change. There was not one bill left."

The kindness shown the survivors would never be forgotten. The *Perth* sailor Lloyd W. "Darby" Munro: "The crew were tremendous, wonderful people." Doug Hampson: "They were a fantastic bunch of fellows—bloody wonderful." Jack Flynn: "It was wonderful the way they looked after us." Leo Cornelius: "They couldn't have been kinder or more considerate."

Later, when the survivors were ambulatory, Fluckey interviewed Jack Flynn, Leo Cornelius and others. Flynn recalled that Fluckey asked him if he had seen an aircraft carrier at Singapore. Flynn was able to give him details. Flynn remembered that "he asked me some more questions, and then he called for the steward. This big Negro stuck his head in the door, and the captain said, 'Give Flynn a beer.' And I said, 'Thank you very much, but I don't drink.' He couldn't believe it." After Cornelius was questioned, "Fluckey said, 'Cornelius, how long since you've had a beer?' I said, 'For Christ's sake, it's been a long time.' He told his steward to bring me a beer. I consumed it right there."

The pharmacist mate on *Queenfish* was Harold Dixon, a portly lad of twenty-five. Born in Highland Park, Michigan, he grew up in Windsor, Ontario, across the border from Detroit. In July 1940, age twenty-one, he joined the U.S. Navy. After boot camp and hospital corpsman school, he was based at a Navy medical facility in San Diego. When war broke out, he volunteered for submarines and, following the usual advanced schooling, was assigned to Loughlin's *S-14,* operating out of Panama. He then helped commission *Queenfish.* This was, of course, his first Pacific war patrol. Dixon chose the forward torpedo room for his sick bay. Here there were sixteen bunks and the officers' shower and head. It was ideally isolated.

One by one, the survivors were lowered down the forward torpedo room hatch to Dixon. He gave them a once-over for wounds, then his volunteer nurses escorted the men to the bunks. Dixon: "One man was in a state of collapse and was semiconscious. A second man was likewise unconscious. Two more were semiconscious and disoriented. The remaining fourteen were all in deplorable physical condition. All had a follicular type of skin rash, as if every pore on their skin had lifted. Three or four had sores on the neck, hands and feet. Two had large, deep tropical ulcers. All had from mild to severe conjunctivitis. Their throats were red. Some of their tongues were swollen. Their teeth were in deplorable condition. All were hungry and thirsty."

Dixon first treated the survivors for shock, "applying external heat and giving some of them stimulants in the form of hot coffee." He gave some of them brandy as well, but "it wasn't very well tolerated." Then, of course, sips of water. Later the nurses took the survivors into the officers' shower and, with warm water and soap, got most of the oil off. Dixon treated the conjunctivitis with "saline irrigation and mild silver protein." He gave them all vitamins and sedatives (Nembutal).

Two of Dixon's hardest-working nurses were the motor machinist Tony Alamia (who had provided *Queenfish's* elk's head mascot) and Arthur A. Grandinetti, nineteen, a gunner's mate from Brooklyn, who was assigned full time to Dixon. Grandinetti: "The men were a pathetic sight. It made me angry, disgusted and sick the way the Japs had treated them." Grandinetti (as well as Dixon) worked with the men forty-eight hours without rest. When he finally got to someone's bunk in the crew's quarters, he slept thirty-six hours.

Dixon concentrated most of his early efforts on the four "critical" cases. The two worst cases were the Britishers Cyril Grice of Doncaster and Harry Winters of London. (He was the third Winter or Winters to be recovered by the submarines.) Neither was conscious. Both had temperatures of about 105 degrees and extremely high pulse rates (about 140). Dixon gave them morphine, plasma and glucose in saline. At 0232, September 18, Cyril Grice died without ever having regained consciousness.

The death came as a shock to the *Queenfish* crew. Joseph P. North, twenty-one, a motor machinist and one of the many nurses assisting Dixon, had given one of the survivors a pair of calfskin boots that he'd won in a poker game. Before the war, he had had experience sewing industrial canvas. He volunteered to help the gunner's mate Anthony L. Zangrilli make the burial bag for Grice. North: "I hadn't ever been that close to death. I felt so sorry I didn't know what to do." Grice's body was carried topside in the canvas (weighted with a five-inch gun shell) and committed to the deep with appropriate military ceremony at 1200, September 18 in huge, typhoon-lashed seas. Jack Bennett read the biblical passage.

That evening, in even worse weather, Dixon worked over Harry Winters. "For a time he appeared to improve," Dixon logged. "He vomited twice—something that looked like seaweed." *Queenfish* was rolling "thirty-five to forty degrees." It was difficult to keep a steady flow of intravenous fluids under such conditions. In spite of all that Dixon could do (including a last-minute shot of epinephrine hydrochloride), Harry Winters died at 2325, September 18. The following day, when the seas had

261

abated somewhat, his body was committed to the deep with appropriate ceremony.

Some of the survivors recovered quickly. One was the *Perth* sailor Blood Bancroft. Jack Bennett said: "He was in good enough shape that I was able to interrogate him within hours. He provided us with an eyewitness account of the sinking of the *Houston*, sunk with the *Perth*. We fired off a radio message to Pearl Harbor. This was the first authentic word our Navy [headquarters], and the free world, had on the death of a brave and gallant ship."

The kindness shown these survivors would also never be forgotten. Warrant Officer Smith: "Wonderful. The pharmacist mate worked day and night. And the officers and crew mothered us." George Hinchy: "You couldn't speak too highly of them." Phil Beilby: "We were absolutely overwhelmed by kindness on the submarine." Harry Bunker: "They were marvelous to us."

Blood Bancroft: "I let them know I was a sailor, too, and asked them not to get me mixed up with those army fellows. They reckoned this was great and took me straight down to their quarters, gave me white socks, underpants, skivvy shirt and a dungaree shirt and cigarettes, laid me out on a bunk and said I must be hungry and what did I want to eat? I said bangers [sausages]. The last meal I had on the *Perth* before we were sunk was bangers. They said, 'Right,' and went off to get them. But Doc Dixon came along and squashed that. He said, 'Hey, none of that stuff. We just saved him and you're trying to kill him.' So I had to go back to the forward torpedo room and get the regular treatment."

All day September 18, *Barb* and *Queenfish* had combed the area looking for survivors in mountainous seas. Fluckey logged: "We are now in the tail end of a typhoon. The wind has picked up to thirty-five knots. The seas are very heavy. Believe it will be impossible for any survivors on rafts to last through this night." At 1900 that evening, after darkness closed over the waters, Ed Swinburne gave orders to break off the search and head for Saipan.

For a while, it was a difficult voyage. The heavy seas and winds continued all during the day on September 19. Loughlin estimated the peak winds at 60 knots, the sea State 6 or 7. The two boats remained on the surface, wallowing and rolling at eight knots. At about 1800 that evening, the storm moved off to the southwest; the seas began to moderate, and the boats increased speed to ten knots. The next day, as they approached Balintang Channel, they were able to ring up full speed. *Queenfish*— about five hours in front of *Barb*—had five separate SD radar aircraft contacts that day. She brazened out two of the contacts but was forced to dive for three. Fortunately, none of the aircraft dropped bombs or showed any indication of having seen *Queenfish*.

That night, both *Queenfish* and *Barb* transited Balintang Channel under cover of darkness and entered the open waters of the Philippine Sea. Shortly afterward, *Barb* received an Ultra that a Japanese meteorological vessel lay along the wolf pack's path. Fluckey still had three torpedoes left and hoped to add one more scalp (however small and insignificant) to *Barb*'s belt. He cautioned the survivors that there might be some action in the next day or so. But he couldn't find the ship. The survivors were just as glad.

(6)

The whale factory ship *Kibibi Maru* with its load of survivors weathered the typhoon without notable mishap and arrived at Keelung, Formosa, on September 20. After a day or so, she got underway for Moji, Japan. There were many single U.S. submarines patrolling between Formosa and Moji. The ship was twice forced back to Formosa by submarine alarms. It finally sailed for Japan on September 24. It was another nerve-shattering voyage for the POW survivors.

Ernest Benford: "The first night out was harrowing. There were a number of explosions, some very near, which caused a panic. Most of the survivors rushed for the gangway, trampling over the injured in their attempts to reach the deck. I believe some made it but were beaten down the ladder by guards, once again trampling over the injured. My mates tried hard to quieten everyone, and after some ten minutes we finally settled down again. This mad panic happened at least twice more, once when someone dropped a tin mug on the steel deck

—and each time this happened, the injured were trampled on. That night was one of the most nerve-racking I can remember, our nerves were so shattered. I think I spent the night sitting with my knees bent up, my arms wrapped around them and my head on my arms, trying to shut out the noise."

It was a four-day voyage to Japan. For the POWs, every second of it was agonizing. Many would recall that the convoy was repeatedly attacked by submarines and that many more ships were sunk along the way. However, U.S. Navy submarine records showed no confirmed sinkings from this convoy.

Beyond doubt, one of the escorts, perhaps too small to be included among the confirmed sinkings (limited to 500 tons or more), was sunk. Benford recalled: "I was shaken out of my stupor by a loud explosion. Immediately everyone panicked, and there was this mad rush for the deck that was impossible to control. I was terribly frightened but I think more scared of what the others would think if I showed it. We didn't really recover from this; our nerves were so bad we were almost out of control. We learned from those few who had been on deck that we were sailing close to one of the chain of islands on the southern approach to Japan when one of our destroyer escorts blew up and sank. If it was sunk by a sub, it must have been sitting on the beach on the island, because there was only two miles or so between the destroyer and the island. Once again there was mad panic on board. I believe we sailed off on our own, leaving the destroyer presumably to look for the sub or survivors."

Some of the POWs were topside when this occurred. One was Rowley Richards, who said: "One of the escorts intercepted a torpedo meant for us. It blew up about a hundred yards away. In seconds it was gone. The whaler dropped depth charges and fired guns—the noise was distressing." Wal Williams went on: "The explosion shattered all the windows on our whaling ship's bridge. I thought, 'How lucky we are!' " Arthur Wright: "I saw her hit. Just a terrific roar, a cloud of flame and smoke and in a matter of moments there was no sign she ever existed. Indeed, I had the inclination to rub my eyes, it was so quick. Our luck had held good."

The following day, September 28, the whale factory ship reachd Moji. When the Japanese survivors saw their homeland, Vic Duncan and John Wade recalled, they stood and yelled, "Banzai! Banzai!" When the POWs were debarked—the sick going off first—Duncan remembered, some of them "leaned down, touched the ground, and said, 'Bloody terra firma.'" It had been almost six months to the day since the first, all-Australian Japan Party left Tamarkan, and twenty-two days since they had left Singapore. Of the 716 Australians of the original Japan Party who had left Singapore on *Rakuyo Maru*, eighty reached Moji.

The Japanese in Moji appeared not to have been prepared for the arrival of these 650 men. As Wally Mole told the story: "We walked to the town square. Most of us were without clothing. We were ordered to sit down facing a type of municipal building, with the locals gathering around us and satisfying their curiosity. We stayed there for several hours. Then we were marched to some horse stables, still full of straw and dung. I honestly believe the local Japs could not believe their eyes to see such wretched-looking human beings. Thin, still covered with oil and some poor buggers with dysentery, discharging their excrement as they walked along, supported by those still capable of giving a helping hand. We were so degraded and humiliated that I did not know whether the locals looked at us with sympathy or disgust. I could not care less."

When darkness fell, they were freezing cold. Mole continued the tale: "To our relief, we were rounded up and taken to a large hall. When we arrived there, the Japs asked for all the sick men to go to the other side. They segregated us by putting chairs down the center of the hall. Knowing the Japs, I knew that we were not going to play musical chairs. As I expected, the sick were told they would only be given half-rations. Blankets were issued, one to each man, and we settled down for the night. The next morning, we all marched to the public bathhouse and had a nice bath in one of those big, square, communal affairs with Japanese girl attendants."

At Moji, the POWs were issued new clothing and blankets, split up into work parties, assigned new numbers and sent by train to various camps around Japan. The majority, some 300 (260 British, 30 Australians), went via Tokyo to a camp in northern Honshu, Sakata. The remaining fifty Australians went to Kawasaki, near Yokohama. Most of the rest of the British went to Fukuoka, near Nagasaki.

When they saw the new camps, the POWs were encouraged. They had enclosed barracks, two-tiered bunks, toilets and other luxuries most had not seen since Saigon or Changi. These men were now glad they had chosen or volunteered for the Japan Party and had survived. They were assigned to work long, hard hours in menial jobs in factories and lumber yards and so on.

Many strange things happened to the POWs after their arrival in Japan. One of the strangest befell Ralph Clifton at Fukuoka. One day, out of the blue, he was summoned to the commandant's office. Somehow, word had reached the commandant that in the aftermath of the *Kachidoki Maru* sinking, Clifton had saved the nurse's baby. The Japanese showed their appreciation by awarding Clifton a plastic cigarette case.

However, the good life was short-lived. In every way, it was the worst winter in Japanese history. It was bitterly cold. The submarine blockade was absolute. There was little fuel or food anywhere in the whole nation. The POWs were at the bottom of the priority list for both. They froze and were reduced to killing dogs to augment their starvation-level rice rations. Many *Rakuyo Maru* survivors died of cold and starvation. Among them were eight of the 80 Australians, including Jimmy Mullens and Maxwell Campbell. Allied bombing attacks commenced in the early months of 1945. In April, the Kawasaki camp near Yokohama was completely destroyed by incendiary bombs. The survivors moved to another camp. In July it took a direct bomb hit, killing 30 POWs. Six Australian survivors of the *Rakuyo Maru* were killed, including the *Perth* sailors Tommy Johnson and Pat Major. Of the 80 Australians who had survived *Rakuyo Maru* and reached Japan, a total of 14 died or were killed in Japanese POW camps. That death rate—18 percent—was higher than the Australian death rate on the Railway of Death. The British did not compile statistics on the approximately 570 Japan-based POWs surviving *Rakuyo Maru* and *Kachidoki Maru*. However, it is known that 13 British died in Sakata. The total in all camps might have been thirty. The 540-odd British and 66 Australians who survived were liberated by American soldiers and marines in late August 1945.

PART ELEVEN

"A Very Warm Welcome"

(1)

En route to Sapian, *Sealion* and *Pampanito* rendezvoused with the destroyer *Case* on the afternoon of September 18. The three skippers discussed the possibility of transferring the POWs to *Case,* which had superior medical facilities. But the scheme was finally rejected, Summers logged, "due to rough sea." Pride might also have been a factor. By now, the submariners had a strong proprietary interest in the survivors. They were not anxious to share the credit for having rescued them or to turn them over to strangers. One doctor and one pharmacist mate from *Case* went aboard each submarine for the rest of the trip. These men brought aboard additional medical supplies and clothing.

By this time, *Pampanito*'s pharmacist, Maurice Demers, was a walking zombie. Sustained by amphetamines, he had not slept or eaten for four days and three nights. He had lost weight; his legs had swollen up "like balloons." He welcomed the medical assistance. After they came aboard, Pete Summers called Demers to the wardroom, gave him two ounces of medicinal brandy and told him to "go take it easy." After the drink, Demers said: "I felt like I'd just come off the Brooklyn Bridge. You know, *Wheeeeee!*"

But Demers did not rest long. As it developed, neither Summers nor Ted Swain had much confidence in the new medical team, and Demers was called back to the wardroom. "Summers was blowing his stack. The POWs were not getting any medical care. The doctor hadn't looked at one patient yet. He had been taking down their names, serial numbers, outfits, home addresses. Ted Swain sent both of them back to the wardroom with instructions to stay there. Summers said to me, 'Can you go back and work on the POWs?' So I kept going. I didn't see the doctor or the corpsman again."

The *Pampanito* nurse Mike Carmody explained: "Those

269

guys hadn't the faintest idea about a submarine. That doctor told us to give them fresh milk and vegetables. We hadn't had any fresh milk or vegetables since the first week of the patrol. Everybody was hysterical—breaking up."

By now, all but six of the surviving seventy-two POWs on *Pampanito* were off the critical list. Most were up and about, well scrubbed and cleanly dressed, exploring the submarine (the quarantine had been altogether abandoned), making friends with the crew or patiently working on the written reports and "stories" Summers had requested. These literary efforts recounted their experiences in the Malaya fighting, the surrender, the ghastly aftermath at Changi and on the Railway of Death, the voyage on *Rakuyo Maru*, the survival on the wreckage and the rescue. All ended with a salute to *Pampanito*. Typical was that of the British corporal C. "Andy" Anderson: "My hat is off to the sailors of *Pampanito*, and I hope they are successful in all the work they undertake. So good luck, *Pampanito*. Keep it up. We will remember. Thank you for freedom."

Soon Demers became aware of a new—and alarming—medical problem. About two dozen of the survivors had begun to cough harshly. "A lot of cases of pneumonia set in. No one can say exactly what caused it. They were all run-down, highly vulnerable to any kind of virus. I personally believe it was the cold air-conditioning that did it. There was no way I could treat it. I didn't have the proper medicine, and the *Case* people hadn't brought any."

On *Sealion* the pharmacist mate, Roy Williams, was likewise punch-drunk from overwork. By now, all but one of his surviving fifty-one POWs were off the critical list. The exception was a Britisher, Douglass Rolph, who had been brought aboard unconscious. Williams gave him some plasma. "It seemed to perk him up. He opened his eyes. He had a POW buddy pulling for him. But a few hours later he was gone. That was the toughest one for me to take." At 2230, September 19, Rolph's body was taken topside by a burial party, which included Chief of the Boat Utz, Norman Hunter, Raymond T. Behr and others. While Reich, for the fourth time, read the official burial prayer, the enlisted men committed the body to the deep.

The outside medical assistance was not well received

on *Sealion*, either. Joe Ryan was bitter. "The doctor was an obstetrician from Chicago, a really obnoxious guy. The first thing he asks is, 'Where's my bunk?' So we gave him a bunk, cutting us down even further. Then he wants to know who the engineering officer is and how much fuel we had. When Harry [Harold H.] Hagen told him, he said we'd never make it to Saipan. Hell, we had plenty left when we reached Saipan. Finally, our pharmacist says, 'Would you like to see the patients, doctor?' And he said, 'I hold sick call at 0800.' Eli told him, 'You better go look *now*.' Everybody was pissed at this guy." Roy Williams said: "He slept most of the time."

The *Sealion* cook Fredy Messecar also worked like a slave. But he enjoyed it: "I *loved* working for those guys. Boy, did they make a cook feel fine. You couldn't do anything wrong. We built up their diets, little by little, because we were determined their last meal on board would be what we called an 'Australian breakfast'— steak and eggs and apple pie and ice cream. That was a submarine tradition. We always had that as the last breakfast before we reached port."

There was something more, too—a farewell gesture by the crew. Henry Joyce told about it. "The last night out, we had a little party for the POWs. We got some ethyl alcohol and mixed it with pineapple juice and made a punch. Then we went around, woke 'em all up and gave them a drink."

The survivors on *Pampanito* had a different kind of party, as described by Ted Swain: "On our last day out of Saipan, I figured we'd better have a field day. You have no idea how bad that after torpedo room smelled. I asked the fittest survivors to turn to. The Britishers were a little uppity, but they finally went to work. They cleaned the after torpedo room as good as a hospital. It was the cleanest it had ever been."

Sealion and *Pampanito* reached Tanapag Harbor at Saipan on the morning of September 20, five days after the rescue. All but the most seriously ill of the survivors on both boats were permitted topside to observe the mooring. Dressed in Navy dungarees, some with white hats, the survivors were barely distinguishable from the submarine crews. At 0926, *Pampanito* moored to the submarine tender *Fulton*, having been on patrol thirty-five days. At 1110, *Sealion* moored outboard of *Pampanito*, having been on patrol fourteen days since her torpedo

271

reload at Saipan. (The two legs of this patrol would count only as one.) Brass from *Fulton*—including many more doctors—flocked aboard the two submarines.

Soon small landing craft arrived to take the survivors to the beach—to the U.S. Army's 148th General Hospital, commanded by Colonel R. C. Wadsworth. The eleven worst cases (five from *Pampanito* and six from *Sealion*) were off-loaded into the boats on stretchers. Then the fitter survivors began to board the boats. Joe Ryan on *Sealion:* "You should have seen our POWs at the end. Absolutely elated by the whole experience—and, of course, at being free. I've never seen such high morale. They were begging for permission to enlist in the U.S. Navy and make submarine war patrols." Dick Sherlock: "We were all exhausted. Here's something really greatly constructive. It was the highlight of everybody's whole war experience." Pete Summers: "While the small boats for the transfer were arriving, ice cream and fresh oranges were brought aboard, giving the survivors their finest treat in over two and a half years. The five stretcher cases were moved first, then the two boats carrying the remaining sixty-seven men ashore were loaded and shoved off with cheers, thumbs-up and a mutual feeling of friendliness that will be hard to exceed anywhere." Danny Hayes, cook on *Pampanito:* "When it was all over, there were a hell of a lot of proud guys. They did a good job."

Vic Clifford told of the removal from *Sealion*. "They put us on a landing barge. It was the most beautiful sight I've ever seen in my life. To see the Stars and Stripes! I was on a stretcher and just lying there. I cried and cried and cried. And then the bloke next to me started to cry, and then the other blokes started to cry. And the bloke at the helm, he was crying. When we got on the wharf, they pulled the stretchers out and all those big Negroes were throwing cigarettes and chewing gum on the stretchers. They were saying, 'Good on you, buddy.' Even they were crying."

The *Sealion* and *Pampanito* pharmacists and nurses were now completely exhausted. Demers was practically out on his feet. "The old man told me to take a shower and then come to see him. So I took a shower and went to his cabin. He gave me another shot of medicinal brandy. Then I walked to the crew's sleeping compartment and I said, 'I'm going to bed now.' The whole place

272

shut up. The crew just kept quiet. I went to sleep. They could have had a torpedo attack and I wouldn't have known it. Thirty-six hours went by before I woke up. I'd lost thirty pounds." The nurse Henry Joyce on *Sealion:* "I'd lost twenty pounds. I and three others wound up in sick bay with complete nervous exhaustion."

The medical officers on *Fulton,* fearing the survivors might have contagious diseases, recommended that both submarines be thoroughly decontaminated under supervision of a doctor. Reich described this exhaustive process. "All mattress covers were aired and sprayed with kerosene. Thirty-five new pillows were provided. All bunk covers, sheets and pillow cases laundered or renewed. All gear, personal and otherwise, was removed from the after battery compartment and the after torpedo room. The compartments and lockers were disinfected with creosol solution, scrubbed and then fumigated with creosol insecticide. All other compartments were disinfected, scrubbed and fumigated. Mess gear used by the patients was thrown overboard and replaced."

After passing through Luzon Strait, *Barb* and *Queenfish* were again battered by a tropical storm. The wind rose to about 40 knots, the seas to State 6. Both boats were forced to reduce speed to 8 knots. The rolling and pitching went on for twenty-four grueling hours. Many of the submariners were seasick. Blood Bancroft on *Queenfish* said: "We weren't sick at all. But some of the crew were ill. My nurse, Art Grandinetti, was violently ill next to me in a bucket while I was busy eating food."

But the rest of the way was smooth sailing, and most of the survivors recovered quickly. Then, apparently those on *Barb* began to worry about the future. The pack commander, Ed Swinburne, recalled: "The night before we got into Saipan, we discovered these men were raiding the icebox. They were making sandwiches to take with them the next day. They didn't know if they'd get fed again. They weren't going to be hungry again."

Barb and *Queenfish* reached Saipan on September 25. They moored alongside *Fulton,* both having been on patrol fifty-three days. Again, brass (including doctors) descended from the tender, and stewards brought ice cream and oranges. When the landing craft arrived to take the thirty-two survivors to the Army's 148th General Hospital, there was another moving moment as reported by Charles Moore on *Queenfish*. "They had our dungarees and looked pretty good. They got on the boat, and as they pulled off, they gave us one of those British 'Hip, hip, hoorays.' You could sure tell they meant it." Elliott Loughlin: "It was with the utmost feeling of respect for their courage and fortitude that we transferred our passengers on arrival at Saipan."

In the official reports emanating from *Fulton*, the Army hospital and elsewhere up the line, there would be considerable confusion as to the total number of survivors actually rescued by the four submarines. The correct figures were: *Pampanito*, 73 (one died); *Sealion*, 54 (4 died); *Queenfish*, 18 (2 died); *Barb*, 14 (none died). In sum, the four boats had rescued 159 survivors, of whom seven died en route to Saipan. A total of 152 were delivered to the Army's 148th General Hospital, ninety-two Australians and sixty British.

Thereafter the four boats left Saipan for refit in rearward submarine bases. *Sealion* and *Pampanito* went to Pearl Harbor, where their crews enjoyed two weeks at the Royal Hawaiian Hotel rest camp. *Barb* and *Queenfish* went to Majuro Island in the Marshalls, where the crews blew off steam in more primitive surroundings. But, wherever they went, the four crews had an astonishing tale to tell.

Beyond that, the two wolf packs, Ben's Busters and Ed's Eradicators, were judged the two most successful of the war to date in terms of damage inflicted on Japanese merchant marine and navy. The Busters (with three boats) were credited with sinking fourteen ships for 97,119 tons. (Reduced by postwar records to seven ships for 37,634 tons.) The Eradicators (with two boats) were credited with ten ships for 90,800 tons. (Reduced by postwar records to six ships for 51,661 tons.) Total for both packs: wartime credit of twenty-four ships for 187,919 tons; postwar credit, thirteen ships for 89,295 tons. The thirteen ships actually sunk included four men-of-war: Fluckey's escort carrier *Unyo;* Oakley's destroyer and frigate; and Reich's minelayer.

All hands involved in this unique rescue enterprise received unstinting praise from Admiral Lockwood. All four war patrols were, of course, declared "Successful." All hands received the Submarine Combat Insignia, or a gold star in lieu of a second award. Ed Swinburne, Fluckey, Loughlin, Reich and Summers were awarded

Navy Cross medals. This enabled them to award a number of lesser decorations (Silver Stars, Bronze Stars) to their officers and men. The pharmacist mates on the four boats each received a Navy and Marine Corps Medal and a promotion. Demers was commissioned warrant officer, a rare honor in the Navy hospital corps. The swimmers received Navy and Marine Corps Medals. *Pampanito*'s Tony Hauptman received a Bronze Star. The nurses, cooks and others received Letters of Commendation (signed by Admiral Nimitz) with authorization to wear a Commendation Ribbon with their fruit salad. A few men were overlooked. For instance, Robert Bennett on *Pampanito,* a swimmer, received no decoration.

Pearl Harbor's comments on the official patrol reports were glowing. *Barb:* "This patrol is a continuation of the illustrious record of *Barb*." *Queenfish:* "The first patrol of *Queenfish* was an outstanding performance worthy of a veteran ship." *Sealion:* "Another outstanding performance typical of *Sealion*." *Pampanito:* "The Commander Submarine Force, Pacific Fleet, congratulates the commanding officer, officers and crew for this outstanding patrol. The entire submarine force is proud of each officer and man in the *Pampanito* for his kindness and unselfish devotion to the rescued nationals of our Allies in their desperate need."

(2)

Saipan island, invaded on June 15, had been declared secure, after a bloody fight, on July 9. But there were still some Japanese hiding out in the hills and caves. U.S. Marines and soldiers were systematically rooting these out. A few casualties were incurred, but the British and Australians found the 148th Army Hospital, in tents on a hillside, almost deserted. For all practical purposes, the survivors had the place to themselves. The Army doctors and nurses and the Red Cross aides were able to devote full attention to this skeletal, ragtag group of foreign Allies fished from the sea—and the horrors of Japanese captivity.

Later, the hospital's commanding officer, Colonel Wadsworth, filed an official medical report to *Fulton* on the survivors: "Average age, twenty-nine years. Average weight-loss during imprisonment, sixteen pounds. Ninety-five percent had had malaria. Sixty-seven percent had had recurrent dysentery. Ninety-five percent reported, during their imprisonment, recurrent manifestations of vitamin and nutritional deficiencies of one type or another. Sixty-one percent had had tropical ulcers. Upon hospitalization, all were found to be suffering from malnutrition, exhaustion and exposure. One hundred percent showed evidence of vitamin deficiency, varying in degree and extent. . . . All had some type of skin lesion. . . . Five men had either scarring of the cornea or acute corneal ulcers. Undoubtedly, exposure to the sun and oil contributed to their development. Ten percent of the men complained of a sticky sensation on swallowing. . . . Twenty percent had palpable livers. In ten percent the spleen was palpable. Twenty percent of men recovered by *Pampanito* and *Sealion* had an acute bronchitis. Out of twenty-nine chest X-rays, there was one fractured rib and nine cases of acute broncho-pneumonia. There was one case of pulmonary tuberculosis: Richard E. Laws (an Australian rescued by *Sealion*). There were no clinical cases of malaria. . . ."

The professional medical care rendered the survivors by the 148th Hospital was thorough. The Britisher Barney Barnett said: "We had some wonderful nurses. They put us on these beautiful white sheets. We couldn't sleep on beds, so we slept on the floor. The Japs, living in caves, used to come out at night. The story went that they would get in the mess queues and eat dinner and even watched the films. The Americans were edgy. They were firing at everything. We had bullets coming right through the tent. The nurses were trying to build us up. But the food was too rich. We couldn't eat what they gave us. Then we couldn't move our bowels. They gave us all sorts of things. But, still, we couldn't move them at all. I told one nurse, 'Why don't you use dynamite?' She laughed."

The Britisher Laurie Smith had this memory: "I left *Sealion* wrapped in a Navy blanket. After Thailand and Singapore, Saipan looked to be a beautiful place, cheerful and friendly and all the amenities. (Though they were still using flamethrowers on the Japs hiding in the hills.) They issued us U.S. Army summer khakis, comfortable boots, blankets, towels, soap—all the little things that made life worth living. We had food galore. In Albert Hall's case, too much. He and others required laxatives. We were pumped full of vitamin pills. I personally had the undivided attention of a medical orderly wielding a scalpel—cutting into what I considered to be a mere boil on my back. He was so interested in asking me questions that without looking, he dug a hole in my back so large I still bear the scars thirty-five years later. Then I had a toothache. The dentist had to stand on a box with his knee in my chest. I vowed he would never practice in England, and if he had, I would have given everyone a public warning."

The Australian Doug Hampson: "Just when we got to bed, the first comfortable bed I'd had in years, we had an air raid. The matron came along and told us to get under our beds. I said no way was I going to get out of that bed. It turned out to be a false alarm. The next night, one of the nurses was killed by a Jap when she went out to get a drink of water."

Another Australian, Harry Weigand, went on: "It seemed funny to sleep in a nice clean bed with nice clean sheets and pillow slips. With no bugs or lice. It did seem strange to be without them. Uncle Sam did not do things in halves. At times I gave myself a hard pinch to see if I was not just dreaming. I was afraid I'd wake up sometime and find out that I had just had a prisoner-of-war dream. The American nurses were certainly looking after us, treating us swell. If I were a younger man and I wasn't married, I sure would have taken one of the American girls home for a souvenir."

Frank Farmer, still another Australian, added: "We were treated like royalty, and I shall never forget the generosity of the fighting men who were still dealing with isolated pockets of Jap resistance in the immediate area. One night Japs did enter the hospital perimeter, and nightly air raids forced patients to sleep under their beds at times, rather than on them. It was the first time for nearly three years that we had been in a combat zone, and most of us were a little scared that we still might not make it."

In time, the survivors were segregated by nationality. After that, the two groups did not see each other again. The two senior survivors of each group, Sergeant Harry Jones of England and Warrant Officer Bill Smith of Australia, were placed in charge of their respective contingents. Unaware of the 136 men who had been rescued from the lifeboats by the Japanese, these 152 believed they were the sole survivors of the *Rakuyo Maru*, a belief that would shortly cause complications and, in a few cases, unnecessary grief. Those who could get about posed for group photographs. Jones and Smith compiled muster rolls and, via the Red Cross, radio-wired next of kin, informing them their loved ones had been liberated from Japanese captivity. These 152 telegrams evoked 152 separate domestic dramas. One of them involved the Britisher Tommy Carr: "When she got the wire, my mother collapsed from shock."

The senior British naval officer in the Pacific, Captain D. N. C. Tufnell, flew in from Pearl Harbor with some aides. His team, together with American intelligence officers, grilled both British and Australians. The survivors provided a complete history of their experiences since surrender, with notable emphasis on the barbarism of the Japanese and Korean guards, leading to the appalling death rate on the railway. (Lieutenant Yamada was singled out for praise; Lieutenant Tanaka was described as "very bad.") In addition, they provided valuable specific intelligence information such as: location of principal bridges and junctions along the Burma-Thailand railway; exact locations of Japanese naval headquarters, airfields, ammo and fuel dumps, and other installations in Saigon and Singapore; descriptions of shipping facilities (and maritime traffic patterns in those two places), and, finally, exact locations of dozens of POW camps in Burma, Thailand, Indochina and Singapore, so that Allied bomber pilots could be warned to avoid them. Believing that all except they had died on *Rakuyo Maru*, they began compiling vast lists of dead, by *kumis*, for their respective military departments. Tufnell concluded of the survivors: "They were a remarkable crowd of fellows, cheerful in the most, but quiet and subdued, modest and in no way claiming anything for themselves; universally in praise of the wonderful work done by their own doctors and other officers during the past two and a half years, and especially of their reception by their American rescuers." Maurice Demers was officially commended.

Tufnell compiled a very long classified report to the Admiralty in London and to the Royal Australian Navy in Australia. His report landed like a bomb in both countries. Intelligence agencies in both nations knew that the Japanese had utilized POW labor to build a railway linking Burma and Thailand, but it was the first time anyone had heard of the horrors and atrocities. Civilian and military authorities who were cleared to read the report were outraged. There were long debates and official memos exchanged all through both governments over what to do about it—whether or not a public protest would endanger or help POWs still in Japanese captivity.

(3)

What the survivors now wanted most was to get out of the war zone to some sort of civilization and, eventually, home. The British Naval Captain Tufnell discussed with the American doctors and military authorities how best to accomplish this. He even polled the survivors for their views, and Blood Bancroft's reply was typical: "He gave us all a questionnaire to fill in. One of the last questions was: 'Would you like to visit America?' And, of course, we all answered, 'Yes.' It was our impression they were going to fly all the survivors to America and sort them out from there. A brief holiday in the States suited most of the Australians just fine."

But there would be no holiday in America for the Australians. The transportation arrangements Captain Tufnell finally arrived at were that the Australians would go directly to Australia by sea. They would board a liberty ship, *Alcoa Polaris,* leaving Saipan September 28 and sail to Guadalcanal, where other sea transportation would be arranged. The British group also would go by sea, leaving Saipan October 1 on the liberty ship *Cape Douglas* for Pearl Harbor, thence to San Francisco on another vessel, and would travel across the United States to New York, where they would catch yet another ship for England. Some of the Australians were bitterly disappointed that the British survivors would see America and they would not. Blood Bancroft said: "Able Bodied Seaman Collins of the *Perth* called that naval captain a very rude word. He could have been court-martialed."

Only eighty-six of the ninety-two Australians were deemed medically fit to travel. The six to be left behind

279

on Saipan were George Hinchy, Vic Cross, Murray Thomson, Roy Cornford, James Boulter and Jock Hart. The others collected their mounting pile of gear (including dozens of cartons of cigarettes given them by G.I.s) and boarded a landing barge for *Alcoa Polaris.* Harold Bunker: "It was a bit of a battle to get on the ship. There was a swell. And it was hot! With our new skins, it was the first time I had prickly heat. When we got on the *Alcoa Polaris,* there was a nice little lecture about what to do in case we got torpedoed. That got a good laugh."

Frank Farmer remembered that "at the time, such a voyage was not without its dangers as the Japanese Navy still had a considerable number of its fleet operating in the Pacific. Our quarters were cramped, but we were in good spirits and looking forward to meeting our loved ones again. With a sole destroyer as escort, *Alcoa Polaris* took us south to Eniwetok in the Marshall Islands, where we anchored from the third to the sixth of October with the great Philippine invasion fleet all around us. This was the greatest congregation of ships I had ever seen and included the flattops of Admiral Halsey's Fifth Fleet."

From the Marshalls, *Alcoa Polaris* steamed south toward the equator. "We were really just getting our appetites back," said Sergeant James O. Smith. "They had two feedings a day. You'd go down to the mess hall and get your food. When we finished one tray, they'd take it away and bring it back again full. We must have been entertainment for the other troops on board. Once, when we were in line for a meal, I saw a little typewritten notice: 'Due to the presence of POWs aboard, the crew will go on half-rations of ice cream.' I thought that was marvelous of them." Bob Farrands: "When they practiced firing their guns, the ship shook hard. The ship was full of bugs, and the gunfire sent the bugs everywhere! When we crossed the equator on October 8, they had a ceremony—King Neptune reigned—and we all got our shellback cards."

The *Alcoa Polaris* reached Guadalcanal on October 10 after a thirteen-day voyage. The eighty-six survivors were transferred from her to the U.S. Army's 20th General Hospital. Vic Clifford was still on intravenous feeding. "One bottle a day. *Drip, drip, drip.* That plus custards and soft food. In Guadalcanal I went berserk. They had ice cream and peaches. The ice cream wasn't bad, but the acid in the peaches almost killed me. It was awful. And it was back to drip feeding again. *Drip, drip, drip.*"

It now appeared that no further transportation arrangements had been made for the survivors. The Australians waited and waited, army style. Here they had their first contact with the Australian army. An officer issued them a small advance on their pay. Frank Farmer was caustic. "An Australian paymaster was pleased to advance us the equivalent of about twenty dollars, to be duly deducted from the first pay we received in Australia. Twenty dollars! G.I.s in Saipan had offered us fifty-dollar bills!" They were taken sight-seeing. Vic Clifford recalled: "They took us on a tour of a cemetery. Some Marines were there and they were jeering at us: 'Dogfaces!' We were still dressed like U.S. Army soldiers. I wondered what we had done to them. There were thousands of white crosses —as far as you could see. I said, 'Thank you, God.' I'd got out of it. I wouldn't even have had a cross. I would have been fish food."

The Australian government was evidently not able to provide transportation for these war heroes. Once again the U.S. Navy came to the rescue, and Mac McKittrick told how it did. "After we'd been in Guadalcanal a few days, an American captain called us in and said that our government wasn't doing anything about getting us home, so how would we like to go on this U.S. Navy minelayer? We were unanimously in favor."

The minelayer was the *Monadnock,* a 292-foot vessel of 3,000 tons. The survivors boarded her on October 14. There were no suitable quarters for them on such a small ship. McKittrick went on: "We slept on stretcher beds lying among the mine racks." It was a very rough, uncomfortable voyage. Bob Farrands: "The crew had been seven weeks in harbor, and when they came out, they got sick as dogs." John Hocking: "It was so rough that one day we didn't even have ice cream. I got seasick. So did the whole crew." And so the Australians completed the final leg of their long voyage, arriving in Moreton Bay off Brisbane, Australia, on October 18—a little over a month after most had been picked up by *Sealion* and *Pampanito.*

A Royal Australian Navy launch pulled alongside the *Monadnock* before she moored. Commander C. R. Reid, a former executive officer of *Perth,* came aboard and summoned the four *Perth* survivors, Blood Bancroft, Bob

281

Collins, Darby Munro and Jack Houghton, to the *Monadnock* captain's cabin. Here, for about four hours, the survivors were grilled—mostly about names of men who had survived *Perth* and the railway and those who had not. This was the first eyewitness account the Australian Navy had of *Perth,* her loss and the aftermath. Later that day, the four were questioned another two hours at naval headquarters, ashore. After that, they were cautioned not to discuss anything about their experiences, given money, and sent off to their various homes on leave, still wearing U.S. Army uniforms. Jack Houghton, whose wife lived in Brisbane—and who was expecting him but not so soon—was driven home in a navy staff car that night. He was the first survivor of *Rakuyo Maru* —and the Burma-Thailand railway—to reach home.

During these interrogations, the *Perth* men had singled out Vic Duncan for special praise. This started machinery that would eventually lead to Duncan's being awarded the British Empire Medal. The citation, in part: "When the Japanese ship *Rakuyo Maru,* carrying prisoners of war, was sunk by a submarine, Electrical Artificer Duncan, who was amongst the prisoners, immediately took control of No. 2 Hatch. That the lives of most of the prisoners were saved was due to his coolness and good leadership." So far as is known, Duncan was the only Australian on *Rakuyo Maru* to be decorated for action directly related to the sinking.

The interrogation also caused grief in Duncan's family. His wife Elizabeth worked in naval intelligence. Inevitably, she had quickly learned of the *Rakuyo Maru* disaster. Later, she was permitted to talk to Jack Houghton. Duncan said: "He told her I had been in good nick but not to get her hopes up too much because a typhoon had blown through the area. He more or less told her to get used to the idea I'd gone." For several months, Elizabeth Duncan had to believe her husband was dead. But in late January 1945, Radio Tokyo broadcast the names of the eighty Australians rescued from the lifeboats. Vic Duncan was on the list—alive once more.

When the *Monadnock* moored at a Brisbane dock, Australia's number-one soldier, Field Marshal Sir Thomas Blamey, Commander in Chief of the Australian Army, was waiting with a brass band. The public was not invited. The rescue of these men was still a military secret. The band played "Waltzing Matilda" and "Road to

Gundagai," and General Blamey gave them a welcome-home speech praising their courage and cautioning them not to talk to the press. Thereafter, they boarded buses and were taken to a secluded Catholic convent, Stuartholme.

At the convent, the survivors fell under supervision of Major R. E. Steele, formerly a sergeant in the 15th Regiment. Steele had been captured at Singapore and sent to Borneo to work. On June 4, 1943, he and seven other Australian POWs escaped and made their way to the Philippines, where they joined a guerrilla force. Two of the eight escapees were killed, but Steele and five others had recently made it back to Australia. So far as recorded, these six were the only Australians to escape Japanese captivity before the ninety-two survivors of *Rakuyo Maru*.

The survivors spent two weeks in the convent under close military guard. Bill Cunneen was one of them: "You might say we were virtually prisoners of war again." They were once more examined medically and underwent intense interrogation by intelligence personnel. Australia's Chief Justice, Sir William Webb, who was commissioner for the investigation of Japanese atrocities, also interrogated the men. An Australian war correspondent, Thomas H. Farrell, interviewed many of them and wrote dozens of stories, should the Australian government decide to make the event public. They were also required to compile a list of men lost on *Rakuyo Maru*. (Five men had to agree on each lost man.) In off hours, the men watched old newsreels, hour after hour, to fill in the two-and-a-half-year void in their lives, and ate ice cream sent daily from the *Monadnock*. They were issued new Australian uniforms, but Frank Coombes didn't like that. "The American clothes were much better."

Some men paid unauthorized visits to the town. Mac McKittrick: "One night some of the officers from the *Monadnock* came to the convent, and Tobey Johnson and I sneaked out with them. We went into the city. Tobey got drunk. I had a hell of a time getting him back in the convent. He was about twice my size. I dragged him through the graveyard and put him under the showers. I got plenty of abuse for that caper. Those *Monadnock* guys were great. They had ordered us to turn in our U.S. Navy and Army uniforms, but the captain of the *Monadnock* gave each of us a slip that said the uniforms were a gift of the U.S. government and were our property."

The intelligence debriefings continued daily. Ray Wheeler recalled: "Somewhere they had captured this military map of Saigon with all these military installations, but nothing to unlock the code. We were able to unlock nearly the whole thing: what was ammunition, what was petrol. Later they showed us the results of the bombing attacks." Mac McKittrick's memory included this fact: "We were able to tell them where the new Saigon wireless station was and the power station, and the names of the streets that had all been changed." Frank Farmer summed up: "Intelligence officers told me that the sum total of information supplied by the rescued was greater than that gleaned by intelligence throughout the war to that time. There was tremendous satisfaction, too, in pinpointing the established POW camps. This vital information undoubtedly saved the lives of thousands of fellow POWs."

They were soon busy filling out dozens of army forms. Doug Hampson initiated what was probably the most unusual official petition of them all. "I applied for five days' subsistence to cover the period from September 12, when I left the hands of the Japanese on *Rakuyo Maru,* until September 17, when I was rescued by *Barb.* Subsistence was two shillings and threepence per day. After three months fighting with the army, I finally got it. The total paid me was about one dollar and ten cents, U.S."

Though the survivors told of many tales of heroism and gallantry on *Rakuyo Maru* and, later, on the rafts, the Australian army awarded no medals to the army survivors. So far as is known, only the Australian Captain Arthur Sumner was cited. The army reported that he was given "honorable mention in dispatches, posthumously, for services rendered in the Southwest Pacific area during September 1944."

On October 29, eleven days after the first contingent of survivors arrived, a second group of five checked in at the convent. They had flown from Saipan in American aircraft. They were George Hinchy, Vic Cross, James Boulter, Roy Cornford and Murray Thomson. The last man on Saipan, Jock Hart, who had developed double pneumonia and other complications was not well enough to make the trip. He finally arrived in Australia in late

November, all alone. No Australian official bothered to meet him.

After the debriefings, the fit survivors were given three months' leave. Although the government had made no official announcement of the return of these men, the word was spreading on the grapevine. When Bob Farrands got home on November 3, by train, "the town band and every Tom, Dick and Harry and their dogs were at the station. The train whistle was blowing, the band was playing. Fantastic. You couldn't move, there were so many people."

Several were too ill to go on leave. Don McArdle, injured internally by the depth charges, had an operation on his stomach. He was in the hospital for about six months. Richard Laws, who had tuberculosis, was confined to the hospital. Vic Clifford was still quite ill from swallowing oil. He remained hospitalized for about two months. These men were transferred to hospitals near their homes, and eventually all recovered.

While the survivors were on leave the Australian government (in cooperation with the British government) decided to make the story public. On Friday, November 17, Australia's Acting Prime Minister Forde addressed the House of Representatives in Canberra for about one hour. He began with a detailed account of the sinking of *Rakuyo Maru* and the subsequent rescue, then broadened his report to include the horrors and atrocities of the Burma-Thailand railway. He stated that Sir William Webb had concluded on the basis of the facts obtained from the survivors that "the Japanese almost entirely disregarded the rules of warfare concerning prisoners of war."

Forde concluded: "I know that I speak for the people of Australia when I say that they share fully the sorrow and pride of their kith and kin throughout the British Commonwealth who are grieved by these sad events. The Government regrets that these disclosures have to be made, but it is convinced it is necessary that the Japanese government should know that we are in possession of the facts and will hold them responsible. All the rescued men speak of the high courage shown by their comrades. Everywhere and in all circumstances, the Australians have maintained matchless morale. They have shown themselves undaunted in the face of death. The many who have survived privation and disease in the jungle have developed spiritual and physical powers of triumph over adversity and over their captors. Let us look forward to the day of their release."

Forde's report was one of the most shocking stories ever published in Australia. All across the nation the stories of the railway and *Rakuyo Maru* were carried beneath huge headlines. The Sydney *Morning Herald* was typical: JAPANESE LEFT PRISONERS TO DROWN. War correspondent Thomas Farrell's vivid and touching survival stories (though run with all survivors' names deleted) were likewise released and published with the hard news. The coverage caused shock waves from one end of the nation to the other.

It also set in motion a tremendous effort on the part of the next of kin of the 10,000 Australian POWs in Southeast Asia to find out what was known about their loved ones. Inevitably, local papers—ignoring requests from the government—printed the names of hometown survivors. Each was deluged with inquiries from all over the nation. Bob Farrands said: "I was inundated by thousands of letters. People were calling the house and coming by. I finally had to go to Melbourne just to get away from it all."

The survivors finished compiling a list of Australians believed to have been lost on *Rakuyo Maru*. By this time, the list of the original Australian Japan Party given the police chief spy in Phnom Penh on a roll of toilet paper had reached Australia and was an invaluable aid in preparing the list of dead. The list, of course, included the eighty Australians rescued from the lifeboats. On December 11, the Australian army notified the next of kin on the list that their loved ones had "probably" been lost at sea on September 12, 1944. This list was made public.

It was a severe blow for everyone. The experience of Wal Williams' parents was typical. Having heard nothing of him in years, only a few days earlier they had received a copy of the radio message he wrote in Saigon over six months before. This message, of course, led them to assume he (and Max Campbell) was still alive and well. Now, on the heels of that joyous news, they were again plunged into despair by the news of his probable death. Then, a little more than a month later, on January 28, 1945, Radio Tokyo broadcast the names of those rescued from the lifeboats. (The same list Duncan's wife

286

received.) Williams was on the list, confirmed two days later by the Red Cross. Once more his parents were joyous. Max Campbell's loved ones endured the same emotional roller coaster, only to learn later that Max had died in Japan.

The Australian survivors were hailed as heroes all across the nation. There were official public statements of welcome and congratulations from His Majesty King George, His Excellency the Acting Governor of Australia, Winston Dugan, and other dignitaries. That of General Blamey expressed the view of the Australian army: "The rescue of these Australians is one of the great stories of the war. But even greater is the story of the courage, endurance and the unflagging loyalty of the men themselves, during their period of imprisonment and while battling for their lives in the China Sea. These men have set an example to the whole of Australia by the manner in which they sustained their morale under almost impossible conditions. They were always on top of the Japanese. They never bowed to their temporary victors, nor did they accept their capture as a defeat or as the end of the war for them."

The homecomings evoked unimaginable joy—and some heartache. At least three of the wives had long since given up their men for dead and taken up with other men. Perhaps the strangest story of faithful love, empathy and perhaps something even more was that of Jimmy Campbell during his long ordeal on the raft as he told it to his pal Roy Whitecross when Whitecross was liberated after the war. It was Whitecross who had the premonition that Campbell would be torpedoed and rescued and insisted that Campbell stay topside. Whitecross related how Campbell, on the desperate sixth day, had been saved from at last releasing his grip on the boards by hearing his sweetheart's voice crying out to him to hold on. "When Jim returned home," Whitecross said, "he was told an amazing story of terrible nightmares suffered by his fiancée. They lasted for six days and stopped at the very hour he was rescued."

(4)

At Saipan, fifty-eight of the sixty British survivors were deemed fit for travel. On October 1, they embarked in landing craft for the liberty ship *Cape Douglas,* which would take them to Pearl Harbor. Bill Emmett remembered: "We were wearing U.S. Army uniforms. There was a ladder up the side of the ship. Lots of the people were still in very weak condition and couldn't climb. A U.S. Marine on deck thought we were U.S. Army. He didn't want us to come aboard. So, finally, an officer had to shout to him to make him let us on. We got two extra meals a day to build us up. Because we used a knife and fork differently, the Americans would come and watch us eat. One of our blokes did a star turn. He ate his peas with a knife. He got a standing ovation." Ed Starkey: "We used to have breakfast with the Marines, and then we'd have lunch with the officers. Then about five o'clock, we'd mess with the Marines again and about eight, we'd eat with the officers. We used to get big steaks and chicken—and vitamin pills. They treated us all right. They really built us up."

Laurie Smith's story was: "I suddenly started having pains in my chest and difficulty breathing. It hurt so much to breathe that I thought I had a busted rib. The doctor said we had to board the ship the next day. 'Great,' I thought. I'll never forget the group boarding the ship. The landing craft went up and down alongside. It was a question of stepping onto the ladder at the right time. The pain in my chest was excruciating. Any movement made it worse. How the hell I got up those steps, I don't know. But within minutes I was in a bed and officers and orderlies were giving me damn great white tablets and gallons of drinking water and bandaging my chest so tight I really thought they didn't want me to breathe. Apparently I had pleurisy and pneumonia—a cheerful combination. They did a good job. I wallowed in this

288

comfortable convalescence. A Negro soldier in the ship's hospital had found time to gather small matching sea shells. He made a necklace for my wife and she wears it to this day."

The *Cape Douglas* plowed steadily eastward. On October 5, she stopped overnight at Eniwetok Island in the Marshalls. On Friday, October 13, after a wholly uneventful voyage, she arrived off the naval base at Pearl Harbor. A ship's pilot and a British officer came aboard by launch. The British officer was Major Thorpe, deputy assistant adjutant general of the British Army Staff in Washington, D.C. Major Thorpe announced that he was to be the group's escort from Hawaii to New York.

When the *Cape Douglas* moored in her designated slip, none other than the Commander in Chief, U.S. Pacific Fleet, Admiral Chester Nimitz, was on hand to greet the survivors. With him was a Marine Corps band, which struck up a stirring march, "The British Grenadiers." Harry Jones formed his group into a rigid parade. Nimitz, a white-haired, genial man, came aboard with staff and aides, shook hands with the survivors, told them to stand at ease, then gave a little welcoming speech. He updated the survivors on the progress of the war, telling them, as Harry Jones put it: "The tide had turned and the enemy was on the run." Sam Fuller said: "He said that if they'd known that the ships contained POWs, they would have let the whole convoy go."

The British group remained in Hawaii four days, all the while under very strict security. The lid was still on. Like the Australians, they were ordered not to reveal who they were or tell anyone of their experiences. They were taken from the dock in a bus, with a military police motorcycle escort, to a guarded base, the 13th Reinforcement Camp. Here, they were assigned to a barracks and permitted to go to the PX and drink beer. Harry Jones: "An urgent message called me to the PX. On arrival I found ten of my men had drunk their way through over one hundred and fifty cans of beer. The most amazing thing about it was that none of them were drunk. When they realized they had just about drunk a day's supply for the camp, they got up, returned to their beds and went to sleep."

On each of the four days, the group was visited by high brass and entertained by Red Cross representatives and some local citizens. The British Governor General of Fiji called to pay his respects, as did the commanding general, U.S. Army Forces, Central Pacific, Robert C. Richardson. The Red Cross representatives took them on sight-seeing tours (in private cars) to Waikiki Beach, Diamond Head and elsewhere, and to private homes for lunches and cocktails. Issued twenty dollars in pay, they were allowed to go shopping in downtown Honolulu, with one MP guarding every four men. The climax of this reintroduction to genteel civilization was a full day at the beach home of the tobacco heiress Doris Duke. She provided a lavish buffet, swimming pool, a Hawaiian band, hula dancers, hostesses and a photographer, who took a group picture of the happy survivors on the lawn beneath swaying palm trees. As to the female hostesses, Harry Jones remembered: "We were so afraid of them through lack of contact with the opposite sex for some years that they must have thought us complete dead loads."

On Tuesday, October 17, the Hawaiian idyll came to an end. At 0730, the group left the camp and traveled back to Pearl Harbor to board a ship, the 11,000-ton troopship *Orizaba,* for San Francisco. It was another uneventful five-day leg in their long journey. Harry Jones spent the time re-creating his diary from memory. Barney Barnett came down with malaria and was confined to sick bay for two days. Others read, gambled or strolled the decks. On October 22 the ship passed under the Golden Gate Bridge into San Francisco Bay.

There was a welcoming committee on the dock, including another military band, which broke into "California, Here I Come." British Major Baker, deputy assistant quartermaster general of the British Army Staff in Washington, joined Major Thorpe in supervising the group. Again, tight security prevailed. They were put in small boats and taken to a U.S. military base, Fort McDowell, on Angel Island. The survivors did not like this at all. However, when they grumbled at being locked up again, Major Baker assured them they would be escorted to all the high spots of San Francisco.

That very night the survivors got their first real taste of nightlife. It was a high moment for Barney Barnett. "We went out to a place, like a canteen, where plenty of beer was given free. And there were plenty of women. You couldn't go wrong. We had one or two *artistes* there to entertain us. After that, we had dancing. I had one or two drinks. There were three girls from Texas singing. I was asked to sing with them. What a time we had! We got back about two in the morning. It was the end of a perfect day."

The following day, the men were desperately anxious to cut loose in San Francisco on their own. Sex drives, long dormant, had awakened. But it was not to be. Harry Jones: "We were still very much prisoners." When Major Baker announced a Red Cross-sponsored sight-seeing tour from eleven to four, the men were almost insubordinately insolent. They talked the American base commander into extending their passes from 4 P.M. to midnight—to see more nightlife—but Major Baker had that canceled. Barnett's high abated considerably. "We went out until four P.M. and it was the worst day we had. We were taken on buses around San Francisco. We didn't like it. We wanted to go out on our own. We were glad to get back to camp. We had tea and went to the PX and got drunk. Then we went to bed, glad the day was over."

The next day, October 26, Major Baker announced they would be leaving by train for New York. This was another disappointment. They had been led to believe they would fly. The men packed and went for a walk on the base. Barnett told what happened: "We found out there were some Jap prisoners there. So we went to have a look at them. When we got there, they started throwing things at us. Then the fun started. The lads all started to get over the wire to them, calling them all the names under the sun. They all saw red that day. The Americans turned out extra guards with fixed bayonets. Otherwise, I don't think there would have been many Japs left."

When the survivors left the barracks, they stripped it bare. As Roy Hudson recalled it: "We still had the habit of wanting to take things. We'd all got in the habit of stealing to survive. They had nice sheets on the beds, and small radios on tables between the beds. I didn't do it, but when they ordered us to fall in with our full kits, ever so many of those sheets and radios were in those kit bags. We never heard a thing about it. There was no comeback."

The survivors boarded a small boat for Oakland. On the way, they passed Alcatraz island. Harry Jones said: "We could not help feeling sorry for its inmates, after having tasted prison life ourselves, although on a different basis. One cannot conceive anything so valuable as freedom." At Oakland they went to the train station and climbed aboard a "luxurious" Pullman car, reserved especially for them, on the *Exposition Flier,* bound for Chicago.

The cross-country trip to Chicago took four days. Barney Barnett enjoyed it. "It was a grand journey. Marvelous scenery. We had food in the dining car and a Negro to make up our beds. It was just like being in the movies." Roy Hudson was overwhelmed. "Somehow word about us must have leaked out. At every station, it seemed, there would be huge wicker hampers of food and soft drinks and cigarettes for us. We had so much we couldn't cope with it. What we couldn't eat, we gave to the black attendant in the car." Laurie Smith: "The meals and service were one thing, but the breathtaking scenery was another. The sheer grandeur took your breath away."

The petty thievery habit was still hard to break. Laurie Smith reported: "At various stations, there were train-jumping salesmen selling souvenirs and rings and scarves. I think they wondered what hit them. As POWs, we were trained thieves and extremely devious. I won't name names, but one bloke in particular hadn't got out of the habit. He showed me a whole tray of rings which he was flogging cheaply to the lads."

The *Exposition Flier* pulled into Chicago late on the evening of October 29. The train for New York did not leave until the following morning. That night in Chicago, Major Thorpe and Sergeant Jones lost control of the group. It was real freedom at last. Most of the men slipped off to bars and got drunk. Three went AWOL, including Barney Barnett. "Stan Costello, Dagger Ward and I asked the officer if we could go and have a drink. He wouldn't let us, so we decided to go get a drink ourselves. We went to a nightclub, where we were made welcome. We stopped there all night. Next morning we went to a YMCA canteen, had a shower and something to eat. We met eight girls. They took us to a Russian market. One of the girls, Roberta, asked me where I was sleeping. I told her I'd missed the train and had nowhere to go. She took me home to meet her parents. I stopped with her brother-in-law three days. I met all her bosses at her office. They even offered me a job. I was having such a good time, I wasn't bothered about rushing home."

Harry Jones was "staggered" to discover three of his charges missing. After he and Thorpe had boarded the rest of the group on the New York train, Jones remained behind in Chicago to look for them. He toured the bars. No luck. Then he went to the police and asked them to put out a "dragnet," and to the British consul to alert them to the crisis. Then: "Feeling satisfied I had done all I could, I caught the next train out of Chicago." Major Thorpe met him at the station in New York. It was a tense moment. Both men were bound to be royally chewed out for losing three security-sensitive men in their charge.

The main body of survivors had been taken to yet another military base, Fort Hamilton, in Brooklyn, where they were issued warm-weather Canadian Army uniforms. Yet another British major from the Washington staff was on hand to supervise this phase of the trip. He was appalled to learn three men were missing. For that reason, and others, the group was severely restricted in New York. No sight-seeing tours, no nights out on the town. There was only one social event, as reported by Sam Fuller. "They let us go to this dance in Brooklyn. We had a little bit of a fight with some Americans. Some of our boys were making a play for the girls. One had been drinking and said something out of place. An American bopped him one—rightly so. It caused a bit of a fight, but we smoothed it over."

The transportation to England was announced: the *Queen Mary*, which had been converted to a troopship. The survivors boarded her on November 3. That very day, the three AWOLs, having borrowed money from the British consul in Chicago, arrived in New York. Barney Barnett told of the happy ending: "When we arrived in New York, I was going to take the tube and go out on the town. But a British officer grabbed me and asked where I had been and what excuse I had. I told him I had been having a good time and I had no excuse. He was mad. But he said he wasn't going to put us on charge. He put us straight on the *Queen Mary*." Sergeant Jones was vastly relieved to see them.

There were some 17,000 American troops on the *Queen Mary*, and two movie actors, Mickey Rooney and Bobby Breen. The survivors traveled as celebrities. They had far better quarters than Rooney or Breen. Ed Starkey recalled: "We were quartered on the promenade deck, with the officers. In staterooms. Every night Mickey Rooney and Bobby Breen would come up to our quarters with a case of beer and cigars and candy. Breen would give us a sing-song. Mickey was exactly the same in real life as he was in the movies." Roy Hudson added: "I don't know where they billeted Mickey Rooney, but he didn't have a bath. He asked us if he could take a bath in our quarters. We jimmied the locks on some boarded-up millionaire's suite and showed him the bathroom."

The *Queen Mary* was a very fast ship, so fast she did not have to sail in convoy with antisubmarine defenses. She crossed the Atlantic (by a devious route, zigzagging all the way) in a mere six days. The ocean, as usual at that time of year, was rough. Laurie Smith recalled: "We hit a terrible storm. Crockery and food went all over the place in the dining room. It was as much as one could do to stay in your bunk." Roy Hudson further described the trip. "It was gray, dull and dismal. Huge swells. The ship would roll over on its side slowly. Rails dipped into the sea. We'd stand in the stern and watch the funnels go over. We didn't think it was possible they could get back again. Many of the troops were seasick."

The survivors had yet another tussle with American soldiers, which Barney Barnett told about: "One time we were all in the mess. They played the American national anthem, and we stood up. Then they played the British national anthem, and the majority of the Americans didn't stand up. We started a fight. Imagine, if you will, fifty-some of us fighting about three thousand American troops!"

On November 9 the *Queen Mary* nosed into Greenock, Scotland. The survivors had been led to believe that they would be met by the King. But Captain R. W. Smith of the War Office, who boarded the ship from the pilot launch, informed the group the King had a "chill" and could not be present. Instead, when they went ashore, they were welcomed by a low-ranking, obscure general who commanded the local military district. He read them a message from the King (the same message sent to the Australians):

The Queen and I bid you a very warm welcome home. Through all the great trials and sufferings which you have endured while in the hands of the Japanese, you and your comrades have been constantly in our thoughts. I realise from the accounts which you have already given how heavy those sufferings have been. I know too that you have endured them with the highest courage. We mourn with you the deaths of so many of your comrades. We hope with all our hearts that your return from captivity may bring you and your families a full measure of happiness.

The survivors responded with three cheers for Their Majesties, but they felt let down by the tepid welcome. Tom Carr was one who did. "When we got off the *Queen Mary,* a lady handed us a packet of Senior Service cigarettes. I said, 'Oh, is this from the British Red Cross?' She said, 'No, it's from the American Red Cross.' I was really mad. I thought our own Red Cross would have been there to meet us. The first British prisoners to come back from the Japanese. That really hurt. All the lads felt the same way. They were disgusted." Ed Starkey summed it up: "We were celebrities until we disembarked in England. Then they shunted us off to a shed on the dockside, then out a back door to a train."

The survivors believed that they would be permitted to go home right away. Another disappointment. Like the Australian army men, they were sequestered for a full week of military debriefings. These took place at a secluded, stately country estate, Vache, in Haversham, Buckinghamshire, outside London. Harry Jones felt: "We were virtually prisoners again." Sam Fuller said: "They wouldn't let us out or even tell us where we were. I was fed up. I said if they didn't let me out, I was going."

A dozen men from the War Office descended on Vache. Most of the interrogation was centered on finding out which British POWs in Japanese hands were dead or alive. The group had already prepared long lists during the sea voyages. These were turned over to the authorities concerned. Other experts grilled the group, individually and collectively, for military intelligence information. Harry Jones turned over his diary, which by now amounted to fifteen thousand words, and he felt: "There can be no doubt that the information the intelligence branch obtained from us helped in no small measure to lift the curtain of secrecy that had remained drawn over Singapore, Malaya and Siam for some three years."

The public announcement of the rescue—and the horrors of the Burma-Thailand railway—was carefully coordinated with that in Australia. On November 17, the Secretary of State for War, Sir James Grigg, addressed the House of Commons. His statement was similar to that of

Australia's Acting Prime Minister Forde. He presented a history of the Burma-Thailand railway, the appalling working conditions and death rate, and an account of the sinking of *Rakuyo Maru* and the rescue of the survivors. He expressed admiration "for the way in which the United States submarine crews risked their own safety to rescue men from the sea," and gratitude "to these crews and to the United States authorities for the care and attention given to them at every step." He concluded: "It is a matter of profound regret to me that these disclosures have to be made; but we are convinced that it is necessary that the Japanese should know that we know how they have been behaving, and that we intend to hold them responsible."

As in Australia, the revelations generated massive front-page headlines. To protect the survivors from next-of-kin inquiries, no names were released. But, as in Australia, local newspapers soon began to publish the names and brief accounts of the saga. The British survivors were soon deluged with thousands of letters and phone calls. Ed Starkey was "absolutely besieged by people." Sam Fuller remembers: "I had terrible experiences with people coming up asking me if I knew their relatives." Charles Perry added: "A bloke's sister asked if he were dead. She said she knew he was dead and begged me to tell her the truth. So I said yes. She just went crazy. After that, if I knew somebody was dead, and was asked about him, I just said I didn't know him."

The survivors were issued new British uniforms, paid some money and then granted forty-two day's leave. The reporting-in date was January 1, 1945, but according to Roy Hudson: "We arranged between ourselves that we'd arrive a day late so that we could have New Year's at home." They were driven to London. Those who lived elsewhere were put aboard trains. Now, two months after being pulled from the water, they were, at last, free.

There were fifty-eight moving homecomings. That of George Gould, twenty-eight, was unusual. "My wife and daughter were at the train station to meet me. The whole village turned out. But it was the wrong train. They went home, then met the next train. My little girl wouldn't have anything to do with me. She'd kiss my photograph, but she wouldn't kiss me. I didn't look a thing like my photograph. My hair was all cut off, eyes staring out of my head, lips swollen up." Charles Perry had this homecoming: "I went to my house. No house. It had been bombed out. They had not received the telegram or the wire. So I went to my mother's, twenty yards away. It was two o'clock in the morning. I banged on the door. My sister opened it. She went white. She rushed in and shouted up the stairs, 'Mum. Dad. Charlie's home! Charlie's home!' They came downstairs. I said, 'Where's Maggie?' (My wife.) She was at her mother's. I spent the night with my parents and the next morning went to see my wife. When I went in, she nearly collapsed."

Epilogue

The lives of the men who were rescued from *Rakuyo Maru* and *Kachidoki Maru* and the submariners who rescued them went on. As with any group of men this large and diverse, there were small and large triumphs and tragedies.

After a happy rest and refit in Fremantle, Ben Oakley, who had received a Navy Cross medal, took *Growler* on her eleventh patrol, his third as her skipper. He commanded a three-boat wolf pack, including *Hake* and *Hardhead,* which patrolled west of Luzon. On November 7, Oakley broke radio silence to tell Fremantle that he was having trouble with his SJ radar and urgently required spare parts. An arrangement was made with *Bream,* ready to return to base, to rendezvous with *Growler* and transfer the needed parts.

Early on the morning of November 8, Oakley, whose radar was evidently working at least part of the time, made SJ contact on a small convoy and directed *Hake* and *Hardhead* to join him in the attack. About an hour later *Hardhead* heard an explosion that sounded like a torpedo, followed by depth charges. The convoy turned away from *Growler* toward *Hardhead,* which set up and sank a tanker. For her pains, *Hardhead* was charged by escorts and viciously depth-charged. Before *Hake* could get in, she was also attacked by unusually persistent and expert escorts. They pinned her down for sixteen "harrowing" hours, during which time *Hake* logged 150 depth charges, many close. That night *Hake* and *Hardhead* attempted, without success, to contact *Growler. Bream* could not raise her for the spare part rendezvous. Nothing more was ever heard from *Growler,* and there was no clue to her loss in Japanese records. The speculation within some circles of the submarine force was that the superaggressive "Destroyer Buster" had again taken on an escort—and lost. The loss of the famous *Growler,* the admired Ben Oakley and his crew, was keenly felt in the submarine force.

In Pearl Harbor, Pete Summers on *Pampanito* asked Admiral Lockwood for leave. "I was really run down after that patrol. I couldn't sleep. I was down to a hundred and forty pounds." Lockwood agreed to relieve Summers for one patrol, and Summers returned to the States. Command of the boat went to Frank W. "Mike" Fenno, forty-two, a full captain who had gained fame earlier in the war as the aggressive skipper of *Trout*. Fenno led a four-boat wolf pack to familiar ground for *Pampanito*: Hainan island. Fenno made three aggressive attacks on three convoys and sank two small ships confirmed in Japanese records. After that, to the great delight of the crew, *Pampanito* was ordered to Fremantle, Australia, for refit.

When *Pampanito* pulled up to the pier in Fremantle on December 30, the topside gang was astounded to see four or five of the ex-POW survivors, including Jack Cocking and Wally Winter, standing there, dressed in the Navy dungarees the *Pampanito* crewmen had donated, and grinning from ear to ear. George Strother said: "They wouldn't let the line handlers work. They handled the lines themselves." The chief of the boat, Clarence Smith, observed: "The changes in their appearances were remarkable." Equally remarkable was the fact that the survivors had somehow penetrated the strict submarine security to learn of *Pampanito*'s arrival. They never explained how they did it.

No submarine crew ever had a more hospitable welcome anywhere. Maurice Demers said: "They hugged and kissed me! They took us to their homes. We met their families. *They* hugged and kissed us. They gave us parties. Everything you wanted. Food. Drink. Dance. Whatever. The whole town was ours. It was an emotional experience, hard to describe." Peder Granum recalled: "We were received with open arms. Party after party after party was given in our honor. We will never forget the wonderful time we had there." The yeoman Red McGuire: "We were treated like absolute kings."

Jack Cocking took Tony Hauptman, Bill Yagemann and Bob Bennett under his wing. They went rabbit hunting and to horse races. Yagemann said: "Cocking owned a racehorse, a long shot named Gay Parade. He told me to bet ten on him. So I found a bookie and bet ten pounds. The horse won. Jack asked if he could turn in my winning ticket for me. When I gave it to him, he looked at it and said, 'My God! Ten pounds! I meant for you to bet ten shillings.' The payout almost broke the bookie."

Pete Summers rejoined the boat in Fremantle, sorry to learn that he was losing Tony Hauptman, who had injured his back and required a spinal operation. Summers took *Pampanito* on two more patrols. On the first, he led a two-boat wolf pack and sank two big ships. On the second, when targets were almost impossible to find, she sank none. *Pampanito* returned to the States for overhaul and made no more war parols. Because he had been promoted to warrant officer, Maurice Demers had to leave the boat. After the war, he remained in the Navy until 1963, when he was forced to retire for a physical disability: arthritis. Pete Summers advanced to captain and retired in 1957. Because he had won a Navy Cross, he received a "tombstone" or honorary promotion to rear admiral upon retirement.

Eli Reich took *Sealion* on one more patrol, another spectacular performance. Alerted by an Ultra, Reich attacked a task force of two battleships and two destroyers. He sank the destroyer *Urakaze* and the 31,000-ton battleship *Kongo,* a veteran of the attack on Pearl Harbor. *Kongo* was the only Japanese battleship sunk by American submarines in the war. When he returned to Guam, where Lockwood had established an advanced headquarters, Reich received a third Navy Cross and more high praise from Lockwood. But Reich had had enough. He asked to be relieved of command. Lockwood, keenly disappointed to lose so fine a skipper, appointed Reich to his staff as a strategic planner. Reich went on to a highly distinguished career in the postwar Navy, becoming one of nine submarine skippers to attain the exalted rank of vice admiral. He was also appointed deputy assistant secretary of defense for matériel. In 1973 he retired from active duty.

Sealion, now commanded by Charles F. Putnam, made her fourth patrol in the South China Sea. She sank one big ship, then, to the delight of her crew, was ordered to Fremantle for refit, arriving on January 24, 1945. *Sealion,* too, received a warm reception from the Australian survivors. The chief of the boat, James Utz: "They were standing on the dock when we pulled in." During her refit, *Sealion*'s crew was wined and dined by the survivors, although not so lavishly as *Pampanito*'s.

301

Sealion made two more patrols under Putnam (sinking one more ship), then returned to the States for overhaul. She was still in the yard when hostilities ceased. Her pharmacist mate, Roy Williams, who had made all six of *Sealion*'s patrols, also remained in the Navy after the war, refusing a promotion to warrant officer so he could stay on submarines. After making the famous round-the-world-submerged cruise on the nuclear-powered submarine *Triton,* he retired in 1960.

Gene Fluckey took *Barb* on three more spectacular patrols. On the next, in a wolf pack with *Queenfish* and *Picuda,* he sank three confirmed ships, including the 10-438-ton ex-light cruiser *Gokoku Maru,* and almost got another carrier. For this performance, Fluckey won his third Navy Cross. His next patrol was the most daring of the entire submarine war. Again wolf-packing with *Queenfish* and *Picuda,* he sank three confirmed ships for 18,000 tons (and split credit for another with *Picuda* and *Queenfish*), then penetrated deep into a harbor on the China coast at night on the surface and fired eight torpedoes at a convoy at anchor, achieving eight hits. In all, Fluckey was credited with sinking eight ships for 80,000 tons on this patrol—an all-time record. (This was reduced in postwar records to four and one-third ships for 24,000 tons.) This time he was awarded the Congressional Medal of Honor, one of five given to submarine skippers during the war.

After a long overhaul in the States, Fluckey returned *Barb* to the Pacific for his fifth and final patrol in June 1945. On this patrol, Fluckey created submarine history by sending a commando party ashore on Karafuto and blowing up an eleven-car freight and passenger train. After that, with the war coming to a close, Fluckey relinquished command. In five patrols, Fluckey had won a Medal of Honor and four Navy Crosses, making him the most decorated submariner of the war. His total confirmed tonnage score, 95,360, was the highest of any submarine skipper. Fluckey went on to a fine postwar naval career, rising to rear admiral and often mentioned for the job of chief of naval operations. However, it did not come his way, and he retired to Portugal in 1972. *Barb*'s pharmacist mate, Bill Donnelly, got off after the eleventh patrol while the boat was in the States for overhaul. He remained in the Navy after the war, was promoted to warrant officer in 1953 and retired in 1971.

Elliott Loughlin took *Queenfish* on three more patrols, two operating with *Barb* and *Picuda*. On these two, she sank five and one-third ships for 14,950 tons. On her fourth patrol, Loughlin met professional disaster. He unwittingly sank a Japanese ship, *Awa Maru*, that the United States had granted safe passage because she was supposedly carrying Red Cross supplies to POWs in Southwest Asia. Loughlin was relieved of command, court-martialed and found guilty of negligence in obeying orders. In the postwar years, however, Loughlin went on to a splendid naval career, overcame this black mark on his record and was selected to rear admiral. He retired in 1968. *Queenfish*'s pharmacist, Harold Dixon, made all five of *Queenfish*'s patrols. He too, stayed in the Navy after the war with the rank of chief petty officer. Plagued with ulcers, which he traced back to his ordeal with the *Rakuyo Maru* survivors, he retired in 1960. In 1975 he died.

Following their ninety-day leave, the Australian army survivors were required to spend several weeks in Melbourne going over lists of 8th Division POWs, declaring who was alive, who was dead. After that, most received a discharge and returned to civilian life, married and settled down for their life's work. Warrant Officer Bill Smith became a baker. Neville Thams returned to operating a motion picture theater. Alf Winter and Frank Farmer returned to teaching and James Smith too became a teacher. Later, Smith joined the national government in Canberra as an agriculture expert. He also made an astonishing discovery: his father, a copra planter on Rabaul, who was interned by the Japanese, died when the prison ship *Montevideo Maru*, on which he was being sent to Japan in 1942, was torpedoed by an American submarine. Leslie Bolger joined the government and rose to a high position in the prime minister's secretariat. He tried to return the St. Dominic medal, but Sister Dominic refused to accept it. Philip Beilby became an optometrist specializing in contact lenses and played a clarinet in a dance band on the side. Tony Clive wrote a book on his POW experiences. It was partly serialized in a magazine but never published in book form. Don McArdle became a hair-dresser. His brother James, whom he had last seen in Saigon, returned after the war. Harry Pickett taught and played music.

Bob Farrands became a fireman and rose to be officer in charge of Sydney's main control room. Bill Cunneen bought a 500-acre sheep and cattle station. Leo Cornelius became an accountant. Lindsay Nunan, depressed by a domestic complication, committed suicide—by putting his head beneath a moving train.

Several stayed in the army for varying periods. Ray Wheeler was assigned as an interpreter with Japanese POWs being held in Australia. "I knocked a few of them down." Following a tour to Italy, he got out of the army, worked on a country newspaper, wrote an unpublished novel around his POW experiences and then settled into the commercial printing business. He discovered that his three rolls of film entrusted to his mate Reginald Josephs (who eventually went to Japan) had been destroyed in a bombing attack. Jack Flynn put in another four years in the army. He was sent to Singapore with the repatriation group, where he helped process Australian POWs released from Changi. He saw many of his old mates there and astounded them with his story of *Rakuyo Maru* and the happy (for him) aftermath.

The four navy men were given a choice of remaining in the service or getting out. Jack Houghton and Bob Collins got out. Blood Bancroft and Darby Munro stayed in. When Bancroft reported to a naval installation in Melbourne for duty, he was given a pick and shovel and assigned to help repair a base railway spur! When the base commander learned of this, he "almost hit the roof." He quickly transferred Bancroft to a new unit being formed to handle returning POWs. But navy life no longer held appeal for Bancroft. He applied for a medical discharge and returned to Western Australia. He wrote a slim book on his POW experiences, *The Mikado's Guests*, in collaboration with R. G. Roberts. He re-entered the banking business and has since risen to manage one of Perth's biggest banks. Darby Munro remained in the navy until his retirement in 1966. He was the only *Perth* man to be sunk a third time. After the war, while on a minesweeper, the vessel fouled a mine, blew up and sank. "I was only in the water for a little while. Another minesweeper picked us up."

After their forty-two-day leave, the British survivors reported (one day late, as planned) to a freezing-cold camp in the north of England near Newcastle. Some, such as Samuel T. Whiley, picked up by *Pampanito*, had to be hospitalized for various disorders. Some were immediately discharged for medical reasons. Some were actually retrained to fight in France. But none ever actually left England before the end of the war.

One by one, most were discharged to civilian life, where they married and pursued various careers. Stan Costello, Denny Smith, Ed Starkey, Joseph Bagnall, Barney Barnett and others returned to the mines. Barnett eventually left the mines to become a television production assistant. Alf Allbury, chronically ill, took a civil service job as a telephone engineer and in 1955, while dying of cancer, completed and published an excellent book on his war experiences, *Bamboo and Bushido*. (The jacket was painted by Ronald Searle.) Albert Hall returned to playing professional football but injured his knees, had to quit, divorced and fell into a deep depression from which he never fully recovered. Roy Hudson returned to the Royal Botanic Gardens and later became a high-ranking horticultural adviser to the City of London. Sam Fuller became a noted professional toastmaster, presiding over functions attended by, among other celebrities, every adult member of the Royal Family. Thomas B. Brierly and Leslie Bambridge returned to farming. Bambridge learned that his brother Albert had been killed on the prison ship *Hofoku Maru*, which was sunk by American aircraft off Manila on September 21, the day after Bambridge arrived in Saipan. Norman Ashworth returned to college part-time and rose to be a chartered town planner. Charles Armstrong returned to painting and decorating. Charles Perry returned to cabinetmaking. He petitioned the government for the $15,000 in Malayan currency he had entrusted to Lieutenant Keyes, but the petition was denied. Laurie Smith returned to the paper business. Soon after he got home, Curley Wiles was shot dead in a domestic dispute.

Several men stayed in the British army for varying lengths of service. William A. W. Mandley until 1959, Bill Stones until 1948. Bill Emmett volunteered for two more years in India, Java and Hong Kong. Alfred Ogden, who could not swim and who was rescued by *Pampanito*, was, ironically, drowned in the Han River in Korea in 1951 on a picnic outing. Harry Jones returned to Singapore with the army, was awarded the British Empire Medal (for building the radios while a POW and for his invaluable diary), wrote a book on his war experiences (never published), joined the British Civil Service in Singapore, married a Eurasian (whose mother was Japanese) and eventually retired to Perth, Australia, where he met Blood Bancroft. He died in Perth of a heart attack in 1976.

After the war, the Australian survivors of *Rakuyo Maru* rescued by the Japanese returned home for processing and discharge. They were as astounded to learn that ninety-two of their number had been picked up by the submarines as those rescued by submarine were to learn that eighty had been rescued by the Japanese. Andy Anderson returned to being a golf pro. Frank Johnson drove first a bus, then a taxi. Titch Lemin operated a gas station. Ray Burridge, who learned that his younger brother Frank had died a POW in Borneo, went back to building hospitals. Ian MacDiarmid became a highly successful auctioneer and land developer. Russ Savage rose to a partnership in a large Australian accounting firm and helped to launch a Brisbane TV station. MacDiarmid and Savage married sisters, thus becoming brothers-in-law. Stanley Manning returned to the mining business. Bert Wall became a hairdresser; Clarrie Wilson a sign painter. Wal Williams opened a furniture store, and Doug Mayers went into the earth-moving business. Syd Matsen was thankful that he had returned to *Rakuyo Maru* for a smoke. "I attribute an added thirty years of my life to the fact that I went back for and smoked that cigarette." Vic Duncan stayed in the navy another four years, was commissioned, earned a university degree at night and became a teacher, ultimately rising to be deputy principal of a large Sydney high school. Rowley Richards, the only officer to survive the sinking of *Rakuyo Maru,* opened a medical practice in Sydney and became active in veterans' affairs. The summary of his diary, buried in Corporal Gorlick's grave on Jeep Island, was recovered. He began a book on his extraordinary war experiences, set it aside and recently resumed work on it.

The many British survivors of *Kachidoki Maru* interned in Japan until the war's end returned to England in the fall of 1945 for processing and discharge, Johnny Sherwood played professional football until 1952, when he retired to manage a pub. Roll Parvin also wrote an excellent book on his experiences: *Yasumai!* Tom Parrott became a postman, George Huitson went back to the grocery business. Stan Thompson returned to the dry cleaners he had delivered for before the war. Doug Spon-Smith returned to the meat business and became an inspector. In 1977 his mate Tom Pounder also published a book on his POW experiences: *Death Camps of the River Kwai.* Ernest Benford remained in the army until 1959, rising to the rank of warrant officer. After retirement, he became a technical writer for the Ministry of Defence.

After the war, the Japanese were held accountable for the horrors and atrocities on the Railway of Death. The case against them was based, in part, on the records and diaries of Brigadier Varley, which survived. Many camp commanders and guards were hanged. Others served long prison sentences. Authorities in Britain and Australia halfheartedly investigated the atrocity of the *Rakuyo Maru,* but this crime—leaving 1,182 men in the water to drown—was not ever pursued to the end. Nor was the specific alleged massacre of the Brigadier Varley lifeboat group. The 1,030 men who died in the *Rakuyo Maru* tragedy were not avenged.

Little or no financial assistance was given the survivors in either country. A few years after the war, when the railway was sold by the Allied governments to Thailand (most of it today is in ruins), the net proceeds were divided among the ex-POWs who built it. Each British ex-POW received 75 pounds. Each Australian ex-POW received 100 pounds. All the POWs received, in addition, all the back pay that had accumulated during their imprisonment, ranging from 100 to 400 pounds, depending on rank. This was soon spent—often in foolish sprees. In both countries many disabled and partially disabled men applied for government pensions, but both nations were niggardly in handing them out. Only five of the sixty British survivors rescued by the submarines were receiving any sort of pension in 1978, and the amount these five received was piddling. Strong efforts on the part of veterans' organizations in both countries to persuade the governments to provide financial assistance to the survivors have thus far been unavailing.

After the visits of *Pampanito* and *Sealion* to Fremantle in the winter (or summer, in Australia) of 1944-45, there was little contact between the survivors and the submariners. A few exchanged letters and Christmas cards for some years, but decades went by before there was again face-to-face contact. In 1972, Neville Thams (rescued by *Barb*) met *Barb*'s Tuck Weaver in Sydney. Later that same year on a trip to Europe, Thams and his wife spent a happy afternoon in Portugal with Gene Fluckey and his wife. In 1977, Shorty Bates of *Sealion*, who worked for a time in Australia for Alcoa, met Bill Cunneen and Vic Clifford in Melbourne. That same year, on a visit to the United States, Blood Bancroft and his wife called on one of the *Queenfish*'s nurses, Tony Alamia, in Anaheim, California. Alamia was then in the hospital, recovering from a severe heart attack. By now, Alamia was bald and Bancroft was white-haired. At first, they did not recognize each other. But then the memories rushed back and eyes filmed. Alamia said: "This time the tables were turned. I was in bed, and Blood was fit as a fiddle, exhorting me to get well."

Source Notes

The material in this book was derived from original official documents in the United States, the United Kingdom and Australia; books, periodicals and taped interviews with, or written accounts from, 172 of the participants or their relatives.

OFFICIAL DOCUMENTS

United States

At the Naval Historical Center, Navy Yard, Washington, D.C.:

Barb, U.S.S. Report of Ninth War Patrol, 3 October 1944, 62 pp.; Annex to Patrol Report, "Information Obtained from Rescued Australian and British Prisoners of War," 24 September 1944, 7 pp.; Ship's History, 11 pp.

Case, U.S.S. Ship's History, 6 pp.

Fulton, U.S.S. Report from the Medical Officers to The Chief of the Bureau of Medicine and Surgery, "Experience of Survivors from a Sunken Japanese Transport Recovered from Life Rafts in the South China Sea," 30 September 1944, 12 pp.; Ship's History, 7 pp.

Growler, U.S.S. Report of the Tenth War Patrol, 26 September 1944, 58 pp.; Ship's History, 6 pp.; U.S. Submarine Losses in World War II, *"Growler,"* p. 124-26. U.S. Government Printing Office.

Holland, U.S.S. Ship's History, 6 pp.

Pampanito, U.S.S. Report of Third War Patrol, 28 September 1944, 39 pp.; Annex to Patrol Report, "Rescue of British and Australian Prisoner-of-War Survivors," 28 September 1944, 17 pp.; Letter (Serial 168) "Revised List of Officers and Enlisted Men Who Contributed Greatly to the Successful Rescue of British and Australian Prisoner-of-War Survivors," 3 October 1944; Ship's History, 12 pp.

Queenfish, U.S.S. Report of First War Patrol, 3 October 1944, 55 pp.; Annex to Patrol Report, "Allied Prisoner of War Survivors; Treatment and Disposition," 2 October 1944, 6 pp.; Annex to Patrol Report, "Interrogation of Allied Prisoners of War," 28 September 1944, 5 pp.; Ship's History, 12 pp.

Sealion, U.S.S. Report of Second War Patrol, 30 September 1944, 45 pp.; Annex to Patrol Report, "Rescue of Allied Prisoners of War Aboard the *Rakuyo Maru*," 24 September 1944, 6 pp.; Annex to Patrol Report, "Preliminary Interrogation of Survivors from the *Rakuyo Maru*," 25 September 1944, 4 pp.; Ship's History, 14 pp.

Tufnell, Captain D.N.C., Royal Navy, British Intelligence Liaison Officer, U.S. Pacific Fleet, Pearl Harbor, Action Report, "Rescue of Allied POWs," 3 October 1944, 32 pp.; plus a list of the survivors rescued by submarines.

Tunny, U.S.S. Report of Seventh War Patrol, 17 September 1944, 22 pp.; Ship's History, 13 pp.

In addition to the foregoing, the following were consulted: "Deck Logs" and Muster Rolls" (complete lists of crews) for the aforelisted submarines, at the National Archives, Washington, D.C., and Suitland, Maryland, respectively.

United Kingdom

At the Public Records Office, Kew Gardens:

"British Prisoners of War in Japanese Hands," June 1944, 9 pp. Records of the Chief of Naval Operations, Secret Files C-10-F 24045.

The following are filed under FO-371/41791:

"Arrangements for the Reception and Interrogation of 58 Prisoners of War Repatriated from the Far East," 8 November 1944.

Grigg, Sir James. Statements before the House of Commons, 31 October and 17 November 1944.

Melbourne, Australia, to War Office, London. "Report on Interrogation of 86 Australian Prisoners of War," Most Secret Cipher Telegram, 30 October 1944, 22 pp.

"Parliamentary Statement Regarding 58 Prisoners of War . . ." 15 November 1944.

Royal Message to the Prisoners of War, November 1944.

Australia

At the Australian Archives, Melbourne:

Navy: *"Rakuyo Maru*—Japanese Transport—Loss of." MP 1587/1 File 20S.

Army: "Survivors from Sunken Japanese Transport." MP 742/1 File 255/15/579.

Department of Defence (Navy): "POWs Rescued from Torpedoed *Rakuyo Maru*." MP 1049/5 File 1951/2/99.

Department of Defence (Army): "Rescue of Allied POWs aboard the *Rakuyo Maru* and Following Interrogation." MP 729/6 File 63/401/728.

Statement by Acting Prime Minister Forde in the House of Parliament, 17 November 1944.

Statement by Commander in Chief Sir Thomas Blamey to returning Australian Prisoners of War, including message of greeting from the King and Acting Governor General of Australia, Winston Dugan. Undated.

At the Australian War Memorial, Canberra:

Farrell, Thomas H., War Correspondent, despatches of, relating to *Rakuyo Maru.*

"Sinking of Japanese Ship *Rakuyo Maru*—Report by Australian and British Prisoners of War Recovered by American Submarines." CRS A2663, Written Records File 1010/9/109.

Varley, Brigadier Arthur L. Diary.

BOOKS AND PERIODICALS

The following were found to be pertinent—and useful. The official military histories contain only brief accounts of the sinkings but were invaluable for background. All the periodicals and newspaper citations deal directly with the sinkings. Those books or manuscripts that deal directly with the sinkings are indicated by the name of the ship in parentheses. The Harry Jones unpublished manuscript was kindly made available by his widow, Irene Jones, now living in Perth, Australia.

Adams, Geoffrey Pharaoh, with Hugh Popham. *No Time for Geishas*. London: Leo Cooper Ltd., 1973.

Allbury, Alfred G. *Bamboo and Bushido*. London: World Distributors, 1965. (*Rakuyo Maru*)

Bancroft, A., and R.G. Roberts. *The Mikado's Guests*. Perth: Patersons Printing Press Ltd. (*Rakuyo Maru*)

Barker, Ralph. *Against the Sea*. London and Sydney:

311

Pan Books Ltd., 1972. (See Ernest Fieldhouse, *Rakuyo Maru.*)

Braddon, Russell. *The Naked Island.* London: Pan Books, 1955.

Caffrey, Kate. *Out in the Midday Sun.* Great Britain: André Deutsch Ltd., 1974.

Campbell, Jim. "I Survived a Hell Ship." *Truth,* September 23, 1951 (Sydney, Australia).

Carew, Tim. *Hostages to Fortune.* Great Britain: Hamish Hamilton Ltd., 1971.

Coast, John. *Railroad of Death.* London: Brown, Watson Ltd., 1958.

Craven, Wesley F., and James L. Cate, eds. *Army Air Forces in World War II, India-Burma Operations, 1943.* Chicago: University of Chicago Press, 1948–58.

Fluckey, Capt. Eugene B., U.S.N. "The Terrible Trek of the Submarine Barb." *Cavalier,* December 1955 (United States).

Gilmour, O.W. *With Freedom to Singapore.* London: Ernest Benn Ltd., 1950.

Gordon, Ernest. *Through the Valley of the Kwai.* New York: Harper & Brothers, 1962.

The Grim Glory, The History of the 2/19 Battalion A.I.F. Sydney, N.S.W., 1975.

Hall, David O.W. *Prisoners of Japan.* Wellington, New Zealand: War History Branch, Department of Internal Affairs, 1949.

Jeffrey, Betty. *White Coolies.* Maidstone, England: George Mann, 1973.

Jones, Harry. Unpublished manuscript. (*Rakuyo Maru*)

Kinvig, Clifford. *Death Railway.* Great Britain: Pan/Ballantine, 1973.

Lumiere, Cornel. *Kura!* Brisbane, Queensland: Jacaranda Press Pty Ltd., 1966.

McKie, Ronald C.H. *Proud Echo.* Sydney and London: Angus & Robertson Ltd., 1953.

Maloney, Tom. "Action in the China Sea." *Cosmopolitan,* November 1945 (United States).

Mant, Gilbert. *Grim Glory.* Sydney: The Currawong Publishing Co., 1945.

Morison, Samuel Eliot. *The Rising Sun in the Pacific 1931–April 1942.* Boston: Little, Brown & Company, 1951.

Nelson, David. *The Story of Changi Singapore.* Australia: Changi Publication Co., 1973.

Owen, Frank. *The Fall of Singapore.* London: Pan Books Ltd., 1962.

Parvin, G.R. *Yasumai!* London: Digit Books. *(Kachidoki Maru)*

Pounder, Thomas. *Death Camps of the River Kwai.* Cornwall: United Writers, 1977. *(Kachidoki Maru)*

Rawlings, Leo. *And the Dawn Came Up Like Thunder.* London: Futura Publications Ltd., 1975.

Rivett, Rohan D. *Behind Bamboo.* Sydney and London: Angus & Robertson Ltd., 1946.

Russell, Lord, of Liverpool. *The Knights of Bushido.* London: Cassell & Company Ltd., 1958.

Simpson, Ivan. *Singapore: Too Little, Too Late.* London: Leo Cooper Ltd., 1970.

Sol, Martin. "Pick Us Up, Please!" *Argosy,* March 1964 (United States).

Talbot-Booth, Paymr. Lt. Cdr. E.C., R.N.R. *Merchant Ships.* London: Sampson Low, Marston & Co. Ltd., 1940.

Walker, Allan S. *Middle East and Far East.* Series Five, Volume II, in Australia in the War of 1939–45. Canberra: Australian War Memorial, 1953.

"When U.S. Subs Sank Our POWs." *Parade,* October 1972 (Australia).

Whitecross, Roy H. *Slaves of the Son of Heaven.* London: Corgi Books, 1961.

Wigmore, Lionel. *The Japanese Thrust.* Series One, Volume IV, in Australia in the War of 1939–45. Canberra: Australian War Memorial, 1953.

Ziegler, Oswald L., ed. "Men May Smoke." Final edition of 2/18 Bn. A.I.F. Magazine (Australia).

Interviews

In 1977 and 1978, the authors conducted extensive taped interviews with submariners and survivors or their kin in the United States, the United Kingdom and Australia. A few survivors who could not be found immediately later provided lengthy written accounts. Many submariners and survivors had diaries or letters that were consulted during the interviews. Mrs. James F. C. Lillington provided a long and valuable letter from her deceased father, Harry G. Weigand, written on Saipan shortly after his rescue. Those who contributed:

Submariners

Barb

Donnelly, William E.
Duncan, Capt. Max C., USN (Ret.)
Houston, Traville
Lanier, James G.
Lego, H. Frank
McNitt, Rear Admiral Robert W., USN (Ret.)

Saunders, Paul G.
Schmidt, Rudolph H.
Swinburne, Rear Admiral Edwin R., USN (Ret.)
Teeters, David R.
Weaver, Everett P.

Growler

Bell, C. Edwin
Bialko, Daniel
Bush, Harold A.
Byerts, Mrs. Robert K. (formerly Mrs. Thomas B. Oakley)
Daspit, Rear Admiral Lawrence R., USN (Ret.)

Dissette, Capt. Edward F., USN (Ret.)
Gale, Harold D.
Hall, Capt. Warren C., USN (Ret.)

Pampanito

Bennett, Robert
Bixler, Herman J.
Carmody, Clarence G.
Demers, Maurice
Elliott, Richard E.
Fives, Francis
Granum, Peder A.
Greene, John H.
Hauptman, Anthony C.
Hayes, Daniel E.
McGuire, Charles A.

Markham, C. Boyd
Pappas, Paul
Red, John W., Jr.
Sherlock, Richard J.
Smith, Clarence H.
Stockslader, Edmund W.
Strother, George W.
Summers, Rear Admiral
  Paul E., USN (Ret.)
Swain, Cdr. Ted N.,
  USN (Ret.)
Yagemann, William F.

Queenfish

Alamia, Anthony J. A.
Bennett, Capt. John E.,
  USN (Ret.)
Bledsoe, Samuel H.
Coleman, Douglas W.
Dickinson, Robert L.
Dixon, Mrs. Harold
Fedor, Robert C.
Glazebrook, Wilfred M.
Grandinetti, Arthur A.

Levine, Charles
Loughlin, Rear Admiral
  C. Elliott, USN (Ret.)
Moore, Charles M.
Nadeau, F. Laurence
North, Joseph P.
Penn, Robert D.
Roan, James O.
Wilson, Eugene J.

Sealion

Bateman, O. Thomas
Bates, Joseph C.
Behr, Raymond T.
Brooks, Captain Daniel P.,
  USN (Ret.)

Case, Harold D.
Catalano, William J.
Enos, Anthony W.
Goetz, Alfred K.
Hunter, Norman C.

Sealion

Joyce, Henry A.
Lauerman, Captain Henry
  C., USN (Ret.)
Messecar, Fred
Pagel, Edward F.
Reich, Vice Admiral
  Eli T., USN (Ret.)

Ryan, Joseph F.
Scarano, William M.
Schuler, Fred G.
Utz, James L.
Williams, Roy J., Jr.

Survivors

British—*Rakuyo Maru*

Allbury, Mrs. Alfred G.
Armstrong, Mrs. Charles J.

Ashworth, Norman
Bagnall, Joseph

Bambridge, Leslie
Barnett, Wilfred
Brierley, Thomas B.
Carr, Thomas
Costello, Stanley
Cresswell, Douglas A.
Dunne, Christopher T.
Emmett, William H. R.
Fuller, William H.
Gould, George
Halfhide, Eric C.
Hall, Mrs. Albert E. B.
Hudson, Roy A.
Hughes, Ernest
Johnson, Sidney
Jones, Mrs. Harry
Jones, Mrs. Herbert

Leslie, Adam H.
Mandley, William A.
Ogden, Alfred (Ellen Cunliffe, sister)
Perry, Charles A.
Smethurst, Harry
Smith, Denny
Smith, Lawrence W.
Smith, Thomas
Starkey, Edward G.
Stones, William H.
Taylor, Thomas
Ward, George K. J.
Wheeler, Mark
Whiley, Samuel T.
Wilson, Hugh F.

British—*Kachidoki Maru*

Benford, Ernest S.
Clifton, Ralph
Cooper, Frederick A.
Curtis, Roger B.
Devine, Arthur
Grisbrook, Thomas J.
Hallett, R. S.
Huitson, L. A. George
Juson, Leslie A.
King, Frederick J.

Mole, Walter G.
Parrott, Thomas H.
Peddie, Arthur R.
Pounder, Thomas
Rennocks, Alfred J.
Richards, Fred A.
Sherwood, Henry W.
Spon-Smith, Douglas
Stark, Raymond L.
Thompson, Stanley

Australian—*Rakuyo Maru*

Amoore, John B.
Anderson, Edward W.
Bancroft, Arthur
Beilby, Philip J.
Bolger, Leslie J.
Bunker, Harold T.
Burridge, Raymond
Calvert, Norman D.
Clark, David H.
Clifford, Victor
Clive, A. Anthony
Collins, Robert A. C.
Coombes, Frank J.
Cornelius, Leo G.
Cornford, Roydon C.

Cunneen, D. William
DeSailley, Harold V.
Duncan, Victor R.
Farmer, Francis E.
Farrands, M. Robert
Flynn, John J.
Hall, Arthur W.
Hampson, R. Douglas
Harris, Reginald J.
Hart, Reginald H.
Hinchy, George F.
Hock, Laurence J.
Hocking, John R.
Johnson, Francis B.
Langley, John R.

317

Lemin, Francis A.
Lihou, Eric J.
Loughnan, Kitchener M.
McArdle, Donald F.
MacDiarmid, Ian A.
McGovern, Francis J.
McKechnie, Charles B.
McKittrick, William H.
Manning, Stanley J.
Matsen, Sydney C.
Mayers, Douglas G.
Mayne, William E. T.
Mills, Frederic C.
Miscamble, Ronald C.
Munro, Lloyd W.
Pickett, Harry
Porter. J. E. N.

Ramsey, Harold G.
Richards, Rowland
Savage, J. Russell
Smith, James O.
Smith, William R.
Stewart, Reginald S.
Thams, R. Neville
Wade, John
Wall, Herbert J.
Weigand, Hilton G.
 (via Lillington)
Wheeler, Raymond W.
White, Strachan M.
Williams, Walter G.
Wilson, Cedric C.
Winter, Alfred D.
Wright, Arthur G.

Index

321

325

327

333

The most fascinating people and events of World War II